# *Social Media Field Guide*

# Social Media Field Guide

## A Resource for Graphic Communicators

Julie Shaffer and
Mary Garnett

**Printing Industries Press**
PITTSBURGH

Library of Congress Catalog Card Number: 2010906517
International Standard Book Number: 978-0-88362-686-3

Printed in the United States of America
Printing Industries of America Catalog No. 1790



Printing Industries Press books are widely used by companies, associations, and schools for training, marketing, and resale. Quantity discounts are available by contacting the Printing Industries of America Member Central department at the number below.

**Printing Industries Press**
Printing Industries of America
200 Deer Run Road
Sewickley, PA 15143
Phone: 412-741-6860
Toll-Free: 800-910-4283 x770
Fax: 412-741-2311
Email: membercentral@printing.org
Online: www.printing.org

# Contents

## Dedication

Like most sizable projects, this book involved many other people who have been pivotal to its creation. We sincerely thank everyone who has helped make this book possible and for all our industry colleagues who encouraged and inspired (and critiqued) our work. We appreciate each of you and your valued insight!

- To our families who did not complain when we told them we had (yet another) late-night editing and writing session
- To all the printers and colleagues who shared with us the stories of their sojourns into the social media realm
- To Michael Makin for his support and understanding during a long year of writing and rewriting the book
- To Amy Woodall, our editor, on whom we could always count to save the day

And thank you, reader, for picking up this book to read it. Don't forget the journey continues at the *Social Media Field Guide* website: www.printing.org/socialmediafieldguide.

## Introduction

### What is social media?

"Social media" is one of the those topics that is so hot, discussed ad nauseum by so many "gurus" eager to put their own spin on it, that a single definition is hard to come by.

"Social media are media for social interaction, using highly accessible and scalable publishing techniques," says Wikipedia. "Any website or web service that utilizes a 'social' or 'Web 2.0' philosophy. This includes blogs, social networks, social news, wikis, etc.," says About.com's Web Trends glossary. Duct Tape Marketing calls it "the use of technology combined with social interaction to create or co-create value." The authors of *The Social Media Bible* (Safeko, Brake) add the notion of community to their definition: "Social media refers to activities, practices and behaviors among communities of people who gather online to share information, knowledge, and opinions using conversational media." We've even heard several pundits declare that social media is, in fact, simply "conversation."

**We know it's a misnomer.** We think that "social networking," the phrase used earlier in the evolution of this phenomena then usurped by the more widely used "social media," really is a more apt bucket term to describe what we'll be talking about throughout this book. "Media" refers to a means of mass communication and is a noun, a thing. Conversely, "networking" is a verb, and is the interaction between people to exchange information and develop contacts—a much better way to describe what we're doing via the communication channels on the Web. We don't much like the term "Web-to-print" either, but it's become the commonly used phrase to describe the e-commerce or Web portals that print service providers offer to help customers solve problems. Similarly, while social media is something of a misnomer, we're using it because it is the most commonly used term to describe the use of online communication channels to converse with others for personal or business marketing purposes.

**We're using the term "social media" to describe the use of online communication channels to converse with others for personal or business marketing purposes.**

With myriad books and articles on social media, and commentators and pundits taking a snipe at the topic, what makes this book different and needed? You've told us—through phone call inquiries at Printing Industries, questions at conferences, seminars, and surveys—that you want a concise, not-too-technical primer on the topic of social media. Something like … a field guide!

Those leaders, like you, indicated they are seeking:

- A basic overview of the social media universe
- Customer engagement through social media
- Information about available methods and tools
- Insight as part of the 91% of leading printers who recognize social media is not going away
- Potential company direction and strategies
- Guidelines and focus for their company's marketing strategy
- Practical applications that will solidify your presence in social media
- Help to clarify your path in the online world of social media

So, this book is for you!

## Is the entire book worth reading?

As the authors, of course, yes, we certainly believe that it is. But as realists, we understand that you may want to skim the entire book first, then come back to the sections on topics you want to delve into in more depth.

This is an action-oriented guide to help you immediately, with a step-by-step "get-started guide" (chapter three), a compendium of more than fifteen of the top social media platforms (chapter four), and very granular tips and tricks for using specific social media tools to your best advantage (chapter five). Just looking for print-centric success stories? Skip to chapter six. Want a definition for a buzzword you're hearing about but don't fully understand (how about OAuth)? Look in the glossary. Need an RFP to use when you interview a social media marketing firm? Check the appendix. Want an overview of why you should care about any of this social media stuff? Begin at the beginning; you'll find what you're looking for in chapters one and two.

## Why Julie Shaffer and Mary Garnett?

While there are so many supposed experts in the social media field, we think that, for the most part, there are really just people with more or less experience studying and using it. Think of us as a kind of "advance team" for you—we've been doing the research and diving headfirst into using a wide variety tools to see which are a good "fit" for marketing-focused print service providers.

Julie is the technology geek in the pair and has been delivering social media commentary, analysis, and observations for the last two years and other emerging technology commentary for many years. Mary has been active in publishing, education, and training; with deep ties in the printing community, she looks at the social media engagement topic with the eyes of this community. We have both had moments when we've waxed poetic in our enthusiasm for this subject and others when we've been overwhelmed by the sheer rapidity of the changing social media scene. We both agree that social media is a big time-consumer. We have both been frustrated and overwhelmed—just like you, most likely.

Together, we have researched and reviewed numerous third-party resources; we have discussed and distilled others' experiences. This book is just the beginning of an evolutionary journey. Every day the tools and stories change. Join us and we will move forward together.

## You, the Reader

We are all on a journey together in a social media landscape filled with twists and turns. We like to think of ourselves—all of us—as being on a profitable adventure and we are the advance team. We want you to succeed and experience profitable growth within your graphic communications company.

We have made all efforts to find practical suggestions and directions for you to use immediately. Leap ahead, find activities and information to apply now. Use the suggestions in sales meetings, customer interaction, and research, and above all, use this information to begin to build your business plan to help develop strategies and tactics for your company's social media engagement!

# 1 The Lay of the Land: Take a Look Around You!

## What's to Be Gained?

Renee Berger of **Western States Envelope & Label** told us she began to dabble with social media several years ago. She saw the potential, but like most of us, she wondered how spending time on social networking websites and forums would parlay into some tangible growth for her company. Little did she know that her time investment in social media would result in a whole new revenue stream, not only for her company but also for Western State's clients.

Renee participates in the **Print Services & Distribution Association (PSDA)** social networking site **Printjunkie.net.** Monitoring the conversation there, she tuned in on one thread in which members discussed a problem about the heat of a laser printer causing a letter inside a window envelope to stick to the clear window. Renee wondered if this was an isolated or industry-wide issue, so she decided to put the question to her connections on social media site **LinkedIn.** Her LinkedIn community confirmed not only that this was a universal problem

*Figure 1-1. Printjunkie.net's home page.*

but also that no solution seemed to exist in the marketplace.

This is what social media engagement for business is all about! Who would not want to be able to say that their conversation on an online community resulted in significant new business?

Renee went back to her development team at Western States and challenged them to come up with a solution to this problem. They came through by developing the **Digi-Clear™ envelope**—a new side-seam window envelope with heat-resistant window material that doesn't stick to toner. Suddenly, Western had a brand new revenue stream while solving a known problem for many of its customers, all thanks to Renee's engaging in the *conversation* on a relevant social media site.

## How Do We Get There?

*Conversation* and *community* are indeed two key aspects of the social media phenomenon. As we noted in the introduction, definitions for the terms "social media" vary according to these key aspects.

There are hundreds of such communities on the Internet, which we can clump into several rough categories:

- **Social networking sites**—such as Facebook, LinkedIn, Spoke, Twitter, MySpace, Bebo, hi5, and Friendster
- **Location-based social sites**—Foursquare, Gowalla, Loopt, Snikkr, TripIt and dozens of other geo-social platforms
- **Video and image-sharing sites**—including the likes of YouTube, Flickr, Vimeo, Metacafe, and Blip.tv
- **Social review, news, and bookmark sites—**Yelp, Digg, Reddit, Delicious, FriendFeed, and Newsvine, among many others
- **Virtual worlds—**Second Life, Instant Messaging Virtual Universe (IMVU), and others, plus many toy/gaming worlds

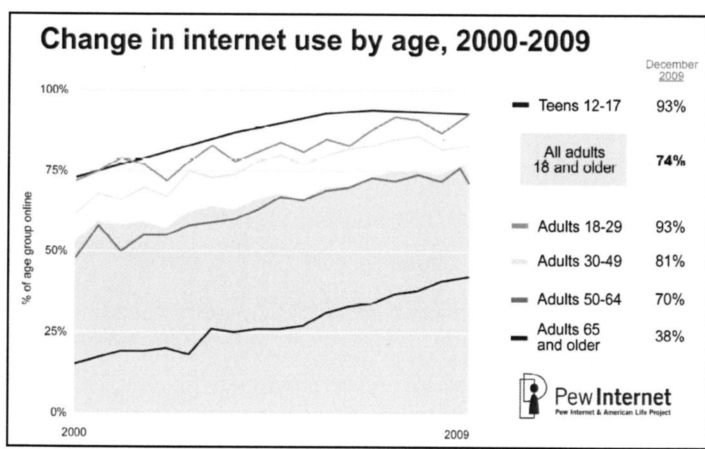


*Figure 1-2.*

- **E-communities or forums**—on every topic, including print's PrintPlanet
- **Blogs**—helped by tools like TypePad, WordPress, PivotX, and dozens more

These are the online places where people virtually live today, and it just makes sense for businesses to talk to people where they congregate and communicate.

**As of this writing there are approximately 6.86 billion humans on the planet—and 1.97 billion of them are online.***

And yes, the main reason to take part *is* that everyone is doing it. Need to be convinced that this is more than a fad? Here are some stats to back up the notion that **social networking is a phenomenon that is likely here to stay.**

First, let's consider how ubiquitous Internet connectivity is today. The website **www.internetworldstats.com** reports the total world population

* *www.internetworldstats.com*

A December 2009 Pew study broke down the demographics of who is online:

- 95% of people aged 18–29
- 87% of people aged 30–49
- 78% of people aged 50–64
- 42% of seniors, over age 65

and the percentage of it that uses the Internet. The penetration of usage is highest in North America, where **more than three-quarters of the entire population use the Internet,** everyone from toddlers to grannies.

The world is undeniably connected via the Web—and it's not just youth that account for this rapid growth of social interaction. The *2010 USC Annenberg Digital Future Study,* reported that 100% of those under age 24 go online, and a June 2010 Nielsen study found that **twice as many users over the age of 50 are using social networks than are users under age 18** (of course, there are a whole lot more people over 18 years of age than under).

Why are we spouting all of these numbers? These are important demographic details for any business looking to use social media as a marketing platform! **You want to be where the people are.** And while we know that numbers can be difficult to evaluate—every source we checked reported somewhat different numbers even when comparing the same subject—**the trends are indisputable.** The trend lines for all types of Internet-enabled technology, including social media use go up, up, and up.

Let's look at some of the trends we see in our connected world.

## Trend 1
## The Use of Social Media Is Ubiquitous

As we just pointed out, people all over the world are using the Internet in ever-greater numbers. And people are using this mass connectivity for social networking. The June 2010 Nielsen study shows that Americans spend almost a quarter of their online time (22.7%) using social media sites, an increase of 43% over

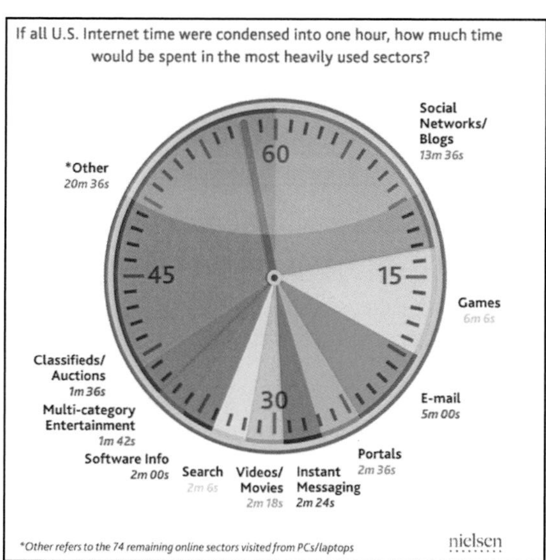


***Figure 1-3.*** *Social media access accounts for a significant amount of users' time spent online.*

the previous year. The study indicates that **using social media may well have eclipsed email** (down 28%) and even instant messaging (down 15%) as an online communication vehicle. Facebook has half a billion users as of this writing, and according to GigaTweet, Twitter was approaching 30 billion total tweets in early November 2010.*

## Trend 2
## Your Lives Are Changing with the Internet and Social Media

A child born in 2001 likely had **Gigglebytes**® classes in nursery school; this course introduced barely talking tots to the joys of computers before they were potty trained! The same child probably had a computer-based toy (such as **LeapFrog**®) at three years of age and then was one of the first to have **Webkinz**® (dolls that come with special codes that lead them to

** Twitter changed the way the company generates unique IDs for tweets, and GigaTweet could no longer count tweets. The final count as of November 6, 2010, was 29,700,500,268.*

computers and what is essentially social media for kids). Today this same child likely has multiple computer gaming systems, at least one mobile device, is a texting expert, and might even have a kid-friendly social network account. Since this child is now nine years of age, you have more than a decade to learn to deal with his or her type of savvy customer—but you really need to prepare now.

In a Pew Internet study, *The Future of Social Relations,* 895 technology stakeholders and critics were asked to look forward to 2020 and consider the Internet's impact on our social world. Some 85% agreed that the impact has been and will be mostly positive. Participant Robert Cannon, senior counsel for Internet law, Office of Strategic Planning and Policy Analysis, Federal Communications Commission, put it this way:

> The tension between the net and social engagement will vaporize in much the same way that thoughts about the telephone network vaporized and it came to be taken for granted. People do not ask if the telephone is an alienating social force. The phone is a utility supporting social life. Likewise, **the net will come to be assumed as a utility for social life.** How else would I know when church starts, when the game begins,

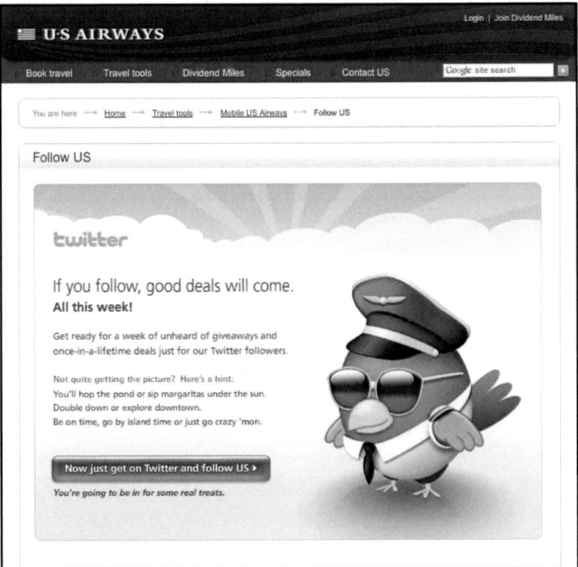


***Figure 1-4.*** *Early adopters of e-commerce, like airlines, now engage on social sites like Twitter offering special deals for followers.*

> where we are meeting for drinks, or what the weather for our trip might be? *[emphasis ours]*

All you have to do is look at your own life to know that **the population's use and commitment to online tools is constantly going up.** It started with going online to buy books, purchase airline tickets, search for houses, and then for more and more retail items. The world of printing was hit with online auctions, online RFQs, and online ordering of printing; now buying print on the Internet is commonplace. As each industry was hit by the wave of online tools, disruptive technology impacted the "traditional" players. Think of the disruptive technology of the Internet over the last decade, which changed personnel, lifestyles, and business practices for bookstores, travel agencies, Realtors, music distributors—and printing businesses! The "thrivers" within online technology are those who learned to leverage the technology to grow their business. The same tactic will work with social media!

**The "thrivers" within online technology are those who learned to leverage the technology to grow their business. The same tactic will work with social media!**

## Trend 3
## All Forms of Communication Will Be Impacted by the Internet and, by Extension, Social Media

Gary Kreps, professor and chair of the George Mason University Department of Communication, in a July 2010 Pew Internet study said:

> The trend to utilize social media to share information will continue to grow through 2010. In fact, these social media are becoming indispensable tools for connecting with others, accomplishing goals, and solving problems. I see the new media becoming more institutionalized and adopted by workplaces, schools, governments, and social organizations as primary channels for communication in the future.

59% of Americans get news from a combination of online and offline sources on a typical day, and the Internet is now the third most popular news platform, behind local television news and national television news. *

According to another Pew Internet study, *Understanding the Participatory News Consumer,* the vast majority of Americans (92%) use multiple platforms to get news on a typical day, including national or local TV, the Internet, local newspapers, radio, and national newspapers. Newspapers are by no means the main news source for the majority (although the study reports that 50% do say they read the local newspaper).

Drops in circulation are nothing new: Since 1945, the number of papers sold per 100 households has dropped steadily, declining in 61 of the last 64 years. Total newspaper advertising revenue declined for 16 straight quarters through June 2010, according to the Newspaper Association of America, albeit the 2nd quarter 2010 declines were less steep than they had been in several previous quarters. Yet, a glimmer of light appears for publications in the form of **e-subscriptions.** The number of daily electronic editions sold by the newspapers at the top of the category rose 40%, according to reports made to the Audit Bureau of Circulation.

By the end of 2010, 10.3 million people in the U.S. are expected to have some sort of **e-reader** device according to Forrester Research in September 2010. *Publishers Weekly* reported in August 2010 that e-book sales in general were up over 200% to date in 2010. Apple announced in June 2010 that the **iPad** has collected 22% of e-book sales since its launch earlier in the year.

---

* *Pew Internet. Understanding the Participatory News Consumer.*

So people are still reading, but the media show continuing signs of shifting from print to electronic.

Of course, "news" comes from many sources other than traditional media outlets. The concept of **"citizen journalism"** or **"community journalism"** is growing along with blogs and Web-based individual commentary outlets. **Technorati,** blog search engine and support organization, reports that there are more than 1.2 million active blogs registered with them, The Huffington Post, the self-described "Internet Newspaper," being number one as of the time of this writing.

## Trend 4
## Digital Distribution of Content Has Expanded to Social Media Tools, Such as Mobile Devices

We're not just sitting in front of our computers to connect; mobile Web connectivity is on a meteoric rise. *Wired* magazine went so far as to pronounce "The Web Is Dead" on the cover of its September 2010 issue. It stated that the Web is eighteen years old, an entire generation has grown up in front of a browser, but **mobile applications are now displacing how the World Wide Web is used.**

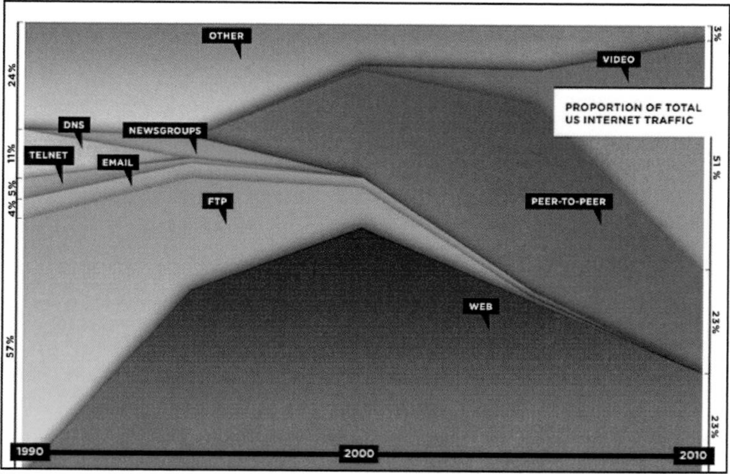


***Figure 1-5.*** *Sources: Wired.com. Cisco estimates based on CAIDA publications, Andrew Odlyzko.*

> **Social networking experienced the strongest growth in app access, increasing 240% to 14.5 million users.**
>
> **Source: comScore, Inc.**

Here are some stats to support this notion. The International Telecommunication Union (February 2010) reports that in 2009 there were 4.6 billion mobile cellular subscriptions globally. Compare that to the number of humans on earth—**two-thirds have a cell phone!** Strategy Analytics (March 2010) claimed that at the end of 2009 almost 530 million users browsed the mobile Web on their handsets. This is predicted to rise to more than 1 billion by 2015.

Digital marketing intelligence firm **comScore, Inc.** reported that 78% of smartphone users accessed a browser and 80% accessed applications in April 2010. The study reported that social networking experienced the strongest growth in app access, increasing 240% to 14.5 million users. Mark Donovan, comScore senior vice president of mobile, stated, **"Social networking is by far the fastest-growing mobile activity right now.** With 20 percent of mobile users now accessing social networking sites via their phone, we expect to see both application and browser usage continuing to drive future consumption of social media."

In celebration of its fifth birthday in May 2010, **YouTube** announced that the well-known online video community was serving well over *two billion* views a day. That's double the number reported in December 2009 and nearly double the prime-time audience of all three major U.S. television networks combined! The viral nature of the Internet is readily evident on YouTube, where even the simplest homemade video, once it catches popular attention, can net millions of views.

Some marketers have learned to harness the power of YouTube, driving viewers through **"promoted videos"** (adopting parent company Google's pay-by-the-view model). Others buy ads on sites like **Hulu.com** that offer free anytime viewing of TV programs or movies (in return for viewing an ad at the start of the program).

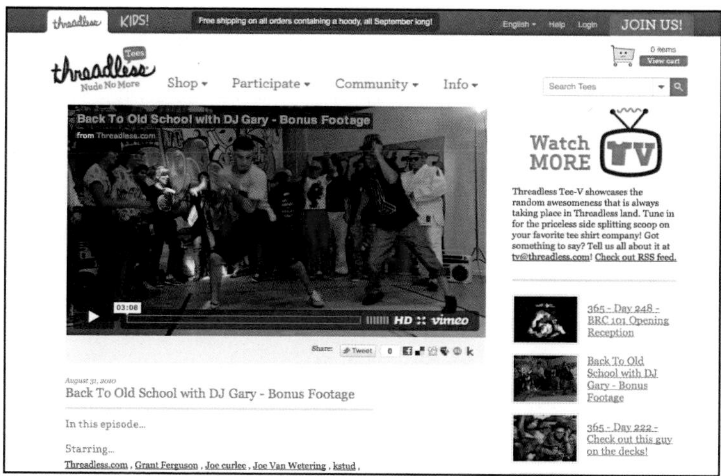


***Figure 1-6.*** *An example of the creative weekly video offerings at Threadless.com.*

Many organizations are posting how-to videos on their websites, like the "How to Change a Bicycle Tire" video on **Trails.com,** a website devoted to outdoor enthusiasts.

**Threadless.com,** a company that prints and sells T-shirts designed through online contests, hosts Threadless TV, a crazy weekly video featuring some of the company's staff people and, increasingly, visiting bands, designers, or other "cool" people. **Vlogs** (video blogs) are also growing, like those found on parenting support site **momversation.com,** sponsored by department store giant Target.

## Trend 5
## Mass Collaboration Will Become a Major Means of Product Development and Problem-Solving

Social media will push this along through **crowdsourcing,** a neologism coined by Jeff Howe in *Wired* magazine, which is the act of taking tasks traditionally performed by an employee or consultant and outsourcing them to a group or community in the form of an open call over the Internet. It's a model for distributed problem-solving. Some crowdsourced projects are offered in the form of a contest—Threadless.com is a great example of utilizing

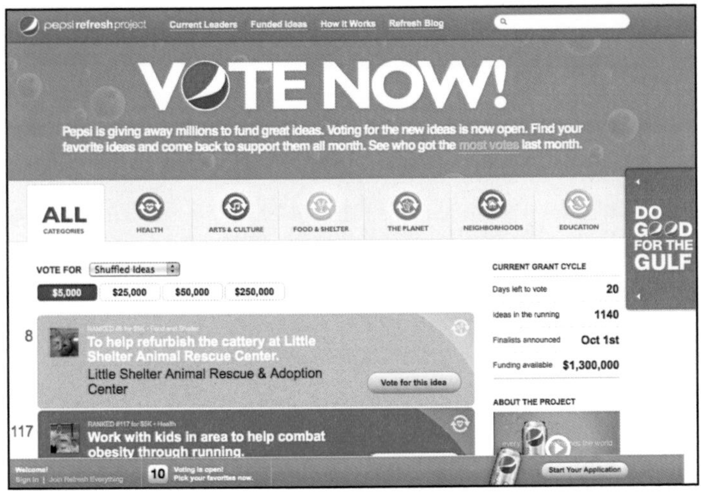


***Figure 1-7.***

contests. Some of these contests result in big money and prestige for the participants.

Take **Pepsi's Refresh Project.** Instead of paying millions for advertising during the 2010 Super Bowl game, Pepsi-Cola Company used the funds for a social media campaign, one that will serve not only as a public relations/marketing boon for the company but also as a charitable engagement that will help potentially dozens of U.S. communities.

Starting January 13, 2010, all legal residents of the United States, age thirteen and older, could apply for a Pepsi Refresh Grant, with up to one thousand proposals accepted per month. Social media platforms drive traffic to the official website **www.refresheverything.com.** Proposals could fall into the categories of arts and culture, education, food and shelter, health, neighborhoods, and the planet. Grants range from $5,000 to $250,000 depending on the scope of the project. People vote on the site for their favorite idea (each person can vote for ten per day), and the winners, based on some final vetting on Pepsi's part, receive the grant. Grants in the $250,000 category tend to go to health-related issues, but some others go for less serious topics. In fact, one went to restore a historic wooden roller coaster at a quaint amusement park in Northwestern Pennsylvania (not far from Printing Industries headquarters)!

Likewise, GE launched its **Ecomagination Challenge** during July 2010, calling it a "$200 million call to action for businesses, entrepreneurs, innovators, and students to share their best ideas and come together to take on one of the world's toughest challenges—building the next-generation power grid to meet the needs of the 21st century." The contest, which ran through mid-September 2010, awarded monies for top ideas in Renewables, Grid Efficiency, and Eco Homes/Eco Buildings.

Just getting started? Don't think you're alone: 65% of surveyed marketers said they've been involved in social media for only a few months or less.

Crowdsourcing businesses have sprung up, matching crowds of potential problem-solvers with organizations with problems to solve. A cynic might say this is a way to get free work from the masses, and it is, but it also allows for rapid team-building to solve a problem and has the potential to uncover previously unknown talent. **In any event, the Internet enables mass collaboration, a trend that will most certainly continue.**

## Trend 6
## Brand Managers and Companies of All Sizes Have Incorporated Social Media Tools into an Integrated Marketing Plan to Grow and Promote Their Businesses

In the *2010 Social Media Marketing Industry Report,* Michael Stelzner, white paper marketing entrepreneur and founder of the **Social Media Examiner** website **www.socialmediaexaminer.com,** explores how marketing professionals are using social media. The free study is chock full of interesting statistics, based on the responses from 1,350 marketing pros, most of them, like printers, representing small businesses. The study reports that **an overwhelming 91%**

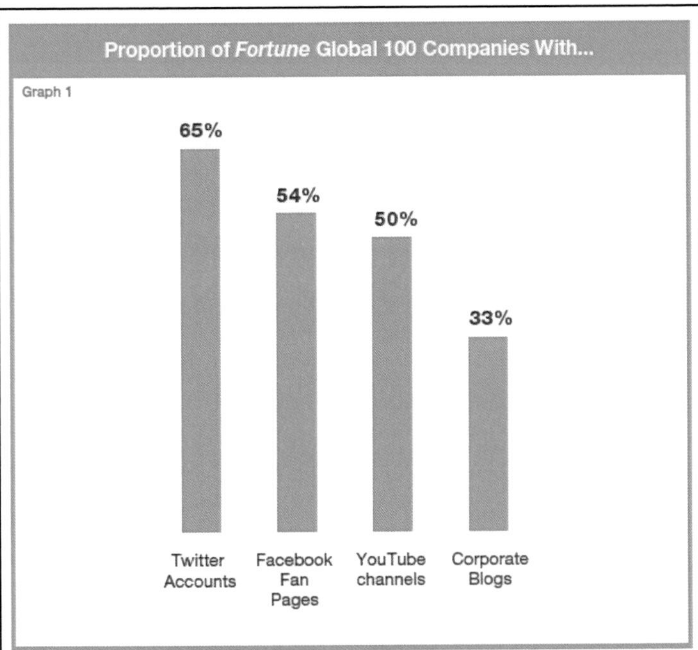


***Figure 1-8.*** *Burson-Marsteller study data showing the activity of large global firms in the social media field.*

**said they were employing social media for marketing purposes,** and more than half (56%) put six or more hours a week into social media engagement. Many were relative newbies to the effort, with 65% of the participating marketers saying they've engaged in social media marketing efforts for a few months or less. So **even amongst professional marketers, the game is relatively new.**

While the Stelzner report is telling of what the smaller marketing organizations are doing, Burson-Marsteller reports, in *The Global Social Media Check-up 2010,* large global firms are in the game as well. Of *Fortune* Global 100 companies, 65% have active Twitter accounts, 54% have Facebook Pages, half have YouTube video channels, and a third have corporate blogs. The study shows that these corporate accounts are actively maintained,

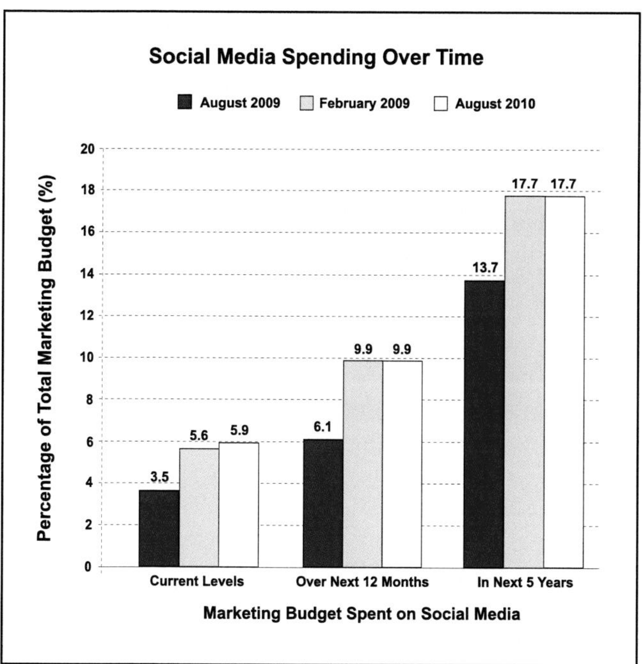


***Figure 1-9.*** *Marketing budgets for social media, as reported by Duke's Fuqua School of Business and the American Marketing Association.*

with 82% of the Twitter accounts updated in the week preceding the study. The 2010 study follows up on a similar study the year before and shows the number of fans for corporate Facebook Pages has increased exponentially over the intervening year.

Then, of course, the most important indicator that social media is critical to marketing efforts is that **this is where money is being spent.** Duke's Fuqua School of Business and the American Marketing Association reported in their *CMO Survey* of 2010 that marketing budgets for social media grew from 1% to 9% in just one year's time (August 2009–August 2010) and is expected to rise to 17% in five years (a number we feel is modest at best).

This last trend is the real reason we've written this book. **Social media as a marketing platform is growing, becoming not just viable but also an essential part**

**of reaching out to customers and, ultimately, selling our products or services.**

## Summary of Thoughts before We Continue on This Path

The social media terrain may be marked or unmarked; we may get lost and traverse dead-end paths—but we cannot wait for clear-cutting, marked trails, and direct routes if we want to stay ahead of the competition.

**Savvy business people are studying and creating social media strategies. Are you?** No one recommends that you jump in before you do your homework, and the following chapters are part of that homework.

But first, remember the trends:

- ✓ The use of social media along with the Internet will be—or rather, already is—ubiquitous.
- ✓ Everyone's lives are changing with the Internet and social media.
- ✓ Communication itself is changing with the Internet and social media.
- ✓ Access of social sites through mobile devices will continue to increase, and video will be used more and more as an online communication tool.
- ✓ Crowdsourcing will be on the rise.
- ✓ Companies large and small are including social media in their marketing plans.

Let's begin the journey!

# 2 Why Make the Journey?

One Sunday afternoon, we were reviewing big corporate **Twitter** accounts, just to see how they were using the platform. We happened upon the **Home Depot** account and noticed a lot of comments aimed directly at specific Twitter users. One congratulated a gentleman on becoming the mayor of his local Home Depot through the location-based social platform, **Foursquare.** He'd noted that accomplishment on Foursquare and from there posted the news on Twitter, where the Home Depot PR staff who monitor the account picked it up and sent him the message.

The folks at Home Depot were obviously **monitoring mentions of the company name.** We also saw a tweet from Brandi, of Home Depot, congratulating another person on moving into a new home. We checked out that person's Twitter feed and saw that she'd been commenting over several days about how she

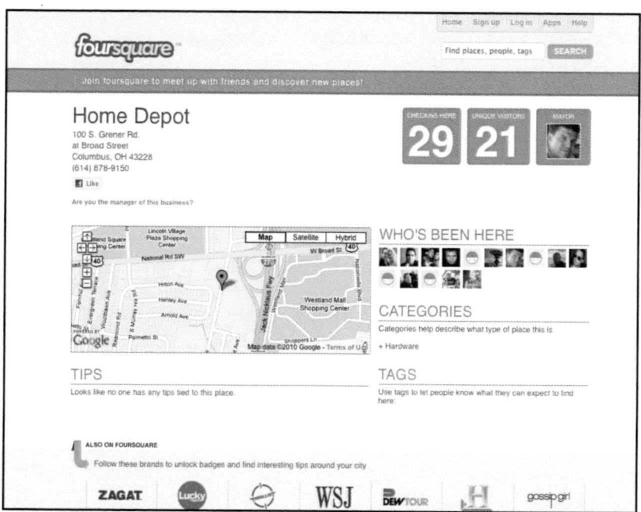


***Figure 2-1.*** *One Foursquare user visited Home Depot enough to become its "mayor"—and got noticed by Home Depot's social media team.*

When it comes to social media interaction, there are no normal work hours—people will engage at all hours of the day.

was painting and cleaning her new place, culminating in the announcement that she had moved in. So in addition to monitoring the words "Home Depot," the staff were also **watching for other keywords** that might be used by potential customers, like "moving," "painting," and "repairing."

We were impressed by this interaction, not the least because it was all happening in the space of about three hours *on a weekend!* When it comes to social media interaction, there are no normal work hours; people will engage at all hours of the day—and Home Depot apparently made the commitment to monitor and engage well outside of normal corporate business hours.

But why would Home Depot bother to write a nice note to everyone who mentions Home Depot on Twitter? The answer goes to the core of why any company would or should be using social media to engage with their audience. Twitter gives Home Depot the opportunity to speak directly to their customers from a corporate level. **It's like a direct feed into the minds of their audience.** By engaging with customers directly via social media channels, Home Depot is working toward the primary goals of social media marketing. What are those goals?

## Goals of Social Media Engagement

While the specific reasons for businesses to engage in social media marketing differ depending upon whether a company is in the business-to-business (B-to-B) or business-to-consumer (B-to-C) space, large or small, the basic goals are similar. If we were to boil these down to their core essence, the three primary motivators for engaging in social media are **to build brand awareness, to nurture relationships and build brand loyalty,** and these all lead to the main goal, which is **to ultimately to drive sales.** We will break this down a bit further, but these motivators are really the bottom line when it comes to reasons for businesses to engage in social media.

Facebook = 500MM+ App Downloads

Vibrant Developer / Application Platform Ecosystem = 500K Apps*, +10x Y/Y

| Category | # of Applications | % of Total | Top 100 Apps' Monthly Active Users (MM) | # of Apps w/ 1MM+ MAUs |
|---|---|---|---|---|
| Games | 13,537 | 23% | 418 | 56 |
| Lifestyle | 4,778 | 8 | 42 | 8 |
| Utilities | 4,604 | 8 | 59 | 8 |
| Education | 2,279 | 4 | 66 | 5 |
| Entertainment | 2,015 | 3 | 76 | 11 |
| Business | 1,981 | 3 | 5 | 1 |
| Sports | 1,431 | 2 | 5 | 0 |
| Just For Fun | 400 | 1 | 44 | 10 |
| Friends & Family | 61 | 0 | 37 | 3 |
| Overall* | 59,427 | | 752 | 102 |

Note: Category breakdown per Facebook, one application can belong to multiple categories or belong to no category; Overall* statistics per AppData, which reports a lower active apps count than Facebook's reported 500,000+ apps "built to date".
Source: Facebook, AppData as of 1/10, Morgan Stanley Research. 47

Morgan Stanley

***Figure 2-2.*** *Games are a big draw for Americans when they are online, according to Morgan Stanley research.*

Big corporations are embracing social media at an astonishing rate. PR firm Burson-Marsteller asked the *Fortune* Global 100 companies how they were using social media and came up with these results:

- 65% have active Twitter accounts.
- 54% have Facebook Pages.
- 50% have a YouTube channel.
- 33% have a corporate blog.

Those who use these new social outlets are not merely setting up sites and letting them lie fallow. While not all may be as prolific as Home Depot, the study shows that 82% tweeted in the "past week," and 68% posted an update on a Facebook Page. The motivation for individuals and consumers to take part in social media is not the same at all. **People engage in social media primarily to communicate,** whether that be with friends and family or with other like-minded individuals on any number of topics. They may also wish to sell (**Facebook Marketplace** is a growing part of the platform), to learn, or to play games. The June 2010 Nielsen study *What Americans Do Online* indicates that online games account for more than 10% of all time spent online. According to a recent Morgan Stanley study, games are bigger than any other app category—both for the social Web and for mobile devices.

### 1. Brand awareness/elevation

Brand awareness refers to the **elevation of your company's name, value, and capabilities** in order to place it at top of mind with a customer. Assuredly, building and maintaining brand awareness is a chief concern for any marketer, especially for the big consumer brands.

A great B-to-C example is the now famous "Old Spice Guy" campaign that took an "old," decidedly non-trendy brand of men's scented hygiene products into the social media mainstream. "The Man Your Man Could Smell Like," Isaiah Mustafa a.k.a. "Old Spice Guy," viewers saw on TV commercials early in 2010 later interacted with individual people through Twitter, YouTube, and Facebook, recording almost two hundred personalized videos with messages for those who commented on the social sites. **This amazingly "new" way of mixing new and old media became a major brand lifter.** Many

***Figure 2-3.*** *Old Spice used social media to raise their brand awareness as part of their "The Man Your Man Could Smell Like" campaign.*

were quick to call this a marketing stunt and condemn it to failure, but Nielsen reported sales increased 55% in the three months following the campaign's social kickoff and sales doubled in July 2010 alone, making Old Spice the number one body wash for men. While some point out that this was due more to coupons and discounts for the product, there is no doubt that in terms of brand awareness, the Old Spice Guy campaign was a winner.

If one of your current customers was considering a new marketing program, would your company be top of mind?

For a printer, building brand awareness means to capture your customer's attention so that when he or she thinks of a partner for a cross-media campaign, your company or sales rep is thought of first. If one of your current customers was considering a new marketing program, perhaps involving a personalized campaign and dimensional piece along with an email campaign, would your company be top of mind?

While social media platforms offer many eyeballs, and **brand-building is cited as a top reason to engage in social media,** some pundits believe that the sheer number of platforms are creating so much static that audiences are in an information overload state. In a September 2010 article in *Advertising Age,* Chris Perry, president of digital communications at PR firm Weber Shandwick, warns that "the rapid rise in use of blogs, branded social network sites and video syndication has created a far more fragmented and inconsistent online presence and voice for many brands now engaged in social media." This is something marketers as a whole will have to contend with as our social media engagement deepens.

### Grow the Network

"Growing the network" refers to **increasing the number of people who are in your sphere of influence** in your vertical market. In thinking of the traditional concept of the "sales funnel," growing the network would be increasing the number of people who could or would enter the funnel (and ultimately,

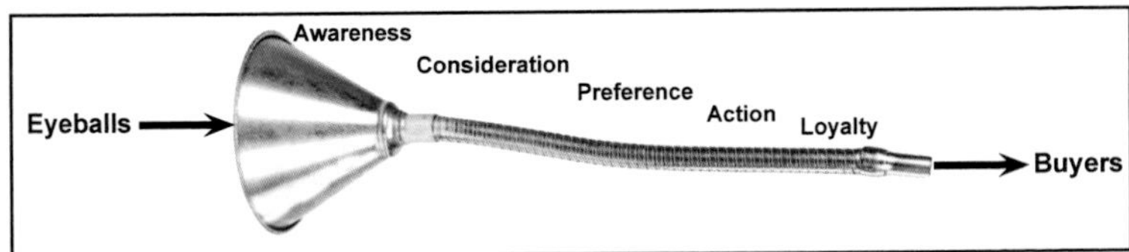


*Figure 2-4. Visualize the process of growing your network by thinking of the number of people who see your message, are pulled in, and then are narrowed down to becoming loyal customers.*

it is hoped, increasing those that emerge on the other side as customers).

By maintaining a presence and then engaging people where they congregate—which today is on the Internet, via whatever physical device we use to access it—we are certainly growing our network. **The most obvious and easily measurable place to see our personal and business contact network grow is through social sites,** especially LinkedIn but also Twitter, Facebook, or any other social gathering space. As a company becomes more adept at building social communities, the ability to expand its network also develops.

### Search Engine Optimization

**Search engines are the new Yellow Pages** and the current way to be "found" by prospective clients. Most people who are searching for a new vendor or supplier of a service will query keywords or phrases on Internet search engines such as **Google, Bing,** or **Yahoo.** A March 2010 Neilsen study comparing U.S. search rankings shows Google and Yahoo searches account for 79% of all searches, while a Yellow Pages search is at a mere 0.2%. In an effort to combat these kind of stats, the Yellow Pages Association initiated a study in 2009 and found that 65% of those queried reference Yellow Pages (print and Internet) first for a local search (compared to 58% citing a search engine).

Search engine optimization, or SEO, refers to undertaking actions and activities to secure a first-page listing when keywords related to the company are entered into the search engine. Tips and techniques for SEO will be discussed further in chapter three.

## 2. Nurture relationships

To increase the relationship aspect of a customer bond (and decrease the emphasis on "price-only" criteria for your interaction), you can **nurture the relationship through social media tools which amplify the avenues of contact** with your customer. So if you participate in a blog where you solve problems or suggest alternative actions, the customer sees you as an authority or a consultant for solutions to campaign issues. If you reveal a personal interest, such as biking, a customer might feel a connection with you if this is a mutual hobby, again increasing the value of the relationship.

**By participating in a blog where you solve problems or suggest alternative actions, the customer comes to see you as an authority or a consultant for solutions.**

Home Depot, when congratulating customers on a new home or other home-based activities via Twitter, is certainly developing its relationship with them. Pepsi's Refresh Project is literally nurturing people and communities around the world with its funding of life-improving projects. Is Pepsi top of mind to anyone in competition for one of its grants each month? Without a doubt, and the good will generated among grant beneficiaries will go on for years to come.

Small businesses can do this too: **printers solve problems for customers every day**—why not get the word out through how-to video clips, a blog, or an advice/chat area on your corporate website or portal?

## 3. Build brand loyalty

### Provide Value to Customers as a Thought Leader

There are a lot of possible answers to what provides value to customers—but at the foundation, it is your ability to give them what they need. If a company representative uses various social media tools to share thoughts that are positive and are seen to offer solutions to the customer's problems, pain points, or concerns, then the rep is offering value to the client. If the comments or recommendations are of a high quality and share advice, examples, and observations on trends, his or her role as a thought leader or a person of authority increases. All of these efforts will also help to grow the relationship with the ultimate goal of reaching the customer with more sales opportunities.

**Like it or not, your customers are talking about your company, your service, and your problem resolution on various social media tools already.**

Thought leadership can be as simple as providing educational information for your customers (think tips for file preparation or ideas for a PURL campaign). Large corporations are involved in the concept of "thought leadership marketing." Pepsi's "Refresh" program is an example of a thought leadership marketing initiative—replacing simple advertising and marketing efforts with a funding campaign that will provide money for social programs to help people and communities.

### Reputation Management

Like it or not, your customers are talking about your company, your service, and your problem resolution on various social media tools already.

Harris Interactive measures corporate America's "reputation quotient" based on an annual survey of 30,000 people. Google ranks #3 in the 2010 list, along with older product-based companies like Johnson & Johnson. The list shows how reputation can swing up and down based on public opinion, current events, or less easily defined metrics. Microsoft—that company which many seem to love to hate—actually ranked #7, ahead of Apple (#12) in what could in part be something of a "halo effect" based on Bill Gates's foundation work. Comcast, a company plagued with numerous reputation-damaging social media slams—including one damning video posted on YouTube which shows a service technician sleeping on the job—ranked at #50.

To monitor—and manage—your own company reputation, first you need to **find out where most of your customers have a presence** and then you need to keep an eye on those sources. Reputation management of your company can also be followed through alerts you receive any time your company name is mentioned on the Internet. You will also want to query various search engines with the names of prominent people in your company to be aware of comments or discussions related to them that may be on the Internet. Reviews by customers are also on the Internet and **you should know what is being said so you can quickly address any public relations issues** brought before these audiences.

In summary, by focusing on the goals of (1) building brand awareness, (2) nurturing customer relationships, either new or current, and (3) building brand loyalty, we can see that they lead to the primary goal of (4) driving sales.

## B-to-C—Reaching the Goals

Because so many businesses are using a multitude of social media tools, as a consumer you should be familiar with many of the business-to-consumer examples out there. Perhaps they will inspire you to develop your own business-to-business strategy, and you can also use these experiences to build your knowledge base when working with your customers' marketing efforts. Within one B-to-C sample you might recognize a print or service component that your company can provide.

### Mobile marketing and print products

*Deliver* magazine shared the experience of **zpizza International,** a chain with 86 stores nationwide, which planned to create an integrated campaign combining **direct mail, email, and mobile text** to promote its loyalty club and thereby increase the number of repeat customers.

**Goal:**

> zpizza wanted to have 1,000 users who would order pizza more than once a month and spend $50 or more at one or more of their locations. The focus of the campaign was to increase the number of members in their loyalty club and thus bump up the opportunity for repeat business.

**Campaign Tactics:**

> Two stages of mailings were sent three months apart to "consumers" who lived near each of their 86 locations.

This included 2,800 mailers for each store (240,000+) in the first round and 3,000 mailers for each store (258,000) in the second round.

Their mailers contained a scratch-off card that would expose a code the recipient could text to zpizza to collect a prize. Prizes included free items or coupons, as well as gift certificates, free pizza for a year, or a cash prize.

The mail component was considered critical to the success of the campaign since it was a tangible item that opened a dialogue with the prospective client.

The card element provided the "call to action" that motivated recipients to respond via text message. Their contact was rewarded by an immediate response from zpizza by text message directing respondents to check their email to see what they'd won. This email also took advantage of this contact to invite the respondent to join the loyalty club.

**Comments:**

One aspect zpizza thought was vital to the success of the campaign was that no purchase was required to take part and receive a prize. This emphasized that joining the club was a reward and an attempt to transform the relationship. The mail component also was considered critical to the success since it was a tangible item that opened a dialogue with the prospective client.

**Results:**

The mailing stirred the audience to action. The first mailer generated 500 text-message responses and the second 1,400 responses, both with a redemption rate of about 1.5%. The loyalty club sign-up increased by 20%, and the program was considered a success.

## B-to-B—Reaching the Goals

In chapter six, you'll find stories about print and marketing service providers who have undertaken social media marketing efforts. But for now, let's take a look outside the industry. Here are a few that stand out as excellent examples of setting clear goals for social media engagement and implementing those plans.

### Brand awareness & increasing sales

There are numerous examples of businesses that build brand awareness with social media, but **Gary Vaynerchuk** is one example worth reading about since he both built a brand and increased his sales through social methods. And, while Gary worked on building business brand awareness for his family wine business, he also created his personal business brand. He is an incredible example of going into a field with many, many other wine distributors—with big names and huge budgets—and he did it!

He built his brand and, with a very small budget and name, grew the family business from $4 million to $60 million in five years.

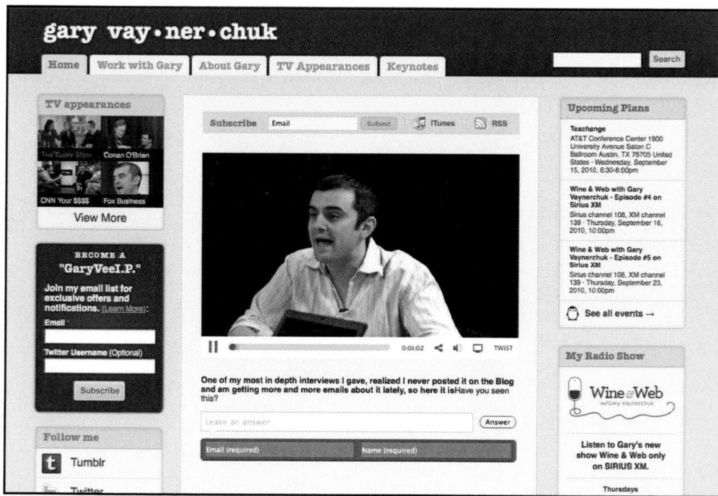


*Figure 2-5. Gary Vaynerchuk mixes traditional promotional vehicles such as television and print, but his renown can largely be attributed to his use of social media tools.*

His efforts gained notoriety by focusing on the Internet and leveraging the tools of Facebook and Twitter. Now 80,000 people view Gary's site daily. With appearances on numerous shows such as NBC's *Today Show* and CNBC's *Mad Money* and articles galore, Gary has become a unique example. It was a lot of hard work building his image as a trusted authority on wine, but he did just that. Check out his site at **garyvaynerchuk.com.**

**Goal:**

Increase the brand of his family-owned wine store and sell more wine.

**Tactics:**

Gary worked to build a persona as a wine expert using social media tools such as a blog, Twitter feeds, and YouTube, as well as webcasts on topics of wine, wine tasting, recommendations, etc.

He also did his homework and created a wine library, capitalizing on years of working in the business; in other words: he knows his "stuff," everything about the content—wine.

Next was the creation of an online sales capability through his one-stop shop on the Internet.

**Results:**

Sales increased from $4 to $60 million, and online sales grew 50%. New revenue streams were developed in public speaking, book writing (including a ten-book deal), and as expert wine consultant for Virgin America.

## Nurturing customer relationships

**MarketingSherpa** (www.marketingsherpa.com) is a research organization specializing in tracking and measuring marketing tactics. Its findings are made available to members of the organization and sometimes in reports made available through partners. The following are excerpts from the report *MarketingSherpa's Top 7 B2B Case Studies for 2010,* provided courtesy of Internet marketing software provider, Hubspot Inc.

**Goal:**

Create strong relationship with hard-to-find prospects.

**Tactics:**

With the plan to create a blog and join other online conversations, BreakingPoint set up a monitoring system to scan the Internet, the blogosphere, online forums, and communities to find relevant conversations in their industry and their audience before starting their own blog. Tools such as **Tweet Scan** and **Google Alerts** were used for industry terms, and **BoardTracker.com** was utilized to monitor various forums.

They used their own blog to break stories which generated links from other sites, and Twitter delivered shorter, more frequent updates to supplement the company blog. Again, a key terms search on Twitter helped them to find conversations, competitors' names, and industry research. **LinkedIn Groups** were created because targeted customers used LinkedIn, and this is where they were able to start conversations.

**BreakingPoint used Twitter to search their "key terms" to find conversations to participate in, study their competitors' activities, and research their industry.**

Other steps focused on increasing website traffic, such as increasing press release frequency to one per week, the use of a press release service, as well as social media sites. They promoted social media channels on the company website and in staff email signatures. Last, they measured social media accounts and traffic.

**Results:**

After six months, unique blog page views increased, and they gained numerous Twitter followers and members in their LinkedIn Groups. A 155% increase in unique Web visitors was reported, and so staff believed the goal was achieved.

## Building brand loyalty

MarketingSherpa also presented a case study on **IBM Cognos,** a company which was seeing what most cross-media providers, printers, and suppliers are observing in the marketplace: lengthening sales cycles; departure of key contacts through mergers, acquisitions, and staff reductions; reduced supplier lists; and mailing lists not generating sales leads.

**Goal:**

Increase response rates and reduce cost per lead by becoming a recognized thought leader, generate demand, and support the sales team.

**Tactics:**

IBM Cognos explored several methods to achieve their goals, including: revamping the website with more offers, releasing white papers, utilizing online demos, hosting events, and participating in online communities. They organized efforts around customer verticals, i.e., finance, health care, and retail.

Prospects filled out contact information for the offers, which led to growing their list, and a new lead-nurturing program was developed based on the new customer list. IBM Cognos was able to extend numerous touches to their list with additional relevant content and to create new offers based on prospect profiles.

They also conducted statistical analysis of their marketing interactions, and with more than 200,000 such interactions, the prioritization of additional tactics and investments began.

**Results:**

Some interesting findings from these activities were that online demos had the highest rate of opportunity creation, face-to-face events had the largest impact on close rate and size of the deal, and ten days was the cycle of the opportunities.

After implementing this plan, the company realized both new leads and reduced costs per lead. More than 11% of visitors to the website complete the registration form, a vast improvement over the 3% average industry capture rate. Of course the numerous touches played a large role, but it all began with the revamped and newly optimized content on the website.

## How Print Service Providers Are Using Social Media

In a review of industry social media surveys, there is no doubt that many printers are using various social media tools with a variety of results. Printing Industries of America asked a series of questions on how printers are using social media in the *Third Quarter* 2009 *Print Market Update.* We'll update this study for comparison over time and make the results available on the *Social Media Field Guide* website (www.printing.org/socialmediafieldguide).

The following comments were submitted in the third quarter of 2009 and will form a baseline for future comparisons. In the survey, printer categories are *All, Sales Leaders,* and *Sales Challenged.* From these categories we discovered the following.

### 1. Use of Social Media for Business

- 35% of All Printers (All)
- 38% of Sales Leaders (SL)
- 40% of Sales Challenged (SC)

**Comment:**

The figure of 40% seems to match with informal, anecdotal observations in seminars, webinars, and "water cooler" conversation. But usage is paralleling the increase in the general population; therefore, the number may be low. The differences between Challenged and Leaders is statistically similar given a margin of error.

### 2. Use of Social Media Tools

| | All% | SL% | SC% |
|---|---|---|---|
| Facebook | 64 | 72 | 61 |
| Twitter | 48 | 39 | 61 |
| Blogs | 28 | 22 | 33 |

**Comment:**

Next surveys will include LinkedIn since people widely consider that the most-used fourth social media tool.

### 3. How Printers Are Using the Tools

| | All% | SL% | SC% |
|---|---|---|---|
| Employee Communication | 6 | 11 | 6 |
| Communicate with Current Customers | 73 | 83 | 61 |
| Networking with Colleagues & Peers | 36 | 39 | 22 |
| Marketing | 72 | 67 | 78 |

**Comment:**

These numbers are more interesting because they begin to indicate how printers are using social media, and they can be used to form a basis to set expectations and plan for specific results.

While this particular survey indicates printers spend 9% of sales on selling expenses, including marketing and advertising, the most currently relied-upon tools are personal sales calls, Internet/Web pages, Yellow Pages, newspaper/magazine advertisements, and telemarketing respectively. Over the years Printing Industries will monitor the results to see if and when social media tools begin to show a ranking on advertising/marketing results for printing companies.

## Gauging Your Social Media Readiness

As an individual and as a company it is important that you determine your baseline of social media readiness. The book *Groundswell: Winning in a World Transformed by Social Technologies* uses terms and descriptions to help you peg your professional readiness as well as your company's readiness. A look at the following ladder graphic (Figure 2-6) with the descriptions of the terms can help you to find your own and your company's levels of usage, as well as to categorize your customers. The questions in the following social media inventory can be used with the ladder and terms comparison too.

The terms in the ladders have been used by various authors but are considered to comprise the following levels of users, starting at the bottom of the ladder:

- **Inactives**—use none of the activities of social media
- **Spectators**—read blogs, watch peer-generated videos, and listen to podcasts

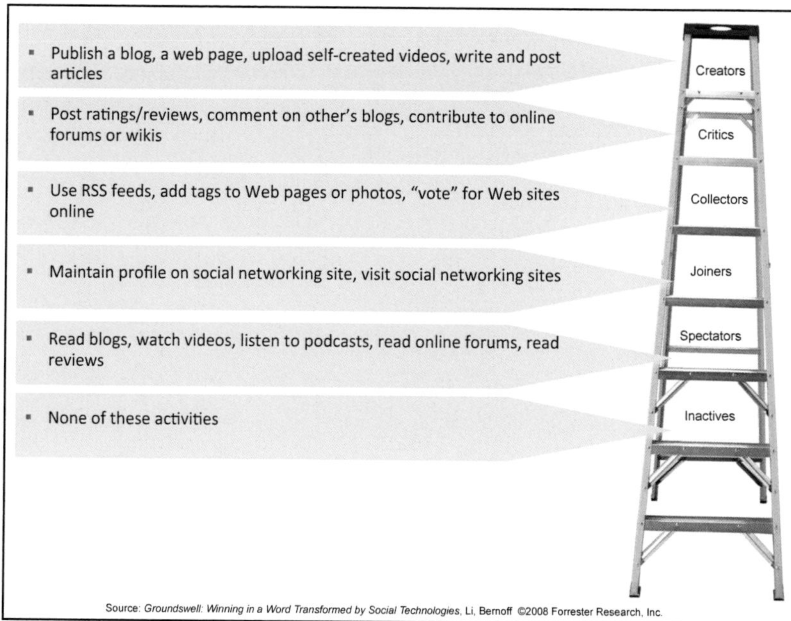

Publish a blog, a web page, upload self-created videos, write and post articles
Creators
Post ratings/reviews, comment on other's blogs, contribute to online forums or wikis
Critics
Use RSS feeds, add tags to Web pages or photos, "vote" for Web sites online
Collectors
Maintain profile on social networking site, visit social networking sites
Joiners
Read blogs, watch videos, listen to podcasts, read online forums, read reviews
Spectators
None of these activities
Inactives
Source: Groundswell: Winning in a Word Transformed by Social Technologies, Li, Bernoff ©2008 Forrester Research, Inc.


***Figure 2-6.*** *Forrester Research Social Technographics Ladder. Use these category descriptions to determine where you and your company fall in terms of social media familiarity.*

- **Joiners**—use social networking sites
- **Collectors**—use RSS feeds and tag Web pages
- **Critics**—post comments, ratings, and reviews
- **Creators**—publish Web pages, publish a blog, and upload video/pictures to sites

## Social media inventory

You can use or modify the following inventory developed for this field guide. First review major categories in the inventory. Use the categories listed, adjust or delete them, or add your own. Then take stock of where you are and where your company is in terms of social media engagement. Now do the same for your customers (individual contacts and the company itself) and maybe even for your competition.

After you complete the inventory for yourself, your company, and a few customers, you'll be in a better position to draw some conclusions.

## Questions to consider from the results of your social media inventory—A conversation starter

When you're reviewing these inventories, think about whether your company is ahead, behind, or equal to most of your customers in the use of various tools.

If your company is preparing an implementation plan, the comparison will guide you in regard to how soon and to what extent you should move toward involvement on a particular site.

- How does your personal inventory compare to the company inventory?
- Which staff members can be on the advance team in social media due to their current experience with social media tools?
- If several staff people are using a certain social media site, that may be a primary starting point for the company. Keep in mind the big four: Facebook, Twitter, LinkedIn, and blogs (generic name used here since there are so many branded sites, e.g., WordPress).

## Social Media

**Directions:** Check each social media tool you and your customer use. You can report on up to 20 customers at a time. Enter their name in the cells highlighted in yellow and they will appear in the graphics on the following pages.

| Media Tool | Frequency, Extent of Use | Company Profile | Customer Profile: Customer 1 | Customer 2 | Customer 3 | Customer 4 | Customer 5 | Customer 6 |
|---|---|---|---|---|---|---|---|---|
| 1. Email | | | | | | | | |
| | *1 to 1 communication* | ☐ | ☐ | ☐ | ☐ | ☐ | ☐ | ☐ |
| | *Groups & Lists servs* | ☐ | ☐ | ☐ | ☐ | ☐ | ☐ | ☐ |
| | *Personalized and Email Campaigns* | ☐ | ☐ | ☐ | ☐ | ☐ | ☐ | ☐ |
| | *Use for customer campaigns* | ☐ | ☐ | ☐ | ☐ | ☐ | ☐ | ☐ |
| 2. LinkedIn | | | | | | | | |
| | *Company/group accoount* | ☐ | ☐ | ☐ | ☐ | ☐ | ☐ | ☐ |
| | *Groups on site* | ☐ | ☐ | ☐ | ☐ | ☐ | ☐ | ☐ |
| | *500+ participants* | ☐ | ☐ | ☐ | ☐ | ☐ | ☐ | ☐ |
| | *Discussions 3 x per week* | ☐ | ☐ | ☐ | ☐ | ☐ | ☐ | ☐ |
| | *Upgrade to business plan* | ☐ | ☐ | ☐ | ☐ | ☐ | ☐ | ☐ |
| 3. FaceBook Page | | | | | | | | |
| | *Company site* | ☐ | ☐ | ☐ | ☐ | ☐ | ☐ | ☐ |
| | *Pictures, Links, Updates* | ☐ | ☐ | ☐ | ☐ | ☐ | ☐ | ☐ |
| | *Fan base 500+* | ☐ | ☐ | ☐ | ☐ | ☐ | ☐ | ☐ |
| | *Updates/discussions 3x per week* | ☐ | ☐ | ☐ | ☐ | ☐ | ☐ | ☐ |
| 4. Twitter | | | | | | | | |
| | *Company account* | ☐ | ☐ | ☐ | ☐ | ☐ | ☐ | ☐ |
| | *Monitor and Post* | ☐ | ☐ | ☐ | ☐ | ☐ | ☐ | ☐ |
| | *Followers 500+* | ☐ | ☐ | ☐ | ☐ | ☐ | ☐ | ☐ |
| | *Updates/tweets 3 x per week* | ☐ | ☐ | ☐ | ☐ | ☐ | ☐ | ☐ |
| 5. Instant Messaging | | | | | | | | |
| | *SMS/phone text* | ☐ | ☐ | ☐ | ☐ | ☐ | ☐ | ☐ |
| | *Use VOIP* | ☐ | ☐ | ☐ | ☐ | ☐ | ☐ | ☐ |
| | *Access social media via PDA* | ☐ | ☐ | ☐ | ☐ | ☐ | ☐ | ☐ |
| | *Use SMS in customer campaings* | ☐ | ☐ | ☐ | ☐ | ☐ | ☐ | ☐ |
| 6. YouTube/Podcasts/Videos | | | | | | | | |
| | *Monitor only related sites* | ☐ | ☐ | ☐ | ☐ | ☐ | ☐ | ☐ |
| | *Post & comment 1-5 x per yr.* | ☐ | ☐ | ☐ | ☐ | ☐ | ☐ | ☐ |
| | *Regular post, comment, 6+ per year* | ☐ | ☐ | ☐ | ☐ | ☐ | ☐ | ☐ |
| | *Post on company and video share sites* | ☐ | ☐ | ☐ | ☐ | ☐ | ☐ | ☐ |
| 7. Build & Manage Online Surveys | | | | | | | | |
| | *use less than ten times per year* | ☐ | ☐ | ☐ | ☐ | ☐ | ☐ | ☐ |
| | *use weekly* | ☐ | ☐ | ☐ | ☐ | ☐ | ☐ | ☐ |
| | *use 52+ per year* | ☐ | ☐ | ☐ | ☐ | ☐ | ☐ | ☐ |
| 8. Blogs | | | | | | | | |
| | Read & monitor others, related | ☐ | ☐ | ☐ | ☐ | ☐ | ☐ | ☐ |
| | Comment , participate | ☐ | ☐ | ☐ | ☐ | ☐ | ☐ | ☐ |
| | Originate blog, active | ☐ | ☐ | ☐ | ☐ | ☐ | ☐ | ☐ |
| | Originate multiple blogs | ☐ | ☐ | ☐ | ☐ | ☐ | ☐ | ☐ |
| 9. Web-Based Meetings | | | | | | | | |
| | *Participate* | ☐ | ☐ | ☐ | ☐ | ☐ | ☐ | ☐ |
| | *Develop & manage for customers* | ☐ | ☐ | ☐ | ☐ | ☐ | ☐ | ☐ |
| | *Develop & participate for company* | ☐ | ☐ | ☐ | ☐ | ☐ | ☐ | ☐ |
| | *Include video conferencing* | ☐ | ☐ | ☐ | ☐ | ☐ | ☐ | ☐ |
| 10. Company Website | | | | | | | | |
| | *Offer social media links* | ☐ | ☐ | ☐ | ☐ | ☐ | ☐ | ☐ |
| | *Video training, downloadable training/client* | ☐ | ☐ | ☐ | ☐ | ☐ | ☐ | ☐ |
| | *Online customer service* | ☐ | ☐ | ☐ | ☐ | ☐ | ☐ | ☐ |
| | *Customer Dashboard* | ☐ | ☐ | ☐ | ☐ | ☐ | ☐ | ☐ |
| | Total | | | | | | | |

*Directions: Check each social media tool you and your customer use. You can report on up to 20 customers at a time. (Visit www.printing.org/socialmediafieldguide for the full-page form.)*

- How does the company social media inventory compare to key customers' inventory? The comparison may help direct the company's future involvement.

  For example: If you find that numerous customers are active on a particular site, that is a pointer to where your company should monitor and participate as well.

- What is the social media participation of your primary vertical? Check out Appendix A at the back of the book, titled "Social Media and Five Vertical Investigations," where we have shared research on a few vertical markets.

### Quality vs. quantity of fans, blog posts, etc.

A measurement of success for a social media tool use is frequently indicators that change, i.e., page views, number of fans, number of posts, number of uploads of pictures, etc. However, the real emphasis should be the *quality* of the relationship within the social media tools.

As an example, if your company has 3,000 fans, what level of knowledge do you have with these fans? Does the fan base get bigger but the relationship is distant? Depending on what you are promoting or attempting to achieve, the quality of the relationship may be the better indicator of the success and the ROI of your time.

## Summary of Thoughts before We Continue on This Path

In this chapter, we talked about the many things that a well-thought-out social media engagement plan can do for an organization. Among them:

- ✓ Increase brand awareness/elevation
- ✓ Help grow your network/sphere of influence
- ✓ Nurture relationships
- ✓ Provide value to your customers
- ✓ Lead you to become a thought leader
- ✓ Monitor what's said about you and your company

- ✓ SEO—drive people to your business site
- ✓ Increase sales—the holy grail of all social media marketing

If you haven't done so already, take the social media inventory for yourself, your company, and maybe a customer contact or two. Check out how verticals are using social media, and visit a few sites to get a feel for how the conversation is flowing there.

# 3 Starting the Trek

It's rare to find anyone today who has not created a profile in at least one of the most common social networking platforms. Yes, there are individuals with professions that require a great deal of discretion—attorneys, law enforcement, physicians, or school teachers—who don't take part in social media in order to avoid any unpleasant personal revelations that might have a negative effect on their jobs. But the average professional person is certainly versed in how to join a social network like LinkedIn or Facebook.

**Do you know what's being said about your industry, your customers, your products, your company, or even about you personally? Do you really know how your brand is perceived?**

When your goal is to make social media part of your company's business development or marketing efforts, however, **creating a profile on specific social platforms is not the first step.** It's not even the second. In fact, we put the process of actually creating your company's social presence *at step number seven* in what we've defined as a ten-step process for a successful launch of your business's social media engagement. These are some big steps, so get your hiking boots on and follow us!

## Ten Steps to Starting Your Business's Social Media Plan

### Step 1: Stop, look, and listen

One generally doesn't jump into deep water without knowing how to swim. Sure, there are some who espouse the "sink or swim" mentality, but with the social media pool brimming with so many people splashing around, the most likely outcome of this approach is floundering and maybe even sinking out of sight. **Before you jump into the social stream, it's really important to listen first.** Do you know what's being said about your industry, your customers, your products, your company, or even about you personally? Do you really know how your brand is perceived?

We've established that one of the key reasons to be involved in social media is to promote your brand. **We all have a personal brand in additional to our business brand. It's critical to know where both stand and to protect them.** We've all heard stories about people who have committed virtual hari-kari by showing just a bit too much of their private lives through their personal social media interaction—usually by being tagged in a posted photo doing something, let's say, less than professional (or even illegal).

But even if you're very careful to never shoot yourself in the virtual foot, it doesn't mean that there isn't someone else out there—a competitor or disgruntled ex-anything—gunning for

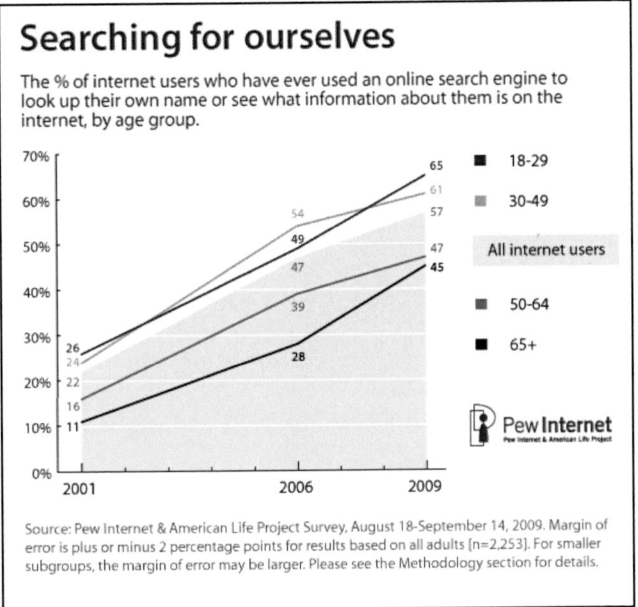


***Figure 3-1.*** *More and more people are using search engines to find out what information is tied to their names.*

you. And you could become the victim of a password breach or phishing scheme that can post reputation-damaging messages under your name. You need to be aware if this should happen in order to address it as quickly as possible.

Have you "Googled" yourself? Between 2% and 19% do so regularly or at least once in awhile. It's not a bad idea to keep an eye on what information is readily available about you and your company.

**Keeping your brand squeaky clean requires some work, but there are many tools to help you** monitor your personal brand and your company or product's brand. Start using them, beginning with the very simplest and most obvious.

**Google Search**

According to a Pew Internet study on reputation management (released in May 2010) 57% of adult Internet users now use search engines to find information about themselves (Figure 3-1). But while the majority has "Googled" themselves, only 2% say they use a search engine to look up information about themselves on a regular basis, and 19% say they do so only every once in awhile.

**So begin your online reputation management effort by doing a search for your company name via Google and perhaps another search engine or two.** Do a search for your own name too. To better see what might be said about you in a professional capacity, search for your name along with your company name (a search for *Julie Shaffer, Printing Industries of America,* for instance, gives a far better picture of what's said about Julie professionally than just a name search). You'll want to do this for your key staff as well to see if you may have some professional reputation issues among them. And you should do the same for your competition and your customers in order to potentially find out what they have, and what they want, respectively.

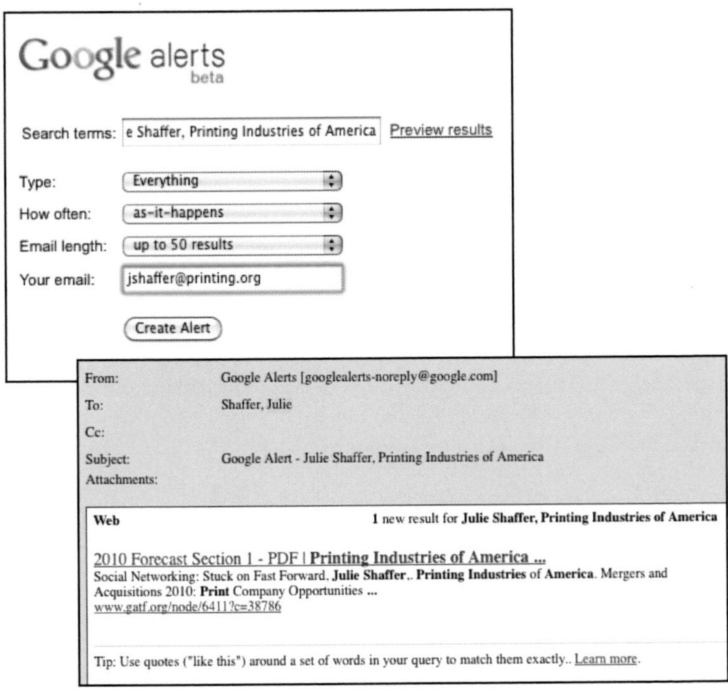


***Figure 3-2.*** *A setup for a Google Alert, and the resulting email notification.*



### Online Reputation Monitoring Services

Google offers a terrific, free way to monitor all of the previously mentioned areas through **Google Alerts,** a service that's still tagged "beta" even though it's been around for several years. Google Alerts are simply emails that will be sent to you when Google detects new results for the search terms you establish. You can set up as many as you wish, so you might, for example, **set up a Google Alert for your company name, your name, your competition or news relevant to the industry,** a key term, or any of your customers. You can choose how often you wish to get these emails, and if you have a Google account (it's a good idea to have a Google Gmail account that isn't tied to a corporate email server to use as your "social media" email address—a Google account lets you log in to and manage other Google services like Reader, iGoogle, AdWords, and Web History) you can have the Alerts come to you in the form of an RSS feed which you can monitor via **Google Reader.** You can also have the list of Alerts exported in the form of a simple CSV (comma separated value) file in order to keep track of them in a spreadsheet or customer relationship management (CRM) system.

**RSS feeds** are indeed a great way to monitor topics and see what's new all in one place. RSS (**Really Simple Syndication** or **Rich Site Summary**) is a Web publishing technology that allows users to automatically receive new digital content—such as blog entries, news headlines, audio, and video—from a provider. **RSS feed readers** can be application- or browser-based, and many offer expanded features beyond just searching for keywords, like statistics-based filters and the ability to post to your own blog from the reader. Of the dozens of RSS feed readers on the market, many are free or offer a free version with a reduced feature set.

If you are interested in an application-based reader, one that you can monitor from your desktop instead of through a browser, remember some are Windows- and some are Mac-oriented. **NewzCrawler,** for example, is a Windows-only reader while **NetNewsWire** works with Macs, iPads, and iPhones.

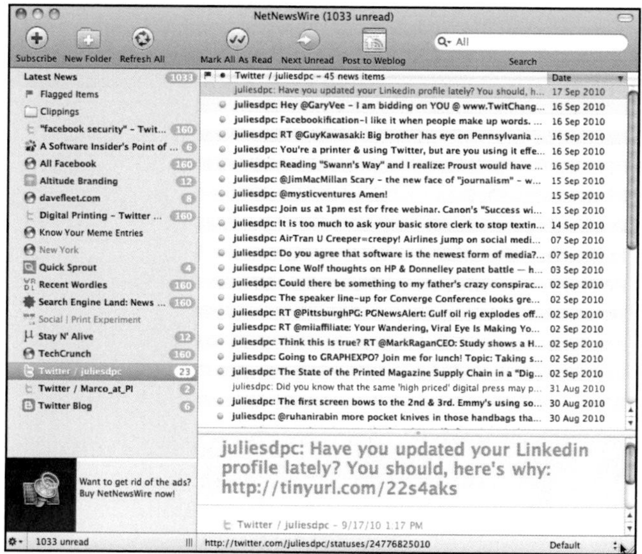


*Figure 3-3.* *Monitoring mentions via NetNewsWire.*

**Google Reader** is a free and simple browser-based way to keep track of RSS feeds, and it's available to anyone with a Google account. You can choose to display an RSS feed in Google Reader or via **iGoogle.** Another nice free browser-based dashboard is **Netvibes** (www.netvibes.com/en) that lets you create an instant dashboard on any topic or customize a dashboard of your own. **Alltop.com** is a fairly new RSS aggregator site, with preset feeds for hundreds of topics (try *Printing*) and the ability to choose from the many feeds Alltop monitors to build our own. You can even suggest that the people at Alltop include your RSS feed on the site, but the Alltop site managers select which feeds they wish to include on a very subjective basis.

> There are services that not only keep you apprised as to what's being said about you in the social stream, but also offer measurement of the effectiveness of your social media efforts.

On the personal brand management front, there is **Naymz** (www.naymz.com), a personal brand builder that helps individuals build and manage a common profile to use across many different social media sites. Along the same lines is **Yasni** (www.yasni.com). Both of these services can be thought of in the spirit of LinkedIn, although they offer a way to monitor one's reputation across multiple social networks.

There are well over one hundred online reputation monitoring solutions on the market, with varying levels of service and cost. Some of the services are free or very low-cost, including **Yotify** (www.yotify.com), a tool that sends out what the service calls "scouts" to track for search items. Yotify offers preset search options for some specific sites, like **Craigslist** and **YouTube,** but allows users to search for any keyword. It's social, offering the option to create a profile on the site and encouraging users to invite friends to help find whatever is being tracked. **Social Mention** (www.socialmention.com) is a social media search aggregator that monitors more than one hundred social media platforms and generates topical information into a single stream.

(It was while monitoring "hot topics" here that Julie found out one of her favorite graphic novel writers, Harvey Pekar, passed away.)

Most of the "for-pay" monitoring solutions offer a free version to make trying the service more digestible for new users, with more sophisticated options available at different price points. **Trackur** (www.trackur.com), for example, offers a service similar to Google Alerts for free, but provides far more sophisticated dashboard-based monitoring, with costs ranging up to $377 per month. **Radian6** (www.radian6.com) offers detailed social monitoring services, delivering results to the dashboard in real time. The cost of this service starts at $500 per month per topic profile. Using a service like this can point out who is the most influential voice on a topic or within a vertical. The service is also a full-fledged aggregator, so users can schedule posts.

**Your name (company or personal) is critical to "owning" your brand—do you have Facebook or Twitter handles that match your real name? If not, there are ways to check availability or register a name even if you haven't started building your sites.**

Radian6 is one of a class of **services that not only help you listen to what's been said about you in the social stream but also offer measurement of the effectiveness of your social media efforts.** (Spoiler alert! That's number 10 in this list!) Radian6, for example, provides feedback on how a company's social interaction impacts measurable criteria, like inbound links and positive comments. A few other online reputation management tools include **Giga Alert** (www.gigaalert.com), **whos.amung.us** (http://whos.amung.us), and **Purewire Trust** (www.purewiretrust.org).

It's critical to "own" your brand, and a big part of that brand is your name and your company name. This is something we all had to learn when we build our first websites almost twenty years ago. There were (and still are) companies that snatch up and register domain names, forcing you to deal with them and buy the right to the one you want (or lurk on **Network Solutions** and hope they forget to renew so you can pounce on your name of choice should it become available). Well, when it comes to social networks, the same can be true. If you got into the game early enough, you had the option to get a "vanity" URL on Facebook or Twitter that matched your real (or company) name. Many common names have already been taken at this point, however. There are ways to check or register the name you want, even if you haven't gotten started building your social media sites (remember, that's not until step seven!). **Namechk** (http://namechk.com) lets you check to see if your vanity URL or username is still available across dozens of popular social media sites. Do the same at **Knowem.com** and use the service to reserve your desired social media brand names—for a fee. (The company charges $99 for 150 sites, up to $599 for 300.)

**Social "Security"**

Signing up for a profile on nearly any social media platform requires you to indicate that you agree to the "terms of use" of that product. This is pretty much the same as when you install software on your personal computer. The thing is that few people actually read these terms of service for true installable software, much less for creating a profile on a social networking site. They simply sign and start using the software, and, as a result, many may be operating in breach of their agreement.

Take Facebook, for example. If you want to see the Facebook "Statement of Rights and Responsibilities" all you have to do is click on the tiny, tiny link "Terms" down in the bottom right of corner on the Facebook site. Here, you'll find it expressly stated that **having more than one personal profile on Facebook is strictly against the rules.** "Having two identities for yourself is an example of a *lack of integrity,*" says Facebook founder Mark Zuckerberg in the book *The Facebook Effect.* So people who try to segment their private and professional identities by maintaining a personal and work-oriented profile is *verboten* (we would certainly not go so far as to agree with Mr. Zuckerberg's assessment that doing so reflects on one's integrity, however!). Most people are merely protecting their own privacy, a notion that has become increasingly alien in the Facebook universe.

**Privacy and security are very big issues in the social media realm,** and schemes to part unsuspecting users from their passwords so hackers can access and use individual sites for spamming or malicious purposes has become an ever-bigger problem for everyone. While it's a bigger problem for bigger brands, **logo highjacking (brandjacking), cybersquatting,**

**email scams, trademark abuse,** and **patent infringement** are all nasty forms of brand corruption—and another reason why it's critical for us to listen up and monitor what's being said and done about us, and on our behalf, in the online world.

**If knowledge is power, you'll enhance yours just by doing a little (maybe a lot) of listening and staying attuned to what's being said about you, your company, your clients—and your competition.**

Oil company **BP** has had its share of woes throughout 2010 (in the understatement of the year), and while the brand is tarnished through the company's own doing, social media brandjackers haven't helped. In May 2010, not long after the Gulf oil spill crisis, someone set up a Twitter account as **@BPGlobalPR** and started posting comments that were clear parody, as if they'd come from BP's PR group. Posts on the site include some outrageous comments such as: *We've eliminated the huge turtle surplus in the gulf. Next on our list: dolphins, whales, and reporters http://ow.ly/26x6u.*

Twitter's terms of use specifically allow Twitter users to create parody, commentary, or fan accounts, so anyone is open to being parodied on the site. While Twitter offers guidelines for parody accounts that warn "the profile name should not list the exact name of the subject without some other distinguishing word, such as 'not' 'fake,' or 'fan,'" Twitter won't generally do anything to prevent a parody site unless someone files a complaint via a "ticket request" on the site. We'd imagine a letter from a major law firm might get someone's attention too.

So once again, **monitoring to protect your brand is critical.** For Twitter, this is as simple as checking for a phrase or your company name through **search.twitter.com** or through any of the many, many monitoring applications, including Julie's preferred desktop application **TweetDeck** (tweetdeck.com), online monitor **TweetBeep** (http://tweetbeep.com,) or **Monitter** (http://monitter.com/) to name just a very few.

While big companies with problems the entire world knows about are more likely to be besieged by this kind of brandjacking activity, no one is immune in our social media world. The

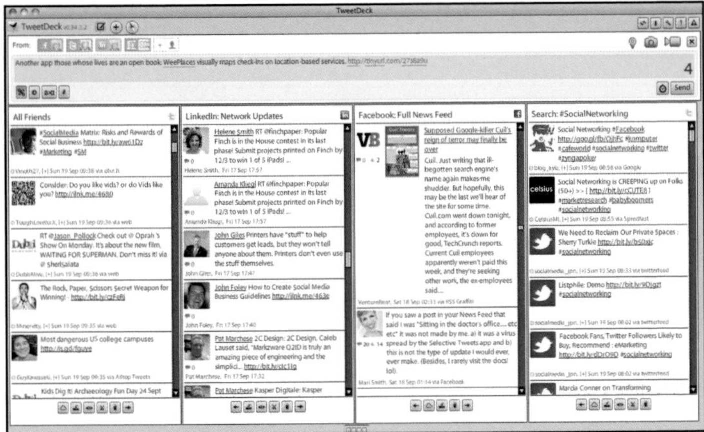

**Figure 3-4.** *TweetDeck allows you to view multiple account feeds at once.*

CMO Council's 2009 report *Protection from Brand Infection* (executive overview available at no cost at **www.cmocouncil.org**) explores how marketing executives for global brands are dealing with online reputations risks. The study identifies some of the top tactics brandjackers use including **"typosquatting"** (using a misspelled company name to siphon the poor spellers from the legitimate site), **search engine marketing abuse** (when a brand is used as a keyword for some other site or placed throughout competing sites to fool SEO engines into giving that site a higher ranking), **pay-per-click sites, phishing, malware,** and good old-fashioned **spamming.**

We can't repeat it enough, when it comes to brand reputation and protecting yours, stop, look around, and listen!

Remember, you can use all of these approaches to monitor what your current clients, the clients you want to go after, and your competition are up to and talking about. If knowledge is power, you'll enhance yours just by doing a little (maybe a lot) of listening.

### Step 2: Get educated

There are so many how-to resources for social media engagement and marketing it can be overwhelming to filter through all the junk (like "How to get 12,000 Twitter followers overnight!") or even to read all of the commentary from reliable sources. One of the reasons we've written this book and built the corresponding website (www.printing.org/socialmediafieldguide) is to help you sift through all of the material out there and come up with some gems you'll be able to use in your own social media trek.

Here are some of the best online resources, people and blogs, groups/forums, events, and research reports and books we've found that can help anyone interested in continued learning on the topic of social media engagement and social media marketing.

**Research Organizations and Websites**

- **Social Media Examiner (www.socialmedia examiner.com)**—This "free online magazine" was ranked as one of the world's top one hundred business blogs within months of its October 2009 launch.
- **Mashable (www.mashable.com)**—An "online guide to social media" and one of the top ten blogs in the world, Mashable features breaking news on Web-centric happenings, products reviews, detailed how-to articles, marketing tips, and viral videos.
- **The Pew Research Center's Pew Internet & American Life Project (www.pewinternet.org)**—The Pew Internet & American Life Project produces some of the best demographic information on American citizens' online activities.
- **All Facebook (www.allfacebook.com)**—All Facebook is "the unofficial Facebook resource." It's a website that acts as a clearinghouse for any news or information about Facebook.
- **Experian Hitwise (www.hitwise.com)**—Hitwise developed proprietary software that Internet service providers (ISPs) use to analyze website logs on their network.
- **TechCrunch (www.techcrunch.com)**—TechCruch is a network of tech-focused sites including **Crunchbase** (www.crunchbase.com), a free database of technology companies, people, and investors.

- **Search Engine Land (http://searchengineland.com)**—Search Engine Land is a news and information site covering search engine marketing, searching issues, and the search engine industry.

**Authority Measurement**

Forrester research shows that 500 billion impressions on products and services are made by people on their peers each year.

In chapter two, we talked about the notion of peer influence and reviewed Forrester's Social Technographics Profile. Forrester analysts have further developed the concept of the Online Peer Influence Pyramid that builds upon three types of online influencers: **Social Broadcasters, Mass Influencers,** and **Potential Influencers** (see the infographic for more detail on how each of these differ). Forrester analysts report that the Mass Influencer group is comprised of just 16% of the U.S. online population, but make up about 80% of the influence impressions and posts about products and services in social channels. (Interesting how the old 80/20 rule seems to apply everywhere!) Forrester claims there are 500 billion impressions about products and services a year, made by people on their peers. Now **there is a huge pool of data upon which conclusions can be drawn about the online influence of a person, product, service, or company.**

A growing number of authority measurement services have come to market to help users analyze just how much authority influence any particular persona has at a given time. They each use their own metrics to come up with results, so each may show a different level of influence for any particular persona. Still they are a great way to discover who or what "matters" in the social media space. Here are two:

- **Klout (http://klout.com)** reviews the level of influence of any Twitter username, based on analysis of twenty-five variables, including things like following/follower ratio,

***Figure 3-5.*** *Guy Kawasaki, a well-known blogger, shows an extremely high rating on Klout.com.*

number of retweets, and how many of your follows are reciprocated. Be warned: if you're just getting started with Twitter, you have to be ready to see that you have a low influence on Twitter. Fear not—you're on the road to greater influence right now, if you want it! Other Twitter-centric measurement services include **Twitalyzer** and **Twitter Grader.**

- **PeerIndex (www.peerindex.net)** joined the peer influence measurement space when the website was unveiled in late July 2010. PeerIndex's algorithms mine data from Twitter, Facebook, LinkedIn, and blogs to rate people on three main criteria: their authority, activity, and audience. PeerIndex has a premium version, which can be used by bigger brands, but anyone can enter their own name or company to see where they stand in this service's ranking. On launch, it was heavily skewed toward IT and tech influencers, and especially focused on Twitter activity.

## Blogs Featuring Social Media Experts

Naturally, most of the professionals/consultants who have become experts in social media marketing use social media to further their own brand recognition and to teach. Following their blogs and social pages is a good way to keep a finger on the pulse of what others in the field are doing. Here are just a few (you'll find detail on each of these in the Appendix B.)

- **Chris Brogan (www.chrisbrogan.com)**—President of New Marketing Labs; Co-author of *Trust Agents*
- **Mari Smith (www.marismith.com)**—Social Media Consultant, Speaker, and Trainer; Relationship Marketing Specialist
- **Chris Garrett (www.chrisg.com)**—Blogging and Internet Marketing Consultant; *The Business of Blogging and New Media*
- **Scott Monty (www.scottmonty.com)**—Blogger and social guru for Ford Motor Co.; *The Social Media Marketing Blog*
- **Technorati (www.technorati.com)**—The "search engine for blogs"

### Social Media Groups & Forums

A forum is a place for online discussion on a specific topic. While that sounds a lot like a social media site, forums predate social networking, at least in the way we think about it today. **Discussion forums** are frequently centered on products (often high tech or software), and many have a technical support focus. Discussion forums are typically moderated by a host and include rules of engagement for participants, including reminders to keep discussion free of insults and on topic (contrast that to the often incendiary anonymous comments posted at online news or blog sites today). Social media-oriented discussions tend to take place on Facebook Pages (Social Media Marketing Network), topical blogs, or within social media platforms, such as LinkedIn Groups, mentioned below.

- **LinkedIn Groups**—We'll talk more extensively about some LinkedIn best practices in chapters four and five, but we wanted to mention here that LinkedIn Groups are a great way to quickly gain insight into the minds of many people on specific topics, such as social media marketing. Among the groups you should consider joining, there is one, **Social Media Marketing,** that boasts almost 85,000 members. **ThoseinMedia,** a group for, yes, media professionals, has more than 73,000 members. Then there is the group **Marketing Communications,** which has 29,000 members. LinkedIn Groups are a fantastic way to keep up with conversations on relevant topics, and, if you've been shy to start taking part in online discussion, this is a good place to stick a toe in the group discussion waters.

**LinkedIn Groups are a great way to quickly gain insight into the minds of many people on specific topics—and to keep up with conversations on relevant topics.**

- **Sphinn (http://sphinn.com/)**—Sphinn is a curated site, described as an "Internet News & Discussion Forum," with a decidedly marketing-centric spin (no pun intended). It offers stories posted by the site's editors on topics such as analytics, SEO, SEM, social media, and vertical search. Registered users can post news stories as well. There is a Comment tab, where visitors can see all the comments on each topic in one place, with links back to the original story. Any registered user can start a discussion, comment on existing stories or discussions, or submit a news story. The idea is that marketers can put their own "spin" on news stories or topics of interest to the community. All users are part of a **searchable directory,** a good way to build contacts in the community. The site editors post a **"discussion of the week"** for all members to take part in if they wish. Users can keep up to date with Sphinn goings on via an RSS feed or the Sphinn newsletter.

### Books

Since social media is one of the hottest topics of the day, there are many books on the topic—so many that it can be difficult to read them all. We could only recommend those that we've read ourselves, but someone recently posted a question on the Social Media Marketing LinkedIn Group asking: "What is your favorite book on the subject of Social Media Marketing?" The question got more than four hundred responses, and we found that every book on our short list was mentioned more than once.

You'll find a longer list of the books recommended by the members of the Social Media Marketing LinkedIn Group in Appendix B.

- *The New Rules of Marketing and PR: How to Use News Releases, Blogs, Podcasting, Viral Marketing & Online Media to Reach Buyers Directly* 2nd Edition, by David Meerman Scott
- *Groundswell: Winning in a World Transformed by Social Technologies,* by Charlene Li and Josh Bernoff
- *The Long Tail: Why the Future of Business Is Selling Less of More,* by Chris Anderson
- *The Social Media Field Guide,* by Julie Shaffer and Mary Garnett (OK, we appended the list to add this one, we admit it.)

### Step 3: Know your audience

- Do you know who your target audience is? Who your current clients are? Who you would like to have as a client?
- Do you specialize in a particular vertical market?
- Do you offer a specific printed product (books, financial reports, postcards, business cards, packaging, labels, envelopes, etc.)?
- Do you work within a particular city or region and wish to become a voice in the area?
- Do you have a personal interest or hobby and wish to connect with like-minded people?

Your audience can be the customers you have now, a vertical you serve, a group that you want to serve, or even your peers in the printing or marketing industries. **Before you can start your conversation with an audience, you really have to determine who that audience is** (or at least start with a specific group and evolve into a relationship with others over time).

We talked about the Forrester Research Social Technographics Ladder in chapter two, and it bears reviewing from the perspective of your audience. As you may recall, the user "rungs" of this ladder identify how people use social media from top to bottom; these include **Creators, Critics, Collectors, Joiners, Speculators,** and **Inactives.**

Since research shows younger men in the U.S. are more likely to upload content to a video site, you'll want to note that this might not be the best vehicle to use to reach an older demographic.

There are demographics associated with these steps on the ladder, accessible through the online profile tool posted on Forrester's Groundswell website, http://www.forrester.com/Groundswell/profile_tool.html. It's a simple tool with which you can view how people use social media based on age, gender, and location. A look at Figure 3-6 shows that younger men in the U.S. are far more likely to upload content to a video site, for example, than older men. If your audience is an older demographic, you'll want to tailor your message and media to that audience.

In *The New Rules of Marketing and PR,* author David Meerman Scott stresses the importance of the **"buyer persona"** when it comes to Web marketing. A buyer persona is a segment of people within a particular target market who share common demographics and interests. Scott says, "an effective web marketing plan requires an understanding of the ways your buyers speak and the real words and phrases they use. This is important not only for building a positive online relationship with your buyers, but also for planning effective search engine marketing strategies."

He cited his work with Shareholder.com to create a Web strategy to reach buyers of that organization's new Whistleblower Hotline product to help companies comply with Rule 301 of the Sarbanes-Oxley legislation (an Act which deals with overseeing financial reporting in corporations, Rule 301 covers the handling of complaints or whistleblowers—something print service

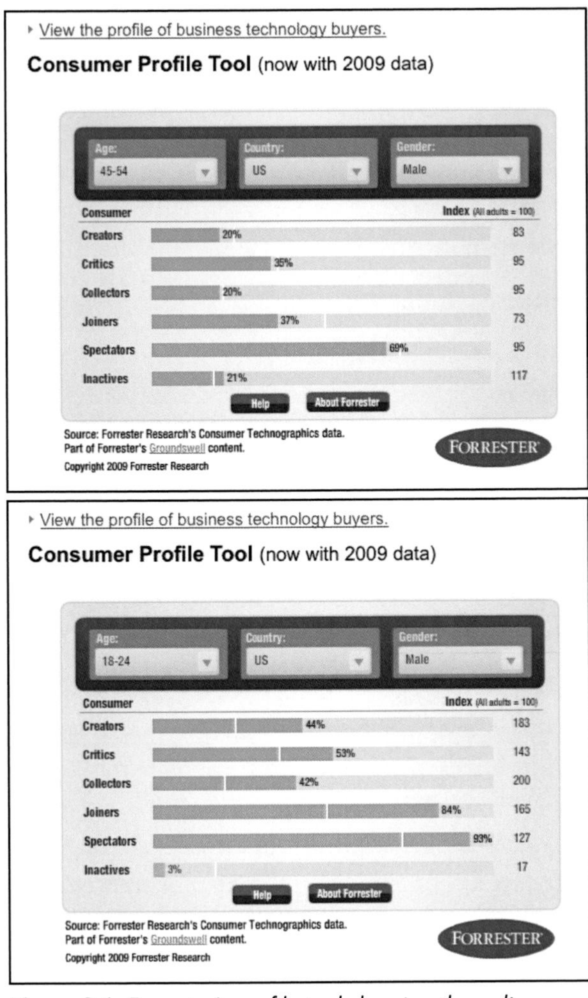


***Figure 3-6.** Forrester's profile tool showing the online activities of technology buyers in various demographics.*

providers, or PSPs, serving that market have to understand as well). From his research on the topic, he found key phrases that would resonate with that audience, such as "SEC mandates" and "complete audit trail." Loading the Shareholder.com website with these key phrases increased its search engine ranking, making it number one for searches on the phrase "whistleblower hotline," and made a new product launch a significant success.

You too will want to **uncover the language that resonates with your audience,** not only later, when you begin your social media presence, but also in the audience discovery phase. If you want to reach out to a particular vertical market segment, a great place to get to know what's important and topical to the people who are entrenched in that space is through the niche social media sites that serve that market. In Appendix A, you'll find a detailed examination of the social networking and industry association sites for five of the top vertical markets that are significant print consumers. But let's look at an example of what we're talking about. Here is a look at some of the organizational websites and social media sites that focus on the restaurant industry.

**Finding the Foodies**

One of the first places to get intelligence about an industry is with that industry's association(s). In the restaurant world, that would be the **National Restaurant Association** (www.restaurant.org). The National Restaurant Association is heavily involved in many social media sites, with a presence on Facebook, Twitter, LinkedIn, Flickr, and YouTube. We learned from a video posted on YouTube that "off-premises" (i.e., mobile food trucks) services are a growing part of the restaurant industry.

**To grow your audience and influence, you need to know where your customers and potential customers congregate so you can reach out to them on their turf.**

How can a local restaurant market this kind of service? Just think about the print possibilities: vehicle wraps, flyers, coupons, menus, and signs around some new menu items or a seasonal offering. That's the sort of program a forward-thinking print service provider/marketing service provider (PSP/MSP) can help develop for restaurateurs in their region. The National Restaurant Association has a Twitter presence (**@WeRRestaurants**) with tidbits of interest to restaurateurs.

**FohBoh** (www.fohboh.com) is an online community for the restaurant industry. FohBoh has created an online environment where people can come together to share ideas, get feedback,

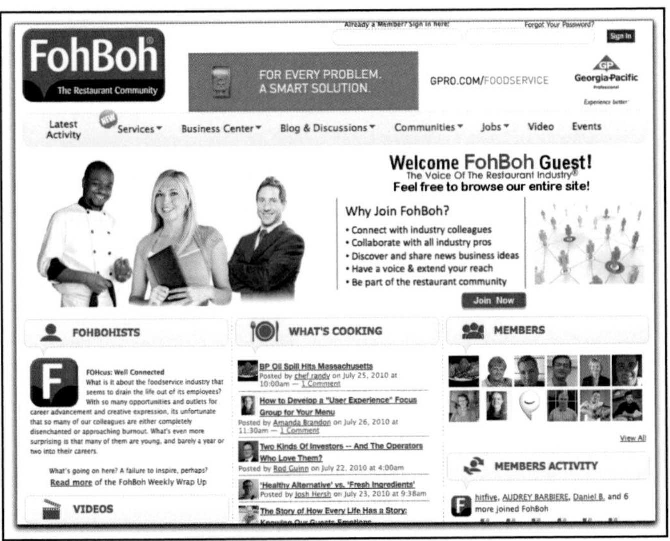


***Figure 3-7.*** *FohBoh.com is a good example of a specialized social networking site focused on a specific industry.*

make friends and new business connections, learn, and do business. In addition to the social networking options it offers, FohBoh provides links to business development services, like investors, and new technologies like mobile guest management products (where "your table is ready" calls come through a guest's mobile phone, replacing the buzzer devices you see at many restaurants today).

It's also important to know where your audience hangs out in the virtual world. If you're already taking part in a social networking platform, like LinkedIn or Facebook, you have a certain number of friends already established there. But to grow your audience and influence, you need to know where your customers and potential customers congregate. Salespeople should be encouraged to link up with their customers via social media, keep track of their interests, and potentially build a greater rapport with them. **LinkedIn connections are especially important, because it's one of the few social media platforms that lets users download their connections to a database,** so you'll know which of your customers are engaged with at least one social media platform. With this information, you can invite these folks to connect with your company via other social media, like an invitation to view a special new "how-to" video you've posted on your YouTube channel.

## Step 4: Know yourself (and your company)

*Excuse me,* you may be thinking, *but I certainly already know myself and my own company, thank you very much.* We can't speak for your self-awareness (if you're interested, there are dozens of self-awareness quizzes online, such as this one at http://www.higherawareness.com/free-personality-quiz.php), but you really have to look at your own company with an open eye.

You might have uncovered some outside perception issues back in Step 1, when you looked at what's being said about your company on the outside. But it's just possible you may have some internal issues that aren't widely known which could come to light once you open your virtual front door. Once you jump into the social stream and start that open communication process, there's a good chance that any previously unhappy customers or employees may join the conversation and bring these issues to light. Better to know about them and be ready in advance.

Have you done an employee survey lately (or ever)? Employee satisfaction surveys can be a very effective way to check the honest mindset of your staff, especially when the surveys are

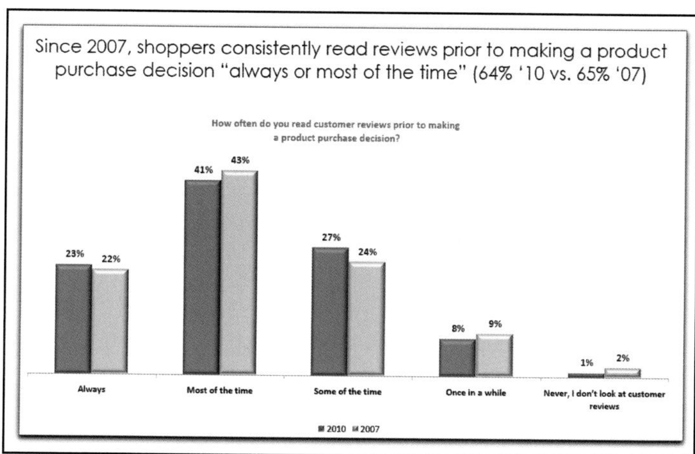


***Figure 3-8.*** *Customer reviews have a significant impact on potential customers' behaviors, as reported by Power Reviews.*

anonymous or conducted by a third party. If you don't have a full-time human relations staff person, it's easy to find employee satisfaction surveys online, along with companies that can help you administer them and analyze the results. You can find free survey templates at **www.biztree.com, www.surveyshare.com,** and **www.createsurvey.com,** among dozens of other websites.

**Do you conduct employee satisfaction surveys? These can provide a great opportunity to peer into the honest mindset of your staff—and uncover possible perception issues both inside and outside your doors.**

If you have built a general Web portal or branded portals for customers, do you have a place for customers to post reviews? A March 2010 study of 1,000 consumers by Power Reviews found that **user-generated reviews had the highest impact on buying behavior** (more influential than social media, mobile alerts, or community forums). The study indicates that 63% of shoppers consistently read reviews prior to making a purchase decision.

You should also be aware of any rejected jobs, customer complaints, or malfunctioning equipment in your shop. **Being self-aware and knowing anything that might be said about you or your company is a critical step in building your online presence.**

## Step 5: Determine how social media fits into your business plan

We talked in chapter two about all of the great things social media can do for businesses. So what do you want it to do for you and your business? Just doing it because everyone else is can be a reason, but it's not the best one. Before you can really start your social media plan, you have to have, well, a plan! **Making the decision to invest time and effort into social media should be done based on some analysis.**

### SWOT Analysis and Social Media

A SWOT analysis is a basic tool that can be used for nearly any decision but particularly a critical business decision. Most people have experienced a SWOT analysis at some point, if only in a business or a management class. It's certainly well covered on the Web, with over 200,000 Google references cited for the terms "SWOT" and "social media." Yet it isn't all that common to find that many businesses haven't run a SWOT analysis recently—maybe not since they put together their first business plan.

Here's a little background on what a SWOT analysis is. You use SWOT as a way to examine strengths (S), weaknesses (W), opportunities (O), and threats (T). A SWOT analysis is a look inside, at yourself or your organization (strengths and weaknesses), and outside, at the market (opportunities) or competition or business environment (threats). Key people will discuss options for a critical decision or direction based on the SWOT. Using a SWOT is an excellent mechanism to flesh out all of the issues and ramifications surrounding a topic. Optimally, it provides a framework that can yield all types of, and very detailed ideas on, the topics.

#### From the Field

***A Conversation about SWOT Analysis***
*John Hamm, President, John Hamm & Associates*

A great way to learn about the challenges and opportunities facing your business is by examining it in detail by performing a SWOT Analysis (Strengths, Weaknesses, Opportunities, Threats). A SWOT analysis is quite often a very useful tool to ascertaining a realistic view of a business's present situation. It is from this SWOT analysis that you will be able to plan your future actions to strengthen your company and plan for its future growth and success. In trying to determine one's strengths and weaknesses, it is important to recognize that strengths and weaknesses are internal to your business and largely under your control, while opportunities and threats are external elements that influence your business for better or worse.

### On the Path of SWOT for Social Media

**Goal:**

Determine social media readiness for ABC Company.

**Preparation Needed:**

- Identify and agree to your company social media goal/s:

________________________________________

________________________________________

________________________________________

________________________________________

________________________________________

- Engage and improve your current customer relationship (yes, which leads to further business).
- Recruit new customers for the company.
- Protect and expand the company brand.
- Position your company as a thought leader, coach, and expert in an area: __________________________.

Other:

________________________________________

________________________________________

________________________________________

________________________________________

________________________________________

Notes:

________________________________________

________________________________________

________________________________________

________________________________________

- Think about how to measure change or movement in this goal.
- Appreciate that social media is an investment of time and resources and your company goal may migrate over time but you need a touchstone goal in the beginning.
- Identify and invite participants who should be part of the SWOT discussion.

- Key leaders—be sure influencers and implementers are part of the team.

Others?

- Investigate customers' social media profiles—focus on the top 20 (or 10 or a number you can comfortably research) accounts to start.
- Investigate competitors' social media profiles—focus on top market share competitors.
- Read chapter four, "Navigating the Social Media Channels." Be familiar with elements of the top tools that your company may initiate, use, or expand into use.
- Identify any employees who are personally or professionally active in the use of social media tools. Check to see what tools they are using and for any experiences of value or caution.
- Investigate which social media tools are most heavily used in your vertical of interest (i.e., education, insurance, finance).

  Note: You could assign various SWOT participants to check out the various areas for investigation: customers, competitors, employees, tools, etc.

### The SWOT Path

To guide you through the process, the facilitator or leader of the discussion should have questions for each area:

*Strengths*

- Who are your advocates of social media (SM) tools? Who is experienced with SM? Who is passionate about it? Who is willing to try SM?



## From the Field

***On Using SWOT for Social Media***
*Renee Berger, Creative Director, Western Envelope and Labels*

We did use SWOT analysis just recently when we signed up with a company called Shoutlet. They gave us a series of detailed questions that we had to answer about our company and how we are going to use and develop our social media in the future.

- What resources exist in the company to add value to SM? Pictures? Products? Videos? Experts in an area? Potential bloggers?
- What is your current involvement in SM? Which of your current customers are active in SM (and using which tools)?

*Weaknesses*

- Who will lampoon SM in the organization? Who will portray a negative image in SM?
- Who has time for the initiative?

*Opportunities*

- What cost savings may come about?
- What new customers may be targeted through SM?
- How can the sales team leverage SM for new customers?
- Can customer comments and conversations lead to new product development?
- Can your competitive stance be improved?

*Threats*

- What hidden customer service or product issues may be raised?
- What reputation issues/personnel issues may negatively come to light?
- With so many staff members, how can control/messaging be handled?
- Efforts can start but may not be sustained.

**Now for the Actual SWOT Process**

- All the participants discuss the answers to the planned questions. New questions are developed and addressed.
- Decisions are made and an implementation plan is developed.
- Dates and people assigned are agreed upon.

SWOT Analysis: Our SM efforts

Strengths

– Presence on Facebook, Twitter, LinkedIn, two vertical-specific sites and company blog

– Marketing manager monitors sites, five sales people very engaged in social media

Weaknesses

– Infrequent updates on all SM sites

– No videos or YouTube site set up yet

Opportunities

– Build more active community around blog and other SM sites through more frequent activity

– Use our vertical knowledge to engage in those social sites more actively to build relationships

Threats

– Our competitors far more active

– Can we control the message with so many staff maintaining their own accounts?

***Figure 3-9.*** *Sample notes from the SWOT analysis discussion process.*



- Measurements are also agreed upon along with the timeline.

Be open to changing and evolving and consider the plan a guide. The company must remain nimble in the market.

### Step 6: Determine who will do what

OK, we're halfway through the process! The next step is critical: determining **who is going to be responsible for running your social media program.** Who's going to set up that Facebook page? Who's going to engage with the Twitterati? Moderate the conversation on your LinkedIn group?

Unless social media is someone's responsibility, it will be no one's responsibility. Because it can be so time-consuming, and may not immediately be perceived as something critical to the business effort, it's too easy to sweep it under the table day after day until it's soon forgotten. There is nothing worse than a blog site, for example, that hasn't had a new entry in it for six months. This can leave the impression that the company itself is in decline or even dead! So **keeping social media conversations alive is a critical part of any program.**

The commitment to maintaining a social media presence can be extremely time consuming. For the *2010 Social Media Marketing Industry Report: How Marketers Are Using Social Media to Grow Their Businesses,* author Michael A. Stelzner queried 1,900 marketing professionals, asking what sort of time they put into social media. The majority of marketers surveyed (56%) said they used social media for 6 or more hours per week, and nearly a third indicated they spent 11 or more hours per week on social media. Take heart, however, if using social media is new to you you're in good company. A full 65% of the marketers surveyed said they had been involved in social media for only a few months or less. **Now is the time to jump into the stream with everyone else!**

Stelzner's survey also asked marketers if they were outsourcing any aspect of their social media marketing, and only 14% said they were. But that doesn't mean this isn't a growing and potentially viable way to build your company's social presence. There are myriad marketing organizations that now specialize in social media consulting. Most of the bloggers we mentioned in Step 2 are "guns for hire" and make their living actually helping companies start their social media plan. There are also a lot of charlatans and self-described "social media gurus" out there (you might want to check out a funny—but terribly profane—video spoof on YouTube called "Social Media Guru" by Markham Nolan).

**Remember, unless social media is someone's responsibility, it will be no one's responsibility—and there's nothing worse than a site that hasn't been updated.**

### DIY vs. Hired Help

In an article published in **Soshable | Social Media Blog** (Soshable.com) titled "Social Media Strategy: Hire, Outsource, or DIY?", author JD Rucker say the answer is seldom easy. He points out the pros and cons of each of these three approaches. Rucker says **hiring a full-time in-house social media specialist gives a company a dedicated person whose entire goal is to help the company succeed with social media.** It provides complete control over the branding message as well. However, that person may well not be an expert (since it's such a new job type, the most experienced people are being snapped up by the dedicated social media agencies). Or, if you do manage to hire a social media expert, the person will likely not know your type of business well. Then there are all of the issues with any full-time staff person: they are sometimes not there (sick days, vacations), someone has to manage them, and there is the overall employment expense that has to be justified with a measurable return. Measurable return is hard to

> **From the Field**
>
> ***On Developing a Social Media Strategy for Printing Industries of America***
> *Mary Garnett, Executive Vice President and Chief Planning Officer, Printing Industries of America*
>
> Our own strategy developed with an annual planning session where a social media "key initiative" was brainstormed and vetted by the Executive Management Team and later approved by the board of directors. Two point people were assigned and monitored for progress, a budget was associated with it, and eventually we hired a junior staff person to implement some of the details under the guidance of senior people. The key initiative had an internal focus and an external focus. For us that meant, internally, staff needed to get involved personally and professionally with guidelines and a concerted, unified effort; externally, it meant that we would help printers learn more about social media and how to maximize it for business growth. This book, seminars, and articles are all part of the external element of the key initiative.

determine in the social media realm, as we mentioned in chapter two and will discuss further later in this chapter.

**When it comes to hiring a third-party firm** to develop and/or manage your social media program, **Rucker cites these organizations' collective expertise as a major pro and claims outsourcing is often less expensive than hiring.** On the negative side, it can be daunting to filter through the thousands of companies out there to find the right one; once you do settle on one, you've lost a certain amount of direct control over your messaging. An "expert" in a field is going to dig in their heels to defend their own methods and opinions. They are, after all, the "expert" you hired because you felt they could do it better than you could yourself.

**As to the do-it-yourself approach, Rucker cites one big pro: it's cheap because all it costs is time.** And that's the biggest con as well—it takes time and a lot of it. And since most of us aren't social media professionals, a program we put together may not be run as well as it would be by an expert.

**Breaking Your Own Trail**

When organizations really started to jump into social media in late 2008/early 2009, the idea of having a full-time professional tasked with the job of managing an organization's online conversation was just being considered. The social media management task was crammed into the job description of many different kinds of employees, including the Web, PR, and marketing folks. What's happened is that, for many larger organizations, whole new departments of responsibility have evolved, most involving people who were previously in a traditional operational silo.

Take the example of **Ford Motor Co.** We mentioned Scott Monty, Ford's Global Digital and Multimedia Communications director, as a chief blogger in the social media space. The back story of how Ford's social media marketing plan came together is a case study for the blending of efforts of diverse corporate groups to create a more well-formed social media messaging machine. In 2009, Ford saw $2.7 billion in profits, despite huge losses posted the year before. Its wise use of social media helped dissociate Ford from all the news of bailouts and bankruptcies that plagued most of its competitors.

According to an article in *Advertising Age,* Ford pulled together teams from Public Affairs (now Corporate Communications) and Marketing. According to Scott Kelly, Ford's Digital Marketing manager, this team approach was new. "Historically, we had very little interaction with public affairs, but ever since the congressional bailout for the other two automakers, we needed to combine marketing and public affairs forces to get the right message out around Ford so we didn't get dragged down by GM and Chrysler."

**Ford's wise use of social media helped dissociate it from all the news of bailouts and bankruptcies that plagued most of its competitors.**

The central hub of Ford's social effort is called **FordStory.com** (having morphed into that role from a political advocacy site). Ford also launched the **Fiesta Movement,** in which Ford lent out one hundred cars, along with gas and insurance to YouTube bloggers for free. Various media and interviews report that the resultant Fiesta videos netted 6.2 million views and won 42% awareness among the sixteen- to twenty-four-year-old youth demographic. In terms of hard ROI numbers, the effort netted 6,000 reserved cars, well before Fiesta went on sale.

If you're considering hiring a social media expert, how do you know what to look for? If all you want is a pair of hands to do the work of maintaining and monitoring the social media sites, it's no more difficult than hiring any support person: you look for enthusiasm, strong work ethic, ability to learn, and some experience using social media.

If you want to hire someone with more expertise and experience, consider the advice of Andrew Ballenthin, president of Sol Solutions and founder of **Community Marketing Blog** (www.communitymarketing.typepad.com). Ballenthin ran a competition called **Blog-Off II** in late 2009, a contest he established to uncover "social media and marketing experts who know how to command top online social media and marketing performance."

From the results Ballenthin, developed eight qualifications that he feels a true social media expert should offer. These qualifications were published at **Marketing Vox** and highlight eight points to use when considering engaging a social media expert:

1. **A significant business and communications background—preferably a minimum of 3 to 5 years in marketing, journalism or media.** "This forms a foundation for understanding effective communication strategies and implementation."

2. **A history of success in their communications background.** "You wouldn't let a mechanic work from a text book or just on their own car before they safety your car." Look for someone who has proven repeatedly he or she can deliver expectations for program results that have real business value.

3. **A series of measurable accomplishments in social media that can be independently validated.** "Having ten thousand followers on Twitter means you learned once how to create this achievement but an expert is someone who has achieved above average accomplishments several times."

4. **A true understanding of your customer's relationship with social media before proposing a program.** Your customers may not want anything to do with Twitter or Facebook or never have used LinkedIn, Ballenthin says. "An expert should build a vibrant profile of your customer's online behavior and model a program that's good for them versus the latest gadget and trendy sites to go with."

5. **Straight answers when you ask about measuring social media campaigns.** 'Social media is too new to be effectively measured' is a common and erroneous claim, he says. "In marketing we understand that we need a baseline on what we want to change in a business before implementing a new program. If you want to improve retention, cross selling, nurture marketing, prospect acquisition, brand loyalty and use social media marketing to try to achieve that, run the program and measure if there was a difference in these areas or not.

6. **A focus on getting a return on investment.** "This is where mainstream marketing backgrounds are important. An expert should be interested in validating a financial improvement not just giving you cost."

7. **Clear methodologies.** Social media is not new anymore. There've been hundreds of articles and case studies on what

does and does not work and effective processes. An expert should have a clear set of methodologies they work with to get consistently replicable results otherwise you may have a one hit wonder, if that.

8. **An emphasis on integrated marketing.** Social media success rarely happens on its own accord. "Great social media campaigns require databases, emailing, advertising, publicity, industry influencers and more. It's exceptional that social media marketing can just happen because it's a good idea in the right place, other media needs to support effective results."

*"8 Tips for Hiring a Social Media Expert." Marketing Vox. 19 January 2010. http://www.marketingvox.com/8-tips-for-hiring-a-social-media-expert-046003/.*

### Finding a Professional Social "Guide"

In his *2010 Social Media Marketing Industry Report,* Michael Stelzner reported that only 14% of the businesses he queried said they outsourced any aspect of their social media effort. Still, those respondents were all marketing professionals who spend all of their time focused on audience engagement. For a print service provider, even one engaged in marketing campaign management, it might be a good thing to get some expert help from the outside.

How can you find a reputable company or individual to help you kick-start your social media effort? Most of these folks have blogs, and we've noted a few of the best known back in Step 2, but many of them will likely be too expensive for smaller businesses. A Google search for the terms "social media marketing, consulting" yields 98 million results. Narrowed to a particular geographic area—in our test, Pennsylvania—the list narrowed to a mere 1.9 million.

You can use a professional social media platform, like LinkedIn, to narrow the search further, potentially finding some options through your groups or through a connection. We conducted a recent search for people within a 75-mile radius of our headquarters in Sewickley, Pennsylvania, on the key phrase "social media marketing consultant" and found more than 300 individuals, most of whom offer help with social media marketing. Narrowing the search to a first- or second-degree and shared group connection narrowed the field to 95 people.

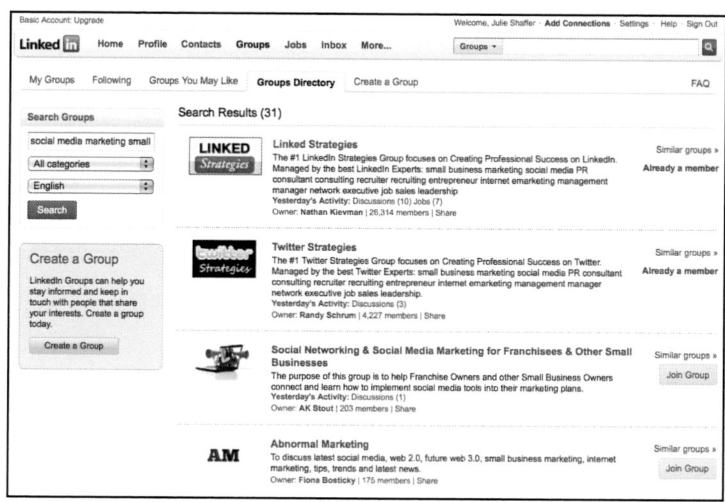


***Figure 3-10.*** *Utilize social media resources like LinkedIn to narrow your search for expert help with your social media plan.*

All of these are people one can communicate with through the basic LinkedIn account. That's one of the things that LinkedIn is quite valuable for: helping narrow a search for a particular type of person or company that can help with a specific need.

When you're talking to any vendor, it's best to have a Request for Proposal (RFP) to add structure to your discussions. One social media consulting firm, **Social Media Group** (socialmediagroup.com) out of Toronto, published an RFP template to help companies that are looking to outside agencies for help. It's generic and should be customized for your needs but offers a good starting point to help structure your search. You'll find a complete copy of the Social Media Group template in the Appendix C and a downloadable PDF version on our website (www.printing.org/socialmediafieldguide).

### Social Customer Service

Your social media efforts may result in a need for increased customer service support because **potential customer issues may be brought up on the social platforms.** You'll have to determine who will handle these issues once they've been brought to the company's attention. You also must have a "chain of notification" as part of your social media business plan.

And speaking of notification, before you initiate your social media presence, you should tell your employees about where the company will be participating in social media. **Begin a culture of transparency inside your organization before you move outside.** Make sure you clue in employees to your new social strategy and let them know their role in it (if any). It is social media, after all, and **you may find your biggest advocates outside your walls are the folks who work inside them.**

### Step 7: Start a presence

After all of the legwork and preparation for launching your social media presence, it's time to deploy. You're standing backstage and the virtual curtain is about to go up!

In a sense, you're going public and a big part of your success, as any actor, musician, or politician will tell you, is to **build a persona.** Should your social media persona be the company itself? Should it be the president of the company? Perhaps it could be a key group of several people within the company, like the sales staff, marketers, production folks, or executive management. You may wish to develop a social presence for a key product, service, or even a contest or event.

> We don't really see a PSP creating a persona around a product, but the idea of centering a social persona around the people in your organization can be a very good one.

Just looking at Facebook, you'll see any number of Pages that are centered not just around an organization, but also on a product, especially in the consumer products space. The company that offers the product creates some of these; fans create others. Take Oreo cookies, for example. **Kraft Foods** created an official fan page for Oreo cookies. The company also created an app that's a kind of survey called the "OREO Cakesters Dunk or Don't Dunk Debate" with a page of its own that people can "Like" containing a link to the app. But aside from these official pages, there are several other unofficial pages that have been created by rabid Oreo fans, such as the Community Page "Oreos and Milk."

Now we don't really see a PSP creating a persona around a product (Hi, I'm Penny Pocketfolder!), but the idea of centering a social persona around the people in your organization can be a very good one.

Take some pointers (no pun intended) from **Point Imaging,** a large-format digital imaging provider, in Hobart, Indiana. Point Imaging is one company in the printing space that grasps the importance of a personal social media approach. Nearly every page of the company's website (www.pointimaging.com) features a friendly close-up of one of its sixty-plus staffers, identified by their name and title. A full-screen panoramic shot of the shop floor lets users click on specific areas of the image, similar to the image on the **Bing.com** search engine, and zoom in for a close-up and explanation of that piece of equipment, often with a movie showing it in action. This is far more interesting than the list of equipment one typically sees on a printer's website and really makes site visitors feel like they're on a catwalk overlooking the floor.

The company's **"What's Fresh?"** blog is one of the most engaging aspects of its site. Marco Perez, Point Imaging's marketing manager, is the man behind, and the face on the front of, the "What's Fresh?" blog and other social media pages. "I initially built our Facebook and Twitter accounts as Point

***Figure 3-11.*** *Point Imaging's "What's Fresh?" blog is just one aspects of its social media efforts that reflect the culture of the company through its posts.*

Point Imaging uses an informal formula when populating its blog, sharing one human interest or entertainment message for every three business-oriented posts.

Imaging," he explained to us. "But I quickly realized that social media works just like the real world. You wouldn't walk up to someone, shake their hand and introduce yourself with 'Hi, my name is Point Imaging' would you?"

While Perez' might be the face that greets blog, Twitter, and Facebook visitors, the messages he crafts reflect the culture Kevin Huseman built over the past twenty years as founder and president. "He knows exactly what is on our website," says Perez. "Kevin encourages outside-the-box marketing and he enjoys using humor and real-life stories to create buzz in Point Imaging."

Perez says finding the best approach to social media can be challenging. "As much time as you spend attracting viewers, you can quickly lose your opportunities by being too pushy or too boring," he warns. "Our ultimate goal is to bring traffic to our website and more importantly, our blog page. **A blog page can be your strongest social media tool. You have driven prospects right to your front door.** Your blog page should be engaging, entertaining, informative, and interactive." Perez uses a formula for the Point Imaging blog site, offering one human interest or entertainment-related message for every three business-related messages.

Point Imaging's foray into social media has driven a 300% increase in website traffic over the past year, with the blog being the top visited page. The site also netted the company a 2009 and 2010 web2award from Printing Industries of America, an annual award program that recognizes excellence in print service providers' websites.

### Taking the Right Path

In chapter four, we provide a review of fifteen social media platforms. There are hundreds of them out there. Where should you be involved? Taking Point Imaging's example, **it's best to**

**get started with the main players in the space because that's where the most eyeballs are.** That means Facebook, Twitter, and LinkedIn for the social networks and, if you can keep up with it, a blog. If you're going to create video content, you'll want to build a YouTube channel with links to your videos on your own website or blog. Images too should be stored on an image hosting site like Flickr then linked to your other social media sites.

Saying that, if you serve (or want to grow your business with) a very specific vertical market, it can be just as or more valuable for you to participate in niche social media that serves that market. In Appendix A, we've included detail on some of the social media outlets for five vertical markets—health care, pharmaceuticals, franchises, insurance, and financial services. Use the guide to find intelligence about verticals and to join in the conversation on those sites.

**CMO.com,** a website for digital marketers, published a chart covering ten social media tools and how each rates in terms of "biggest bang for the buck" on **four of the key social media benefits: customer communication, brand exposure, traffic, and SEO.** We like this chart (Figure 3-12) because it shows, in one quick overview, that **not every social media outlet is created equal,** and some are better than others for specific needs or business types. It shows, for example, that videos on YouTube are very good at search engine optimization and driving traffic to your website, while Facebook is not especially valuable for SEO.

You will find detailed "how-to" material on setting up and using the "big four" social media—Facebook, Twitter, LinkedIn, and YouTube—in chapter five. Whether you are just getting started and need a step-by-step list to show you how, or are looking for some tips for going beyond the basics, you'll find something useful in that section.

You can decide if you want to put a toe in the water and slowly start posting to your social media of choice or announce your presence with a bang, using press releases, mailers, signs, sky-writing (it could work!), or some other more traditional media. If you're going with the big-splash method, you had better be ready to participate on a very regular basis—if you're blogging, for example, have several entries posted with more ready to go

THE CMO'S GUIDE TO:

# THE SOCIAL LANDSCAPE

**2010 IS THE YEAR CMOS WILL HEAVILY INVEST IN SOCIAL MEDIA. HERE'S A GUIDE TO HELP YOU UNDERSTAND HOW BEST TO LEVERAGE MAJOR SOCIAL MEDIA SITES.**

**GOOD!** **OK.** **BAD!**

| WEBSITE | CUSTOMER COMMUNICATION | BRAND EXPOSURE | TRAFFIC TO YOUR SITE | SEO |
|---|---|---|---|---|
| **twitter** A microblogging site that enables users to send 'tweets', or messages of 140 characters or less | Use keyword search monitoring through a program such as Hootsuite, TwitJump or Radian 6 to track what people are saying about you and your competitors. | Offers unique opportunities for Web site integration and to engage with customers in a viral way, helping your company stand out from the masses. | Potential can be large, but promotion is an art form -- promote your brand too heavily and turn off followers, yet don't promote enough and receive little attention. | Value to your site's SEO is limited, but tweets will rank high in search results -- good for ranking your profile name and breaking news, though shortened URLs are of little benefit. |
| **facebook** A social networking site where users can add friend, send messsages and build their own profile | Great for engaging people who like your brand, want to share their opinions, and participate in giveaways and contests. | Facebook brand pages are great for brand exposure. Jump-start your brand exposure through the ad platform, or hire a Facebook consultant to help you grow your brand presence. | Traffic is decent and on the rise thanks to share buttons and counters, but don't expect massive numbers of unique visitors to go to your site. | Little to no value, aside from blogs picking up and featuring your posted links. Not worth the time expenditure. |
| **flickr** An image and video hosting website where community | Unnecessary to spend too much time on this, though properly tagged photosets of company events can help | Participation in industry-related groups might get your photos, and thus your brand, viewed by people with similar interests, | Even if you get tens of thousands of visits to a photo hyperlinked with your URL, click-through rates are among | Heavily indexed in search engines, passing links and page ranks. Also helps images rank higher in Google Images and in |

| | | | | |
|---|---|---|---|---|
| **LinkedIn** A social networking site for business professionals | Not the primary focus, but customer engagement opportunities are possible by answering industry-related questions, establishing yourself as an expert in the field. | Effective for personal branding and demonstrating your organization's professional prowess. Encouraging employees to maintain complete profiles to strengthen your team's reputation is advisable. | Unlikely to drive any significant traffic to your site, though you never know who those few visits might be from -- perhaps a potential client or customer. | Very high page rank -- almost guaranteed on the first page of search results -- especially for your company name or individual employees' names, but that's about it. |
| **YouTube** A video sharing website where users can share and upload new videos | Whether you seek to entertain, inform, or both, video is a powerful channel for quickly engaging your customers, responding to complaints, and demonstrating your social-media savvy. | One of the most powerful branding tools on the Web when you build your channel, promote via high-traffic sites, and brand your videos. | Traffic goes to the videos. If the goal is to get traffic back to your site, then add a hyperlink in the video description, but don't expect traffic to correlate closely with video views. | Very good for building links back to your site because videos rank high. Also a tried-and-true way for your brand to gain exposure. |
| **digg** A social news site where users can discover and share content | Not the site's primary strength, though occasionally an objective third-party writeup as a PR effort, perhaps to counteract bad press or customer sentiment, can be promoted. | Opportunities are huge, especially for promoting objective press/blog coverage of your brand. Make sure content doesn't read like an ad, or your site might be banned for being overly commercial. | The grandfather of traffic spikes, so become active in the community or find someone who is. If your site is corporate, then consider launching an industry blog on a noncommercial Web domain to establish yourself as a thought leader. | Very good because even if your story doesn't become popular, then your page will still be indexed quickly. If your story does become popular, this is likely the best site in terms of getting linked to by bloggers. |
| **su** A social news community where members discover and share webpages | Paid StumbleUpon traffic can be a very targeted method of communicating, but whether you're reaching your existing customers is purely random and costly to determine. | A paid campaign can be good for brand awareness, especially following efforts to get free, organic traffic to your home page. Targeting is very accurate, but keep in mind you're paying 5 cents per visit ($50 CPM). | Enables a diverse range of people to discover your content and share links via the su.pr link shortener on Twitter. Tagging helps, but you don't want the same people repeatedly giving you a thumbs-up. | Very good if your story makes it to the top page for its tag. StumbledUpon's large user base enables many people to find and link to your stories. For vanity name searches, profile pages rank well, too. |

| | | | | |
|---|---|---|---|---|
|  A social news site where community members can vote on stories | Editor-driven and moderated, so this shouldn't be your primary focus. | Noncommercial sites are heavily favored by moderators, so business sites should not waste time in this uphill battle. | Get in the moderators' good graces, and you have a chance to hit absolutely massive numbers -- but it's a long shot. | If you make the front page of Yahoo, then you will get a ton of backlinks, but chances are unlikely unless you are a large, established brand. |
| reddit A social news community where users post links to the site's home page | The community is fickle, and anything perceived as spam will be destroyed. However, look deep into the categorized "subreddits" to unearth small niche communities, and you could get valuable feedback. | Unless you're a bacon company, don't try to build your brand here. You'll end up banned from the site without even realizing what happened. | If Reddit loves you, then traffic is often right up there with Digg and StumbleUpon. Be careful: Push too hard for votes from your friends and risk being banned, but don't push at all and you'll wind up with nothing. | Make the front page and many reputable sites will pick up your story, generating valuable backlinks and extending trust to your site. |
| del.icio.us A social bookmarking site used for sharing and storing bookmarked pages | Site is intended for people to bookmark content. You can see what people tag with your brand name, but communication with them is nonexistent. | Not enough ongoing brand recognition to make it worth your while unless you want to be known for providing reference content for later retrieval. | Not as big as it used to be, but informative, massive reference pieces bookmarked for later use can net you a few thousand recurring monthly visitors. | Pretty much everything about the site helps: When your page is bookmarked, it's a direct link back to your site. When you're on the front page of the site, the big category tag pages are full of trust, which will pass directly to your URL. |

***Figure 3-12.*** *CMO.com charted how ten popular social media tools rated in terms of four key social media benefits.*

so that you have fresh material at hand to let your new audience know you have something to say. We can't say it enough, though: **maintenance, actually keeping up the social conversation, is critically important to success with social media.**

And that leads us to…

## Step 8: Participate

According to Econsultancy's *Value of Social Media Report,* the "big four" social networking sites are Facebook, Twitter, YouTube, and LinkedIn. The study, conducted between December 2009 and January 2010, queried 400 B-to-B and B-to-C companies in 16 verticals about how they are using social media. Based on the responses:

- 85% use Facebook
- 77% use Twitter
- 58% use LinkedIn
- 49% use YouTube

The same report, if conducted in 2005, would have netted an entirely different set of "big" social sites, when platforms like **MySpace, Bebo,** and **Friendster** would have topped the list (and Facebook was then just for college and high school students). **Experian Hitwise** (www.hitwise.com), an Internet research firm with proprietary software that Internet service providers (ISPs) use to analyze website logs created on their network, offers weekly reports on Internet traffic. During the first full week of September 2010, Hitwise showed **MySpace** in the top four list, possibly because the school year had just begun and that demographic was very active that week (**MyLife** and **myYearbook** ranked higher than LinkedIn during that week as well).

What this all means is that **the platform doesn't matter as much as engaging in the conversation** where your audience is hanging out. So, it's critical to stay on top of where the conversation is happening at a given time and to be aware of where the conversation may be shifting.

Whether you are personally the "voice" of your organization, you have a team involved, or you've hired a full-time staffer or third-party company to do it for you, **regular participation is key to any kind of success with social media.** Simply posting sales messages will get you nowhere very fast with social media; no one wants to see a pure sales pitch on Twitter (unless that's the entire purpose of the account, like computer manufacturer Dell's Twitter outlet store).

It can take some work to learn to strike the balance between a marketing message and a relationship-building message. We think the general news feed/status update messages that go out to everyone on platforms like Facebook or Twitter should be thought of as a message on a highway billboard—what would you want to say to a *large* group of your acquaintances? PSPs and MSPs alike use case studies to tell what a great job we do for our clients, so why not post mini case study-type updates, like

**Top 20 Social Networking Websites**

The following report shows **websites** for the industry **'Computers and Internet - Social Networking and Forums'**, ranked by **Visits** for the **week** ending **09/11/2010**.

| Rank | Website | Visits |
|---|---|---|
| 1. | Facebook | 60.68% |
| 2. | YouTube | 16.91% |
| 3. | MySpace | 6.80% |
| 4. | Twitter | 1.08% |
| 5. | Yahoo! Answers | 0.87% |
| 6. | Tagged | 0.87% |
| 7. | myYearbook | 0.66% |
| 8. | Mylife | 0.41% |
| 9. | MocoSpace | 0.32% |
| 10. | Linkedin | 0.23% |
| 11. | Club Penguin | 0.21% |
| 12. | Yelp | 0.20% |
| 13. | Classmates | 0.20% |
| 14. | myYearbook Chatter | 0.20% |
| 15. | Yahoo! Groups | 0.20% |
| 16. | CafeMom | 0.15% |
| 17. | HubPages | 0.15% |
| 18. | BlackPlanet.com | 0.14% |
| 19. | IMVU | 0.14% |
| 20. | CaringBridge | 0.13% |

***Figure 3-13.*** *You'll find weekly traffic stats for social media platforms, search engines and even specific verticals at www.hitwise.com*

"helped XYZ company see a 15% increase in responses—check it out" then link to the full case study on your website. This is a way to draw people back to your central hub site (whether that is your corporate site or a special social media hub), where you can do more overt sales messaging.

**Be cautious when you post. Lawrence Savell warns: "calling something an opinion does not make it so, and words like 'I think' or 'I believe' do not necessarily assure protection for what follows."**

Facebook lets you create groups of friends, and you can use groups or lists to segregate your friends and customize messages to them. So you could create a group around an educational topic or a vertical market and send messages tailored to that audience through that channel; tips of interest that can help them do their job better; or, for salespeople in particular who excel in building personal rapport with clients, send messages on topics you know would be of interest to that individual. If your customer is a runner, scan the running blogs and send a tweet pointing to that blog post. This sort of activity helps you appear to share interests with social networking friends.



### Avoid Legal Hot Water

As we gathered material for this book, we noticed that as time goes on, there are more and more articles about the potential for legal liability based on the participation in social media. In 2009, rocker Courtney Love was sued for defamation based on Twitter comments Love made about clothing designer Dawn Simorangkir.

Celebrities are not the only ones at risk for lawsuits based on social commentary. A social community of scuba enthusiasts, **scubaboard.com,** has been sued, along with more than one hundred of the people who posted on it, for discussion surrounding an *accurate* story about the death of one diver and sicknesses of others, presumably from contaminated air in their tanks. The party identified as responsible for the accident is suing the discussion forum for lost business as a result of the bad publicity. In a litigious society such as ours, stories like this will only multiply.

In an article titled "Minimizing the Legal Risks of Using Online Social Networks," on **Law.com,** attorney Lawrence Savell provides a checklist of some of the salient legal issues that those who use social networking sites must consider, with the goal of increasing familiarity with and sensitivity to these issues so that preventive steps can be taken before a problem develops:

**Are you violating anyone's copyright?** If you are posting content—text, images, audio, video, etc.—that you did not create or do not own, or for which you have not been granted a license or other permission to use by the creator/owner in circumstances where these would be required, you are probably infringing on someone's copyright. An exception applies if your posting qualifies as a "fair use," a fact-specific determination relating to those contexts in which one may use or reference copyrighted material in a reasonable manner without the owner's consent. Common situations in which fair use may be found include criticism, education and parody.

**Are you violating anyone's trademark rights?** If you are using another's trademark, you may be liable for infringement where the owner can establish that your use of its mark or a mark similar to it will likely cause consumer confusion as to the source of the material. There may also be potential liability if the owner can establish that your conduct diluted the strength/value of the owner's trademark.

**Are you invading anyone's personal privacy?** Depending on the jurisdiction, one or more of the traditional types of privacy protection may apply. These include: use (appropriation) of a person's name, portrait or picture for advertising or commercial purposes without prior written consent; public disclosure of private and embarrassing facts; and statements portraying one in a false light (similar to libel). Other privacy proscriptions may be established by particular legislation (for example those protecting children).

**Are you breaching any confidentiality agreements or professional obligations?** Lawyers, doctors, advisers and others in businesses in which they receive client/patient confidences must make sure they maintain such confidentiality.

Possible sanctions may include termination of employment, loss of professional license, potential significant civil liability (such as in the context of trade secret dissemination), or even criminal liability.

**Are you defaming anyone?** Generally speaking, a defamatory statement is a false and disparaging statement about another which causes injury to reputation (or in some cases causes emotional distress). It is a communication which exposes persons to hatred, ridicule (more than a simple joke or satire/exaggeration), or contempt, lowers them in the esteem of others, causes them to be shunned or injures them in their business or calling. Sometimes a person depicted in a photograph may claim that the juxtaposition of the picture with text conveying a negative connotation creates an implicit defamatory assertion. Bear in mind that not just people can be defamed—so can businesses and even products (disparagement). Truth is, of course, a complete defense to such a claim. Statements may be protected if they truly constitute only opinions and are not capable of being proven either true or false. However, calling something an opinion does not make it so, and words like “I think” or “I believe” do not necessarily assure protection for what follows, as a statement may be actionable to the extent it implies a false assertion of fact.

**Are you running afoul of advertising restrictions?** To the extent that your social networking efforts may be viewed in whole or part as an advertisement, you must make sure you comply with all applicable advertising, “deceptive practice,” and “unfair competition” laws and regulations. These may include the FTC’s recent guides which may in certain circumstances require bloggers or other “word-of-mouth” marketers who receive payments or free products or services from the seller to review a product or service to disclose that fact.

**Are you violating applicable regulatory requirements?** If your business is in a heavily regulated industry, be mindful of violating applicable proscriptions. If your business is a publicly traded entity that is subject to SEC regulations, make sure that your efforts do not run afoul of rules such as those regarding public statements.

**Have you made promises to others on your page?** If you make representations or promises to others on your page, make sure you keep them, to avoid potential liability for claims such as misrepresentation or breach of contract.

**Have you read and do you understand the social networking site's terms/conditions of use?** It is critical to review and consider carefully the nature and scope of applicable site use terms/conditions prior to entering into such agreements. Conduct in violation of those provisions could result in termination of your user status or civil liability. In addition, such terms/conditions may significantly impact your privacy and intellectual property rights, as they may include, for example, granting the site owner the right to use any information provided or content posted in any way the site owner desires in perpetuity, or even conveying ownership of such information or material which you would otherwise retain—things you may not want to do.

**Have you incorporated qualified language and appropriate disclaimers?** You may obtain some insulation from certain claims by appropriately qualifying language or posting disclaimers of liability. Qualifying language (with less-than-absolute words like "may") may reduce certain liability risks somewhat, but that does not always carry the day. Similarly, disclaimers are not perfect or ironclad, and the degree to which courts uphold them is not absolute.

**Are you regularly monitoring your page/profile?** Regularly monitoring your online presence is critical, allowing you to detect promptly if your page or profile has been hijacked or modified by another without permission, if messages you did not create but which are attributed to you have been posted, etc.

**Have you checked your insurance policies?** Review your insurance policies to determine if the types of potential risks described in this article are covered. Consider obtaining additional coverage if they are not, such as third-party media liability coverage for infringement and liability costs associated with Internet publishing.

Social networking sites, with the confluence of rapidly developing technology and communication capabilities, expose users to a broad range of potential legal liability. Moreover, certain statutory provisions that may provide critical insulation to site operators against third-party claims such as defamation or copyright infringement may not be available by their terms to site users.

*Lawrence Savell, Esq., Chadbourne & Parke LLP, "Minimizing the Legal Risks of Using Online Social Networks," Law.com, June 28, 2010.*

Savell notes that, while these points are focused on U.S. law, "the global reach of the Internet means that the laws of many jurisdictions may potentially apply, which, among other things, may not be as protective of certain relevant rights as our laws are, and may not provide the liability defenses and privileges that our laws do."

## Step 9: Commit

This step is simple in concept but more difficult in execution. However, you must, to put it in the Nike trademarked phrase, "Just do it!"

There is hardly a blog or discussion on the topic of social media that doesn't have a post on the subject of how often one should post to a social networking site. And the answer depends on who is doing the talking, which of the social media is being employed, and what the message is. Opinions differ as to how frequently to post and what sort of messages to post on social sites.

- **Twitter** —While there is no "common wisdom" when it comes to how often a Twitter account should be updated, we suggest that you **post at the very least daily, with 4 to 10 posts a day as a goal.** There are many automation tools on the market that allow you to create a stack of Twitter posts and release them at specific days and times (**HootSuite, SocialOomph,** and **TweetDeck** to name just three) which can give the impression that you are online continuously, even when you aren't.

  Some well-known social media experts disagree with automating tweets and claim they only tweet live. Entrepreneur **Guy Kawasaki** is a Twitter aficionado, and uses **ObjectiveMarketer** (objectivemarketer.com) to build campaigns to schedule his tweets.

It can be a delicate balance: posting too frequently might be annoying to your followers; posting infrequently may cause them to lose interest and feel you have little to say.

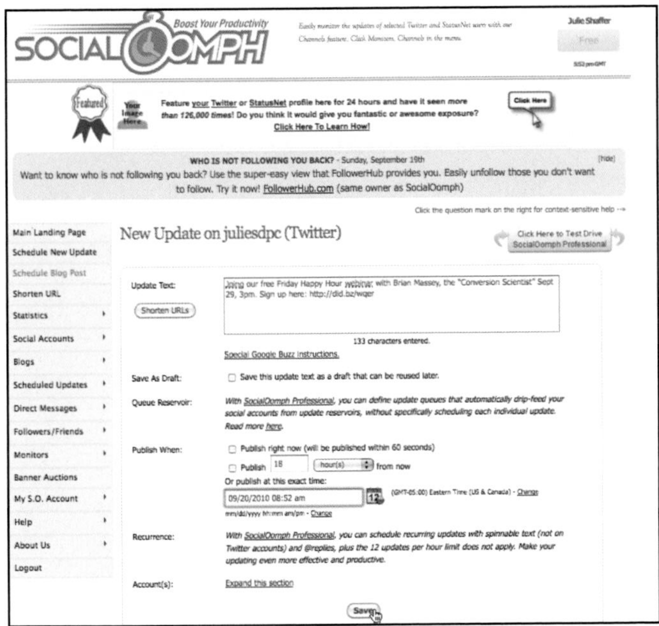


*Figure 3-14. Services like SocialOomph help manage social media engagement with tools to allow users to write entries at one time and schedule them to post at later times and dates.*

In a presentation for the Social Media Summit 2010 "How to Use Twitter as a Marketing Weapon" Kawasaki said he will actually repeat tweets, typically four times throughout the day to hit an audience in all the prime times, much as a newscaster such as CNN would do. So not only does he send many posts per day, he will send the very same post at several times during the day.

While there are no hard-and-fast rules for Twitter, most experts agree that, as with many social networking sites, **Twitter posts should be a mix of on-topic and fun or at least off-topic.** A ratio of 90% topic-centric posts to 10% fun posts is a good rule of thumb.

- **Blogs**—There is some fairly consistent messaging in terms of how often to blog, **most bloggers shoot for 3 to 5 posts per week.** More frequent posts might be annoying to followers and cause them to stop following you. Too infrequent posts cause followers to lose interest and feel you have little to say. So the rule is to stay at top of mind as much as you can without inundating your audience with your dialogue.

A tool like **twitterfeed** is a great option for automatically issuing a tweet whenever you have posted a new blog entry. **One of Twitter's greatest uses is to point followers to more in-depth discussion, like a blog.**

- **Facebook**—While many people say they reserve Facebook for private social networking (and it is a breach of Facebook's Terms of Service to have more than one personal account), Facebook has become a key place for businesses to build Facebook Pages as a kind of satellite website. When it comes to posting an update to one's personal Facebook News Feed, we think that more than a couple of times a day is too much. However, on business Pages, there is often a great deal of dialogue going on daily between the site administrators and the people who "Like" the Page. **Some savvy marketers are using Facebook Pages as a place to hold "live" meetings or question-and-answer sessions with speakers,** much as one would do in a webinar.

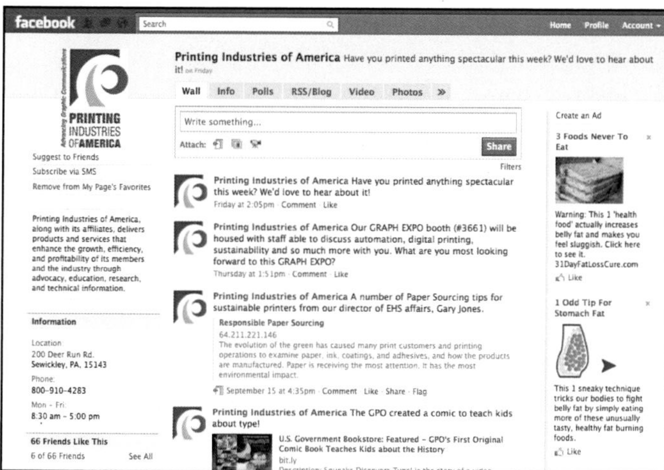


***Figure 3-15.*** *Consider maintaining a Facebook Page as your company's official presence on that platform. A Page can also promote a product or even incorporate a storefront to sell products.*

As Facebook has come to trump Google as a search engine in some respects, it's imperative for every business to have a Page on the platform. Using FBML (**Facebook Markup Language**) or other third-party tools, programmers can customize the look of a Facebook Page to make it match corporate branding and make it stand out from the more generic Facebook Page.

- **LinkedIn**—One of the big mistakes that people make is to think of LinkedIn as an extension to their business card. They will create an account, link up to everyone they know, maybe get and give a recommendation or two, and then let it languish. We offer a good many tips for maximizing the use of LinkedIn in chapter five, but here are a couple of pointers in keeping your LinkedIn account fresh. LinkedIn offers "Share an update" and integration with Twitter, so you can opt to have all your Twitter updates show up as LinkedIn status updates, or only do so with select tweets (by including **#in** in the text). **We've noticed a growing group of our LinkedIn connections using status update almost just as one would use Twitter** (and having their tweets show up as status updates).

### Step 10: Measure success (ROI)

One of the biggest frustrations marketers cite when talking about social media is how difficult it can be to measure the ROI of using it. It's one of the biggest chatter topics on blogs and websites devoted to social media (and there are dozens of those).

There are two kinds of metrics when considering success with something like social media interaction. You have hard measurements, like how many people visit a blog site, and that is actually kind of easy to track through something like **Google Analytics.** But measuring the *value* of interacting through a social network is more difficult to quantify and falls under soft measurements. Sales teams measure how many calls or visits they make to clients and compare that to work coming from the client. Add social media interaction into that mix. Any time a client comments on a post—that's as good as a phone call, right?

### What Do You Want to Track?

You can focus on hard numbers, like traffic driven to a website, number of Twitter followers, or number of sales you can directly attribute to the social program, like "mention this tweet for 20% off." But soft measurements include things like the *type* of comments you get in response to a blog entry. When you get repeat comments from a core group of followers, you know that you are truly engaging with them. But that kind of soft measurement is difficult to translate into a real ROI if measured by dollars brought into the company (unless some of those commenters are actually customers, then you can measure what they purchase and if their purchases have increased since the dialogue started).

Entrepreneur **Jocelyn Arsenault** noted thirty-five social interaction metrics in a recent blog post (www.jocelynarsenault.com), and we think they bear mentioning here. These are the kinds of things that can be measured using a variety of monitoring tools:

1. Alerts
2. Bookmarks
3. Comments
4. Downloads
5. Email subscriptions
6. Fans
7. Favorites
8. Feedback
9. Followers
10. Forward to a friend
11. Groups
12. Install widget
13. Invite/refer
14. Key page activity
15. Love/like
16. Messaging
17. Personalization
18. Posts
19. Profile
20. Print page
21. Ratings
22. Registered users
23. Report spam/abuse
24. Reviews
25. Settings
26. Sharing/participation
27. Tagging
28. Testimonials
29. Time spent on key pages
30. Time spent on site
31. Total contributors
32. Uploads
33. Views
34. Widgets
35. Wishlists

Visit http://www.jocelynarsenault.com/social-media-roi-things-you-might-want-to-track for more detail on using each of these items for measurement.

According to the Aberdeen Group, with impressive research to substantiate the findings, social media monitoring and analysis can assist in reaching several objectives:

- Increased effectiveness in product and service marketing
- General public relations and market research
- Customer support/brand reputation protection
- Intelligence
- New product or service development

In reviewing the study *The ROI on Social Media Marketing: Why it Pays to Listen to Online Conversation,* the main takeaway was that the benefits of social media monitoring were clear but measuring success is not as clear and is "still evolving."

*Note:* While the benefits of reducing risk to reputation, building customer advocacy and top influencers, customer insight generation, and customer service cost reduction were evident, documenting the ROI was elusive. These benefits speak to excellent drivers of each business in all economic environments. One of the biggest negatives to social media monitoring also refers to many other marketing functions: the expenditures are difficult to justify. As with many marketing activities, even if some measurements are apparent—i.e., increase in problems solved— the financial ROI continues to elude businesses. According to this research, increasing customer loyalty is the main pressure to compel a business to allocate the resources for monitoring social media for reputation management.



**Should You Monitor Social Media Platforms to Ensure Your Brand Reputation?**

Yes absolutely. The discoveries online and learning the right tools to monitor will eventually lead a business to the level of resource commitment.

Some of the same tools that you use for listening to what's being said about you (Step 1) are as relevant in measuring the effectiveness of your social outreach program. These simple steps include:

- Receiving Google Alerts
- Regular engine searches for your company name
- Checking your top ten or fifteen customers for any supplier discussions, whether they sponsor a company blog or participate in blogs

Then there's simple counting:

- The number of blog subscribers you have
- How many comments you get
- How many Twitter followers, Facebook friends and fans, and LinkedIn connections you have

These are all very simple and obvious measurements, and they yield some insight into how well your efforts are going. While it might seem obvious that higher numbers are better, that's not necessarily the best indicator of success. For example, if you have 50 followers to your blog and 20 of them actively comment, you have a very high level of engagement with your audience. Conversely, if you have 500 LinkedIn connections and never communicate with any of them, it's little different than having a stack of business cards in a desk drawer.

### Search Engine Optimization—Can They Find You?

Another way to measure success with your program is to see if you've had an increase in page rankings when searching your company name.

Here's a simple exercise: Assume the role of a printing customer, and start a search for "commercial printer any city/state," where the city/state is of your choice—we chose Northern Virginia. Scan the results for yourself or another favorite printer nearby. For us, in less than three-tenths of a second, 125,000 entries were listed for commercial printers. Sure, some of the 125,000 entries were not exactly commercial printers in Northern Virginia but most were; here is what we discovered:

- The first listing in the organic search was a series of geotags on commercial printers with their names and location on a map.
- On top of this listing was an ad to an aggregator of print quotes with a variety of companies receiving our bid.
- The third ad was a business listing directory with numbers for printing companies that we could call.

By page 7 (and more than seventy entries) we still could NOT find our targeted "favorite" printer and stopped looking—we won't name the company to protect the innocent!

Years ago, the **Yellow Pages** were the place to be seen and get chosen by a potential customer, particularly with business-to-consumer companies, i.e., plumbers, electricians, etc. I don't know many people who would have gone to the Yellow Pages for a business-to-business listing for a supplier of any type, but then again, some customers did arrive based on a listing or else businesses would not have patronized the Yellow Pages.

The landscape has changed dramatically. **Today, search engines (with the most common being Google) are the reigning source for seeking and finding companies to do business with in all areas.** While word of mouth is still king in my mind for B-to-B exchanges, some research is likely to involve using a search engine to further investigate a recommended company. With the ease of searches, more people are likely to refer to the Internet now than the Yellow Pages. **Search engine optimization** is the practice of taking steps to get your company higher listings, and a **search engine optimizer** is a person who may be hired to help.



### Why Should You Care About SEO as a Business?

The short answer is so people can find you on the first page of a search, or at least the second page.

Whether the source originates with a word-of-mouth recommendation or a company is seeking a supplier to work with due to locality or product or service specialty, a prospective or current customer is likely to look up your company on a search engine. **Your goal is to have your company listing in or near the top two pages of an organic search.** The organic search is the actual results from a keyword search in a search engine (Google, Yahoo, Bing, etc.). The **organic search** is not to be confused with ads that are placed on the top or right side of the organic search.

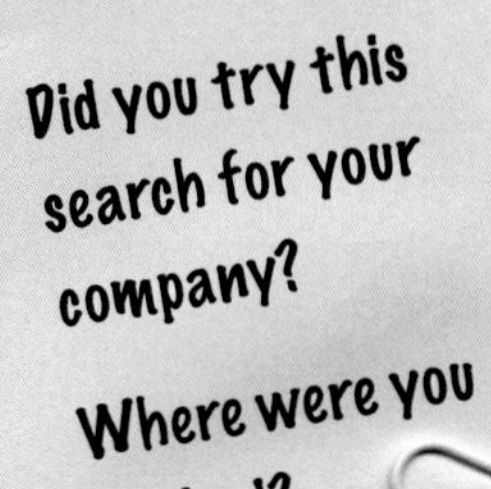

Did you try this search for your company?
Where were you ranked?


**Your Webmaster Is Key**

With most of the elements that can be controlled (many can not), your webmaster is likely to be your main resource for SEO. It is the webmaster who can help content providers to achieve the best success in reaching a higher organic search result. Some of the things that are determiners of rankings in a search engine are:

- Keywords
- Titles
- Description tags
- Links on pages
- Second page tags
- Page content
- Spider-friendly tags

If you have hired a webmaster, talk to this person about search engine optimization. However, a webmaster is not a strategist, so a strategic key person may need to participate in establishing the keywords, titles, tags, etc. The webmaster will eventually become more skilled in the strategic plans, but don't assume this skill without referencing.

Your Internet-savvy sales or marketing employees may also be able to help you with SEO. Certainly content originators need to have some general guidelines to help in the SEO. The main point is that **content, correctly tagged, is your key to SEO.**

SEO tips and guidelines are everywhere on the Internet. There are entire books on and directions for the activity, as well as numerous cautionary articles about hiring a search engine optimizer—specifically those who misrepresent themselves.

Google devotes a multitude of articles and guidelines to SEO, and each search engine has guidelines that will boggle the mind. The methods and details of how to increase the rankings do change, so monitoring your rankings is a must.

**Key Points for SEO**

- SEO is important if you want businesses to find you and increase your company visibility.
- Find a champion of SEO in your company. It's not difficult, but someone must learn all about it, practice it on the website, and continuously monitor the company rankings.
- Search for your own company on Google using keywords that your customers might use and see for yourself. On which page is your company listed? Stop if you don't see yourself in the first two pages—that's a sign you really need SEO help.
- Headings, titles, keywords, meta tags, articles, links, profiles on social media sites, site maps, style, and more—all increase your rankings.
- Content is king on your website if you want to get found.
- Inbound links (links from bloggers, paid links, reciprocal linking, likes and mentions on social sites, for example) increase rankings

## Summary of Thoughts before We Continue on This Path

It takes time and commitment to build a successful social media marketing strategy for your business. Think of this chapter as a blueprint for how to get started and build a strong social presence while working toward your own goals.

Remember the 10 steps:

1. Stop, look and listen
2. Get educated
3. Know your audience

4. Know yourself (and your company)
5. Determine how social media fits into your business plan
6. Determine who will do what
7. Start a presence
8. Participate
9. Commit
10. Measure success

# 4 Navigating the Social Media Channels

When it comes to technology, or even society, it's always interesting to look back just ten years and consider how different things are now. The Internet is not just home to the hottest cloud apps and social sites ... it is also a boneyard of old websites that somehow are still up and functioning today. Just for fun, we found some true living anachronism sites still around that originated a decade ago to show just how much has changed.

Here's a headline from an American Psychological Association page promoting an August 2000 conference: *Internet Is Hot Topic at APA Conference!* From hot to mainstream in ten years. How about all those crazy personal websites, like the famous one from an Istanbul man, Makir, that exclaimed *WELCOME TO MY HOME PAGE!!!!!!!!! I KISS YOU !!!!!* Only on **MySpace** would you find such a horrendous use of HTML today.

This is my page .......
WELCOME TO MY HOME PAGE !!!!!!!!
I KISS YOU !!!!!
I like music , I have many many music enstrumans my home I can play
I like sport , swiming , basketball , tenis , volayball , walk .........


We found an April 2000 report titled *What Is E-Commerce? Presentation of North San Antonio Chamber of Commerce.* So there were people a decade ago, professional people, for whom the entire concept of e-commerce was still new. In the printing industry, print e-commerce sites were all the rage, with the likes of **Collabria** and **Noosh** snapping up booths at print trade shows.

Young upstart search engine **Google** began selling advertisements associated with search keywords in 2000, a fairly radical concept first pioneered by **Goto.com. Blogger** was around, initiating the age of easy blog creation for the nonprogrammer, but there were no social networking sites of the sort we're used to seeing today (although Brett Borders, in his blog **socialmediarockstar.com,** says the true origins of social media date back to **"phone phreaking"**—rogue exploration of the telephone network—in the 1950s!).

Still, the first major social media site of the type we're used to seeing today, **Friendster,** did not come on the scene until 2003. There was no **Facebook,** no **Twitter,** or any of the dozens of other social sites. Many sites came into existence and became extinct in the intervening years. Now let's fast-forward to 2020. Will Facebook be here? Will Google? Those two companies possibly may be, but if history repeats, most of the top players today won't even be around then.

Here are just a few of the names you see in each of the main categories of social media platforms:

- **Social networking**—Facebook, hi5, Twitter, LinkedIn, Buzz, Friendster, MySpace
- **Sharing/collaborating**—Digg, Delicious, StumbleUpon, Reddit, Newsvine, FriendFeed
- **Image/video/presentation sharing**—YouTube, Hulu, SlideShare, Flickr, Fotolog, SmugMug, Zooomr, Webshots,
- **Microblogging** – Twitter, Plurk, Yammer, Tumblr, StatusNet
- **Blogging**—WordPress, TypePad, Movable Type
- **Location-based (social mapping)**—Yelp, Foursquare, Loopt, Gowalla, Brightkite

While we can put these applications into big "buckets," **splintering and crossovers are rampant.** For example, the number one social networking site in the world, Facebook, has trumped all other platforms devoted to image sharing, such as Flickr, and become the number one image sharing platform on the Web as well. **FriendFeed** (notwithstanding its growing irrelevance considering that Facebook bought it last year) can be considered a microblogging platform, a social network, a collaborative sharing site, and like many other social networking sites, a video and image sharing site.

The Top 20 social media sites according to Hitwise shows Facebook as the far and away leader, and Facebook is the most important site for marketers' social media marketing efforts, according to Omniture's *2010 Online Analytics Benchmark Survey.* From a sample of 600 marketers, 69% claimed to be using social media in their marketing efforts. Of those respondents, 63% ranked Facebook as the most important site for that activity, followed by blogs at 40%, and "other" sites at 34%. Just 28% of respondents ranked Twitter as most important (which showed up behind MySpace, the favorite site pundits like to declare dead). But, 88% of respondents said Facebook was either their first or second most important social media channel, followed by Twitter, with 72% of marketers ranking it in the top two.

The data suggest that, overall, marketers focus the majority of their social media marketing efforts on those two networks. The report found that retail marketers were making greater use of social media than those in other categories, with around 80% of respondents in the retail sector using social media channels.

The following section offers a quick reference to fifteen social media sites. Each overview gives a summary of the service/platform, some ways businesses can use it, and a rating on its usefulness for social media marketing with our **Bizometer**—a compass to help you quickly gauge the direction we recommend you take when considering the social media platforms.

If the compass points to the **green bar,** that means this platform is probably **not too important** for your business engagement, but be aware that it exists. The **yellow bar** indicates the platform has **some potential for business engagement,** depending on your audience. The **red bar** reflects those platforms we believe are **essential to any business's social media engagement efforts.**

# Bebo

| URL | www.bebo.com |
|---|---|
| Company | Bebo, Inc. |
| Headquarters | San Francisco, CA |
| Year introduced | 2005 |
| No. Users | 50 million |
| Demographics | Youth |
| Category | Social networking, personal focus |
| Cost | Free |

## The Story in a Nutshell

Bebo was all but dead when AOL, who had bought it in 2008, announced they were dropping it in April 2010. Bebo was a top social networking site early in the game, with a solid and devout audience in the U.K. and Ireland and participants worldwide. But membership dropped from a high of 40 million to 12 million, largely from the wholesale migration of members to Facebook. Bebo got a new lease on life when Criterion Capital Partners LLC bought it and Kevin Bachus, creator of Microsoft's Xbox game system, joined as chief product officer.

Bebo offers most of the usual social networking options, such as conversing with friends, video and picture sharing, playing games, and using apps. The revamped Bebo has added a great deal of integration with email services and other social media platforms in an effort to make it a viable central portal for users to manage all social interaction. Bebo makes money through advertisement display, and the ads are predominant and, many might consider, intrusive.

Bebo has some features like Facebook and MySpace, the latter being the option to apply "skins" to customize the look of your page; hundreds of canned

skins are available, and most are garish and flashing. Bebo's Lifestream Platform and Timeline are intended to let users place their own updates and those of their friends in chronological order. Updates can come from other platforms, including Facebook, MySpace, YouTube, Flickr, Twitter, and Delicious (the list is sure to grow), and the new Social Inbox that provides updates from Gmail, Yahoo! Mail, and AOL Mail. Clearly, Bebo is best used as a way to maintain personal contacts and is geared toward a youth audience. Mobile support has been added in some countries; at the time of this writing it was not yet available in the United States. Bebo offers 30,000+ applications, most in the entertainment and games category. Bebo also offers an Author section, where authors can post their works for others to read and "fan."

## The business case

Considering that Bebo tapped a big name in gaming to lead product development, we can assume the company may center more of its platform around gaming. The future and business case is unknown at this point, but there is an important business story here: the social networking world is full of avarice. People will move from one service to another such that a powerhouse platform one year can be left in the dust as the hordes move to another the next year. It's important to keep tabs on the social media field as a whole to see which are up-and-coming and not to put too many eggs in one social platform basket.

## Similar platforms

Facebook, Google Buzz, hi5, LinkedIn, MySpace, Twitter

# Buzz

| | |
|---|---|
| URL | www.google.com/buzz |
| Company | Google, Inc. |
| Headquarters | Mountain View, CA |
| Year introduced | 2010 |
| No. Users | Not reported (170 million at launch) |
| Demographics | Gmail users |
| Category | Social microblogging |
| Cost | Free |

## The Story in a Nutshell

Google Buzz is a social networking service accessible to users of Google Gmail. Buzz exploded onto the scene in February 2010, with some pundits immediately calling it an über social application that would trump both Facebook and Twitter. Taking advantage of Gmail's huge (170 million-plus) user base, Google pushed adoption by automatically linking people to others based on their IM and Gmail contact lists—but since this information was public: one look at someone's followers on Buzz told you who they emailed and chatted with most. The auto-follow feature has since been eliminated and replaced with an auto-suggest model. Google also stopped automatic connections to Picasa Web Albums and Google Reader-shared items. These measures didn't stop the Electronic Privacy Information Center (EPIC) from filing suit with the FTC, claiming Buzz violated federal consumer protection law. Google entered into a settlement agreement in September 2010 and will establish an $8.5 million fund to pay legal fees and establish a fund for "existing organizations focused on Internet privacy policy or privacy education."

Users access Buzz through the Google Gmail interface, so having a Gmail account is a prerequisite. Users now choose who to follow from their

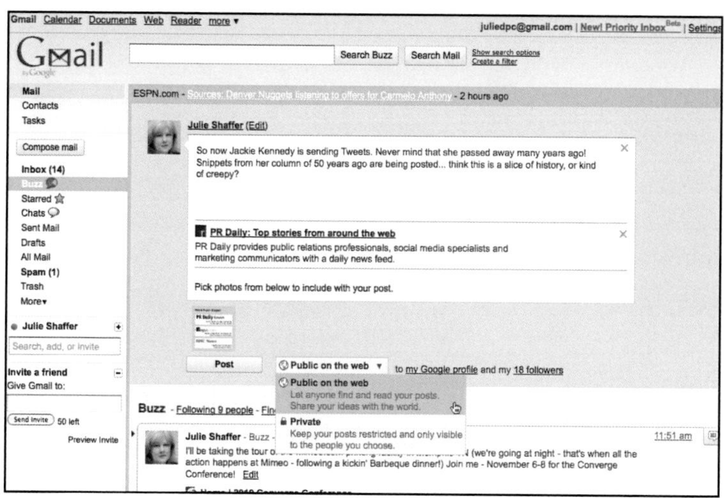


contact list or Buzz user profiles through the Find People option, and choose if their followers can be seen publicly. Unlike Twitter, Buzz does not restrict message size and allows comments to appear in the message stream, much like a blog, making it easy to follow a conversation. Messages are displayed based on immediacy: the most recent comment is pushed to the top of the list. A new version, released May 2010, was written in XHTML and can be accessed in 37 languages from BlackBerry, Nokia Series 60, and Windows phones, Android phones, and iPhone.

### The business case

Despite the privacy faux pas, Buzz has potential to be a decent social media tool, but users have avoided it in droves. PostRank data has suggested that 80% of Buzz traffic comes from other sources (like Twitter posts), so it's not where people go first to post news. Its direct tie into Gmail is a bonus for the millions of Gmail users but not for businesses who typically provide staff with corporate email. In order to use Buzz you have to set up a Gmail account (and the odds of getting an address with your own name, to match your corporate address, is unlikely). Buzz has not taken off as expected, but it's worthwhile to set up a Gmail account if you don't already have one, follow some of the people you link to via other social media, and give Buzz a try.

### Similar platforms

Bebo, Facebook, hi5, LinkedIn, MySpace, Twitter

# Delicious

| | |
|---|---|
| URL | www.delicious.com |
| Company | Yahoo!, Inc. |
| Headquarters | Sunnyvale, CA |
| Year introduced | 2003 |
| No. Users | 8.8 million+ |
| Demographics | Adult professional |
| Category | Social bookmarking |
| Cost | Free |

## The Story in a Nutshell

Touted as the "biggest collection of bookmarks in the universe," this is a social bookmarking Web service for compiling favorite sites and pages for personal use or to share with a community. Now owned by Yahoo, Delicious is a free service. The site aggregates tags into several sections: Fresh Bookmarks, Hot List (a legacy tool), and Explore tags. The Fresh content combines Delicious bookmarks with Twitter conversations to help keep this tool as frequently updated as Twitter.

Delicious is meant to serve as a replacement for the bookmarking option available in any Web browser, making the "bookmarks" accessible from any computer, even a public one. The social bookmarking aspect means users can build networks with other people to keep track of what they are tagging/bookmarking, making collaborative research easier. A user can manage, tag, save, and share websites of interest and see which sites other people are using and how they are using them. While it is a social site in the sense that research can be shared with others, Delicious sharing isn't limited to a specific group of "friends" like Facebook or other social sites.

If you regularly check potential or current customer websites, you can use Delicious

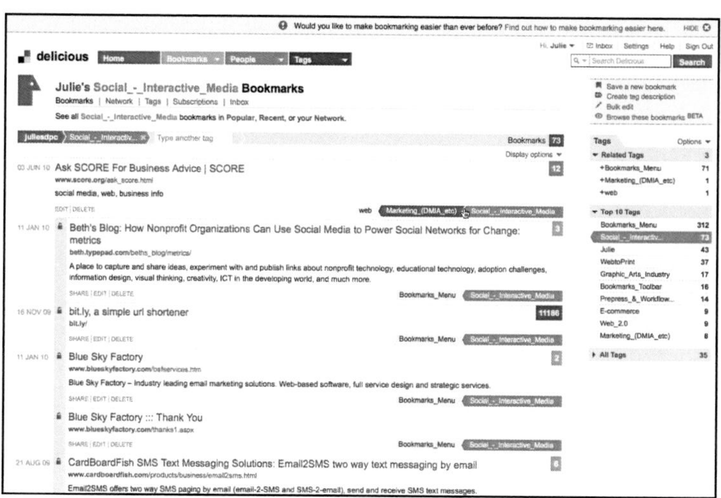


to keep track of them, all in one place. If you are researching a vertical market, for example, you could record links to all related sites in one place for easy referral. Users can also use the subscription option to watch for specific tags. Subscriptions can be bundled into bigger topics, like "social media" or "finance."

## The business case

Similar to Digg and other tagging sites, Delicious has value for research and, for the industrious social media manager, in frequently tagging news about a particular business or topic to increase brand awareness. Note: we say "news about a business" and not "your webpage" because bookmarking a website in order to promote it is considered spamming in Delicious and breaks its Terms of Service. It has the greatest value for bloggers or publishing sites with the Network Badges option, which allows display of details about a Delicious network as part of a website. Delicious is also a great tool for sales and marketing professionals to find out what's happening in vertical markets, on specific topics, or with competitors. When it comes to market research or coming up with ideas for new product development, Delicious is a splendid resource. The process of "tag mining" or searching for the phrases that are most tagged for a specific search-term-generated URL, is a great way to find words people associate with a product, service, or company and provides great marketing insight.

## Similar platforms

Digg, StumbleUpon, Reddit, Newsvine

# Facebook

| URL | www.facebook.com |
|---|---|
| Company | |
| Headquarters | Palo Alto, CA |
| Year introduced | 2004 |
| No. Users | 500 million |
| Demographics | Everyone |
| Category | Social networking, personal and business focus |
| Cost | Free |

## The Story in a Nutshell

Facebook has become the number one and fastest growing social media site in the world. In spring 2010, Facebook overtook Google as the most visited site in the U.S. (these numbers go back and forth daily). According to ComScore, total time spent on the site is 134 billion minutes/month, or about 7.5% of all time spent on the Internet.

Founded by Mark Zuckerberg as an exclusive network for Harvard students, Facebook was an immediate hit, with 30 more college networks added within months. After spurning a buyout offer from then much larger Friendster and receiving millions in investment funding, Facebook opened to high school students, then business networks, and finally to anyone with an email address. Facebook is valued at over $15 billion but has only $150 million in annual revenue.

Facebook's "Open Graph" concept allows websites and apps to share Facebook users' likes in a more public fashion, furthering Zuckerberg's claim that "public is the new social norm." Web publishers are building the "Like" button into websites, as it creates a link back from the person's Facebook Page and allows the site to display the most relevant content to any user based on their friends and likes, driving traffic to the site.

Facebook features a News Feed, where connected users share comments, photos, videos, and links. Games are immensely popular, with entire subcultures evolving around some like Farmville. There are over 550 million applications on Facebook and over 1 million developers; each month, over 70% of Facebook users engage with an app. The Marketplace is a Craigslist-like area to buy and sell goods. Organizations can maintain an official Facebook Page and sub-pages for specific products or brands, of which people become "fans." Businesses can also create Ads targeted to an audience by location, sex, age, keyword, relationship status, job title, workplace, or college. To make it easier to find any Facebook Page, users can create a specific username or personalized URL (www.facebook.com/username).

### The business case

Considering the sheer number of users and time spent on Facebook, it is essential for any public-facing business (B-to-C) to maintain at least one Facebook Page. It's less critical for the B-to-B market, although any product or service around which a group can rally, particularly nonprofits or movements like "green," is a good fit for a Facebook Page. Facebook Ads are easy to create, hit a (broadly) targeted audience, and are relatively inexpensive (you set a daily cost limit). If you opt to pay by click, you only pay when that happens but have the advantage of visibility, much like a billboard, even if no one clicks on it.

### Similar platforms

Bebo, FriendFeed, Google Buzz, hi5, LinkedIn, MySpace, Twitter

# Flickr

| | |
|---|---|
| URL | www.flickr.com |
| Company | Yahoo! Inc. |
| Headquarters | Sunnyvale, CA |
| Year introduced | 2004 |
| No. Users | 32 million |
| Demographics | All ages, pro and amateur |
| Category | Image/video hosting |
| Cost | Offers free and pro accounts |

## The Story in a Nutshell

Flickr is a photo and video organizing site owned by Yahoo. Top Ten Reviews ranks Flickr as the second largest photo sharing site behind Photobucket (which claims 100 million users). While it might have a smaller overall user base than Photobucket, Flickr seems to have a more prominent profile (one often sees links to Flickr accounts on other websites) and is the hosting platform of choice for many bloggers. The platform offers both free and pro accounts (but free accounts are deleted if inactive for 90 days). Users can upload pictures and organize, tag, and share them with others. Flickr was one of the earliest websites to implement tag clouds, which provide access to images tagged with the most popular keywords. The platform offers limited editing capability such as cropping and eliminating red eye; editing is certainly a minor feature. Photos can be sent to friends via email, and a user can join groups, discuss photos, and join blogs related to the photos and videos. The number of photos being posted, tagged and displayed is staggering. On a given moment, one might see 4,000–5,000 images uploaded in a minute's time.

The demographics of Flickr users are very broad. The user profile ranges from individuals using the site for sharing memories of trips,

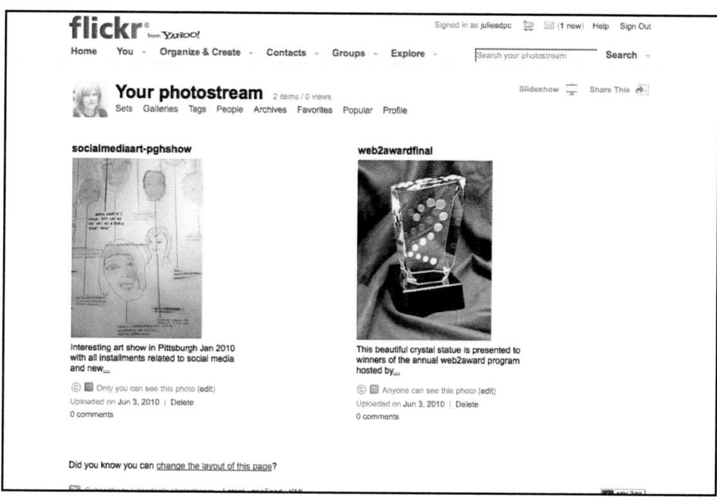


activities, and interests (although Facebook is encroaching here) to bloggers storing referenced images here. Photographers use the site to display photos and get their names and work out to interested parties. Photos can be bought and sold via Flickr, and the company has partnered with Getty Images to offer stock photos. There are levels of reuse made available via the site. You may use some of the photos for noncommercial endeavors as long as there is attribution. Others are copyrighted. Once you find an interesting photostream (series of photos) you can click on Slideshow and watch all the photos in the group. Images can be batch processed with uploader tools available for most operating systems. A iPhone app was added late in 2009.



### The business case

One of the best business uses for Flickr is, as many bloggers have found, to use it as a repository for images referenced in blog and social media sites. In this way, the image on the blog or social site can act as a pointer to an entire related series of images hosted on Flickr. Flickr is a great resource for images, as many photographers, both professional and amateur, host their photos here. Printers may take issue with Flickr, however, as it has entered into partnerships with third parties to offer printing of various forms of merchandise, including business cards, photo books, stationery, personalized credit cards, and large-size prints (including Snapfish, MOO, and Blurb).

### Similar platforms

Fotki, Photobucket, Shutterfly, SmugMug, Webshots

# Foursquare

| | |
|---|---|
| URL | http://foursquare.com |
| Company | Foursquare. |
| Headquarters | New York, NY |
| Year introduced | 2009 |
| No. Users | 3 million+ |
| Demographics | Youth |
| Category | Location-based social networking |
| Cost | Free for user |

## The Story in a Nutshell

Few social media platforms took off with the speed of Foursquare. Foursquare is the most visible of the new crop of geo-social networks, accessible through nearly all mobile device platforms. The original goal of Foursquare was to incentivize people to go out into a city, check into Foursquare to indicate where they are, and share this information with friends. The service is something of a social guide for larger cities as well as a friend-finder and game. Users can earn "badges" for certain activities and for checking into certain venues. Users can also be crowned "mayor" of a business, simply by frequenting it more than other users. Businesses, especially entertainment venues, are starting to run advertisements around this mayor concept.

Foursquare is very young but has already attracted some major corporate partners to use their platform, including MTV, Bravo TV, Starbucks, and Pepsi. Individuals who have downloaded and installed Foursquare on their mobile devices check into locations they visit by accessing the software and indicating where they are (the GPS option makes this easy). Foursquare insists that a person's location is not shown unless they choose to check in. In addition to badges and mayorships, users can earn points through check-

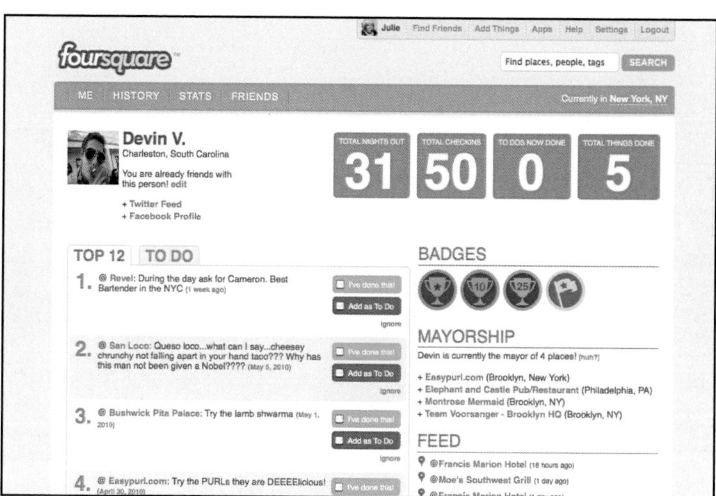


ins. These points rack up on each person's "leaderboard"—which resets every week. Foursquare is working on a model to use points for something other than the pride in a high-scoring leaderboard and has partnered with corporate sponsors to allow users to gather points by visiting certain venues and, when a threshold is reached, the sponsor will make a donation to charity.

The "Find Friends" feature shows a user if people they know are in the area, based on their check-in status, or a user can check a friend's "Top 12" list or "To Do" options.

### The business case

Foursquare sees three types of businesses that can benefit from the service: sole proprietors (small storefronts), retailers, and brands. Any business should set up a business account with Foursquare. If you have a physical location to which you want to drive traffic, it's one of a group of new geo-tracking services that can help drive people there. Foursquare offers businesses a free, real-time Check-in Analytics which shows who has checked in to their business over a time period, with gender, activity check-in times, how many visits were broadcast out to Facebook and Twitter, and top visitors. This can be used to create loyalty programs and reconnect with people who haven't visited in some time.

### Similar platforms

Brightkite, Gowalla, Loopt, Yelp

# hi5

| | |
|---|---|
| URL | www.hi5networks.com |
| Company | hi5 Networks, Inc. |
| Headquarters | San Francisco, CA |
| Year introduced | 2003 |
| No. Users | 80 million |
| Demographics | Youth |
| Category | Social networking, personal focus |
| Cost | Free (but you can pay to remove ads) |

## The Story in a Nutshell

One of the original social media sites, hi5 began losing market share to Facebook and Twitter over the past couple of years. The company revitalized itself by hiring a new management team and focusing on the youth gaming audience. hi5 now specializes in entertainment; this includes games, animated avatars, personalization features, virtual goods and gifts. The service also offers the usual mix of social media capabilities such as photo and music exchange with friends along with messages. The hi5 virtual currency, hi5 Coins, is used for direct user payments for game content and virtual goods. While headquartered in the U.S. the hi5 audience reach is deeper into the Latin America, Europe, Asia, and Africa markets. The service is free and supported by ads. Users can opt to pay to use the service without having to see ads. The hi5 virtual currency, hi5 Coins, is integral to all activities on the site and is used for direct user payments for game content and virtual goods.

Creating a hi5 profile is much like any other social media site, although users can create a semi-customized animated avatar to display on his/her profile. The hi5 Coins are an integral part of the entire hi5 experience. A user can outright purchase Coins, at the cost of $9.95

per 1000, or earn them by playing games. Users purchase virtual gifts, game play, movie views, and other virtual products with these virtual coins. Users receive some free credits to play games each day for free, once they are used, additional time with a game can be added with hi5 Coins. So there is not necessarily a cost to take part in games, but addicted gamesters may find themselves paying for additional play time. The hi5 store offers virtual gifts to give to friends; a virtual iPhone (which is basically an icon) costs 150 hi5 Coins, or around $1.50 if you've paid for the hi5 Coins with real money.

### The business case

This is a site to monitor particularly if your customers deal in the youth market or virtual gaming market or have a high exposure in the countries located in Latin America, Europe, Asia, and Africa. If your customers are game console makers, keep an eye on this site since it seems to be making inroads into the migration of games to a social platform rather than the console use. Some predictions were that the social networking gaming capabilities and attraction will put the consoles into question. The company has been accused of using spam techniques to expand hi5's audience by, for example, sending emails to the contact lists of members (when members open their email contacts to help them find friends with hi5). We kind of like the animated avatar—if nothing else it can be cathartic to set the mood to "angry" and watch it rant and rage.

### Similar platforms

Facebook, Google Buzz, LinkedIn, MySpace, Twitter

# MySpace

| URL | www.myspace.com |
|---|---|
| Company | Division of News Corporation |
| Headquarters | Beverly Hills, CA |
| Year introduced | 2003 |
| No. Users | 130 million |
| Demographics | Young adult |
| Category | Social networking, personal and music focus |
| Cost | Free |

## The Story in a Nutshell

Late in 2010, MySpace attempted to resurrect its declining audience with a redesigned interface and a new logo. It's not likely that this move will significantly reverse the precipitous decline of this platform. Once the dominant player in the social networking arena, MySpace has been in decline for several years and lost its top position to Facebook in 2009. The CEO was ousted in 2009 and 30% of the workforce was cut. MySpace had been a primary driver to websites in the entertainment category, accounting for 35% of such traffic in 2006 but that number dropped to just 9% in 2009 (Hitwise). In early December 2010, owner of the platform, News Corp, indicated it is open to selling the site or partnering with another organization.

Still MySpace remains a popular platform for musicians and entertainers to connect with an audience. Users can create their own pages using HTML into such areas as "About Me," "I'd Like to Meet," and "Interests." Users can form groups with their own message board and common page; specialized options abound, such as MySpaceIM for instant messaging, MySpaceVideo for YouTube-like video sharing, polls, forums, news and classified ads. MySpace is entirely financed by ad revenue and has significant capacity to

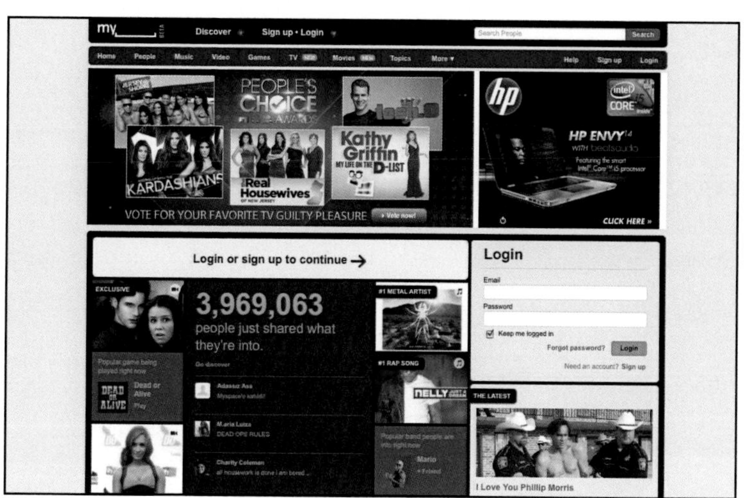


collect data about its users and thus in its ability to use behavioral targeting to select the ads each visitor sees.

MySpace offers users a great deal of freedom in how they design their personal space on the page (hence the name). A complaint about the platform is that a significant number of pages do not satisfy the criteria for valid HTML or CSS established by the W3C (The World Wide Web standards organization). The issue is that poorly formatted code can cause accessibility problems for those using software such as screen readers. MySpace addressed this by adding profile customization tools with some canned themes to make it easier for users to create a personalized space.

### The business case

Outside of the entertainment industry, MySpace does not have a solid reputation as a professional social networking platform. Before Facebook took over the social networking world, MySpace demographic data indicated that half of is users were over thirty-five, but undoubtedly this number will have dropped as people move to Facebook and Twitter. There is some validity to placing ads on the platform, as MySpace has excellent demographic targeting methods, but it has little to offer a business professional in terms of social networking.

### Similar platforms

Bebo, Facebook, Google Buzz, hi5, LinkedIn, Twitter

# LinkedIn

| | |
|---|---|
| URL | www.linkedin.com |
| Company | LinkedIn |
| Headquarters | Mountain View, CA |
| Year introduced | 2003 |
| No. Users | 75 million |
| Demographics | Professional adult |
| Category | Social network, business focus |
| Cost | Base usage is free |

## The Story in a Nutshell

LinkedIn is the fastest growing and largest business-centric social media tool in the world. While half the users are in the U.S., growth is worldwide. The LinkedIn model is that of a "gated community" such that contact with anyone in the system requires either a preexisting relationship or an introduction from an existing contact. Registered users build contact lists of Connections—people they know in business. A user can invite anyone to be a connection, even if that person is not already a LinkedIn user (this is one way LinkedIn expands its user base). So a network consists of your own connections, your connections' connections (2nd degree connections), as well as your 2nd degree's connections (called your 3rd degree connections). A growing area of LinkedIn is Groups, where discussion boards are offering business people a platform to discuss issues of interest. LinkedIn is also a viable tool for researching companies, jobs, and people in specific markets or verticals. LinkedIn offers paid accounts that provide more tools for searching and prospecting.

The first step in using LinkedIn is to build a profile, which many use as a mini curriculum vitae, showing past and present employment and education history. A profile can also show a photo, a person's connections,

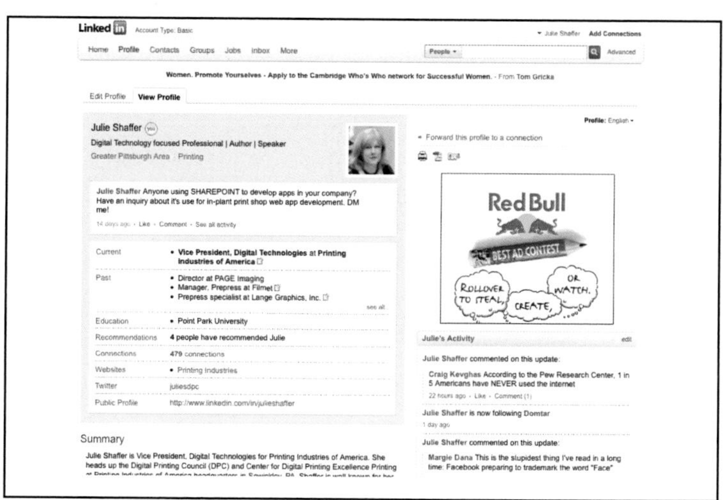


recommendations by other users (a key feature of the site), and Group activity.

LinkedIn offers built-in access to one's Twitter account and the option to share tweets in one's LinkedIn status, a nice way to keep it updated. The site has become a key resource for finding a job (there is a job posting section on the site) or researching potential employees. Aside from personal profiles, LinkedIn provides a platform for company profiles as well, showing key information gathered from LinkedIn members including staff members and new hires (with links to their profiles) past employees, recent activity by staff, as well as general company information. The often neglected Advanced search feature lets users search for people based on job titles, location, industry, geographic location, relationship, company, group, school, and language.

### The business case

LinkedIn is the single most important social networking platform for personal business communication on the internet. Beyond the simple fact that it's a centralized database of business contacts, it can be used as a tool to promote your business, prospect for new contacts, research potential new accounts, find new employees, take part in group discussions, and grow your personal collateral through recommendations and activity on the site.

### Similar platforms

Facebook, Plaxo, Spoke

# Loopt

| URL | www.loopt.com |
|---|---|
| Company | Loopt |
| Headquarters | Mountain View, CA |
| Year introduced | 2005 |
| No. Users | 4 million |
| Demographics | Youth market |
| Category | Location-based social networking |
| Cost | Free |

### The Story in a Nutshell

Loopt is a suite of mobile social-mapping service applications, consisting of three tools: Loopt, Loopt Pulse for the iPad, and Loopt Mix. Loopt is part of the geo-social networking category of social media tools, focused mainly on major metropolitan areas. Users can find Loopt friends through the application and Ping them, which can display their approximate location on a map. Travel-oriented editorial services like Zagat, Citysearch, Metromix, and SonicLiving are incorporated into Loopt, so users can find entertainment events, restaurants, and retail establishments and leave tips or reviews on businesses. Maps, photos, music clips, directions, and connections to other similar sites are available. Users may also snag coupons from participating establishments. Loopt Mix is a purely social tool along the lines of Facebook with users creating public profiles that can be found by other Loopt users. Major mobile phone carriers are partnered with Loopt.

The incorporation of content from travel services like Zagat makes Loopt a decent tool to use when traveling to find all sorts of establishments. Loopt Pulse offers photo directory listings of places, with links to the reviews, so users can actually browse for restaurants or other locations by scrolling through a visual

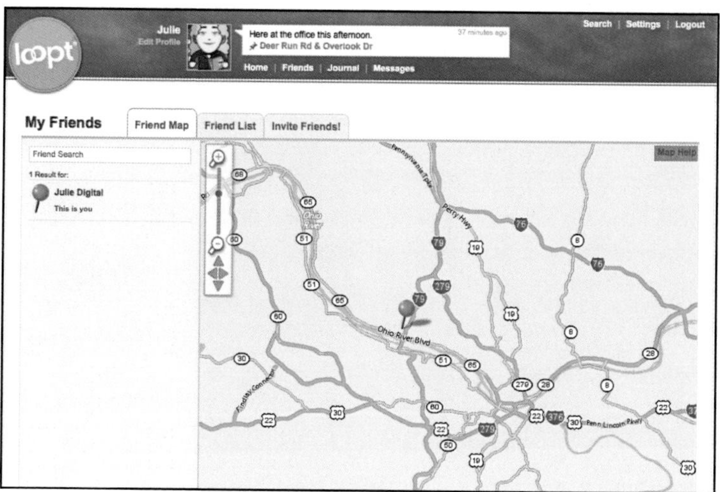


directory. Loopt offers some distinct ties-in with Facebook, tracking RSVPs to Facebook events and allowing users to share favorite places from Facebook. The problem with this and other geo-social networks is that there are already too many of them. You can invite friends to participate, but one of these services is going to have to win out, because people just will not want to use a half dozen different services.

### The business case

The primary benefit of this entire class of mapping, geo-tracking social applications to printers is mainly to provide directions to a business location or event. As with Yelp, Foursquare, and other review-oriented services, it's advisable to keep track of Loopt and what might be said of your business. If you are a storefront, there is some potential, however limited.

Note: After setting up a Loopt account, Julie sent invitations to half a dozen friends. The problem is she used her JulieDPC as her login name, and it showed up in the invite as JulieD—so no one recognized the name, some thought it was spam, and all of them deleted it at first sight!

### Similar platforms

Brightkite, FourSquare, Gowalla, Yelp

# Ning

| URL | www.ning.com |
|---|---|
| Company | Ning |
| Headquarters | Palo Alto, CA |
| Year introduced | 2005 |
| No. Users | 300,000 networks/millions of users |
| Demographics | Everyone |
| Category | Customized social network platform |
| Cost | $20–$500/year |

## The Story in a Nutshell

Ning is a platform that allows people to create their own niche social networks around a topic of their choice. Think of it as a social network of social networks, although users of the sites hosted on Ning do not necessarily know anything about the host platform, as members can use any URL when they create their own network. At its launch, Ning made its source code open, allowing users to modify the application and create their own. As the platform grew and less technically adept users wished to use it, Ning offered customizable templates, which then evolved into a single customizable application aimed at enabling anyone to easily create their own social network. Ning claims to have over 4 million registered members and 2 million Ning Networks.

The company offered a free basic service until July 2010, when it moved to a paid service model, offering three pricing models—Ning Pro, Ning Plus, and Ning Mini—raging from $20 to $500 per year. Ning Mini is the closest version of the application to the previous free model. Limited to 150 members, Mini networks include options for blogs, photos, forums, and embedded video, and administrators can run their own ads. Ning Plus allows for unlimited members and options for chat, groups, events,

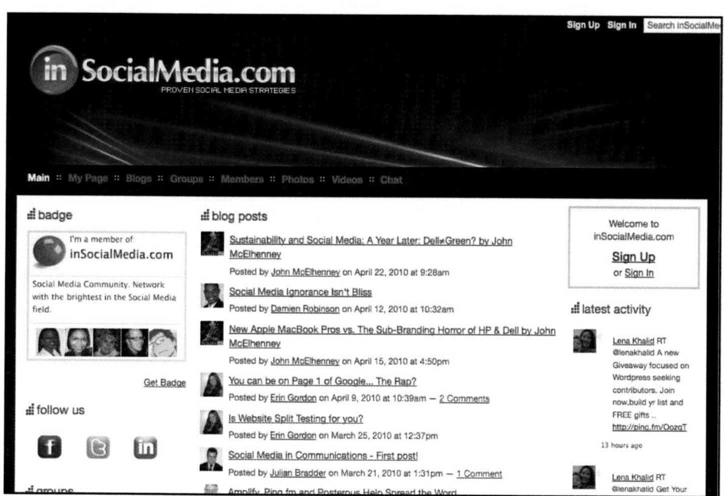


and Ning Apps, as well as advanced customization such as CSS, Javascript, and the Language Editor. In addition to running ads, Plus users can point to their own domain and remove Ning links. Ning Pro adds options for members to upload videos and music and incorporate a branded player plus API access, as well as added storage and bandwidth.

It is easy to review thousands of Ning networks at Ning.com, where they are organized according to broad topics, like music, sports, networking, causes, art, politics, and education (a big constituent of Ning networks). Browsing for ideas on good ways to build and run a Ning network reveals plentiful options, and the platform offers easy setup for the non-technical administrator.

### The business case

Ning offers an easy way to build a community around a topic, product, or idea, so it's a great platform for any organization wishing to do so. As print service providers expand the services they're able to offer clients, adding the ability to create a community social network to, say, a branded portal is an exciting possibility. But even for one's own organization, it could be a great morale booster to offer a network for internal staff to share ideas and build a greater sense of community.

### Similar platforms

BigTent, Facebook, MySpace, SocialGO

# Plaxo

| | |
|---|---|
| URL | www.plaxo.com |
| Company | Plaxo, Inc. (subsidiary of Comcast) |
| Headquarters | Mountain View, CA |
| Year introduced | 2002 |
| No. Users | 50 million |
| Demographics | Adult professional |
| Category | Social networking, business focus |
| Cost | Free and premium |

## The Story in a Nutshell

Plaxo can best be described as an online address book or contact storage site—although it's evolved into the social category. While there are many now, Plaxo was one of the first services that updated contacts. Plaxo says it is to "bring together all your work and personal contacts into a single unified address book." The service lets the user import contacts from other email sources, including AOL, Gmail, Hotmail, and Yahoo, as well as LinkedIn (which is done by exporting and then importing a .CSV file). Syncing with Microsoft Outlook requires "premium" (for pay) membership. When contact information changes, the contact information will change automatically when all sites are synced through Plaxo. Plaxo touts its privacy policy as "one of the strongest out there," clearly in response to the bad press Facebook has been getting on that subject.

A service like Plaxo can be nice, as it is a centralized repository of all of one's contact data, although with so many professionals carrying smartphones today, many have access to email and address lists through the service associated with those devices. One downside mentioned about Plaxo is that the service will periodically send a message to all people listed in a user's address book and

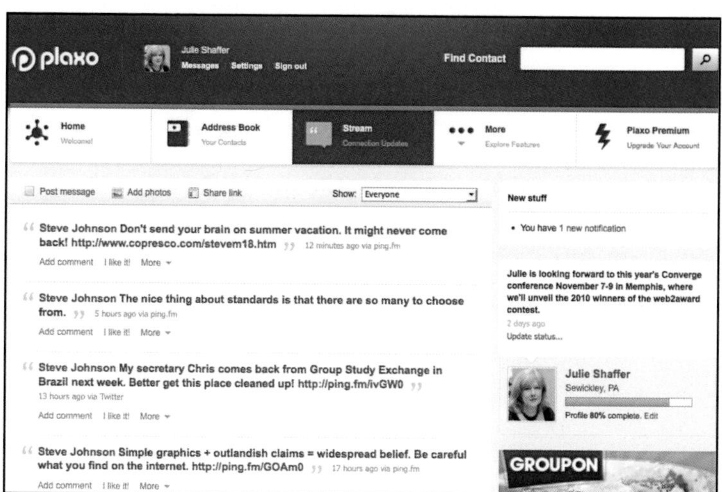


ask to confirm the current information in the contact list—to some this kind of proactive updating is intrusive. The Plaxo interface will feel familiar to anyone who has used other social sites, especially LinkedIn. You can post short messages, links, and photos; review a stream of updates from your contacts; and "like" them as you can in Facebook. One strange feature is the library of ecards, which is a for-pay feature unless you buy the premium service. The Premium service is free for 30 days, but it is not clear what the price is going to be after that in the sign-up page.

## The business case

Why would one use Plaxo when one is already using LinkedIn? The main reason would be for the original purpose, as an online address book, although LinkedIn can also be used in that capacity. Plaxo is just another professional social media channel, and it can't really hurt to have a profile there, although it's not clearly essential.

## Similar platforms

Facebook, hi5, LinkedIn, Spoke

# Twitter

| URL | www.twitter.com |
|---|---|
| Company | Twitter, Inc. |
| Headquarters | San Francisco, CA |
| Year introduced | 2006 |
| No. Users | 75 million |
| Demographics | All |
| Category | Social microblogging |
| Cost | Free |

## The Story in a Nutshell

While Twitter is a microblogging site, it still falls clearly into the category of social media. Users create an identity, and then build a network by following others and being followed. Twitter is a fairly simple service: users write and post ultra-short messages (limited to 140 text characters) called tweets. Tweets can be read by followers and may be open to the public or sent directly to assigned followers. There is no fee in general for using Twitter. Twitter announced in May 2010 that it will update its Terms of Service for developers and prohibit third-party advertising networks and developers from inserting ads into a user's stream, citing that this will "preserve the unique user experience Twitter has created" and ensure the "long-term health and value of the platform." This move will put a number of third-party Twitter ad networks like Ad.ly out of business. A cautionary tale that proves developers building products around social media sites are entirely at the mercy of the decision-makers at the social site, not unlike plug-in developers for any application.

Twitter's growth has been a social Cinderella story. Originally, users appeared to be individuals, which grew to organizations, and now includes a wide variety of people, organizations, and causes. Twitter is more of a culture than one might expect

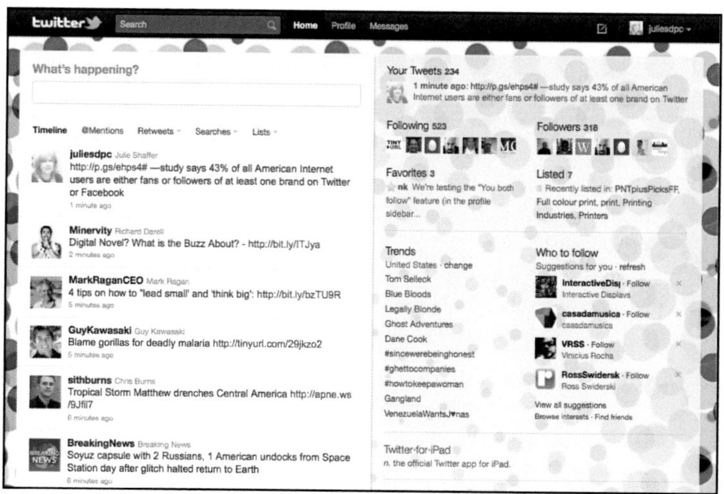


with innovative and inspirational uses. Twitter starts with the simple question, "What's happening?" and people answer this in interesting ways: Surgeons tweeting live from the operating table; simple communications with friends, relatives, and customers; listening to and engaging customers about products and services; a means for employees to communicate within a company. People share links to interesting Internet content, hot topics, photos, videos, and music.

The best and likely the most appreciated business benefit appears to be the new way a business can communicate and form relationships with customers. Proper use of Twitter has the added bonus of building a bigger digital footprint on the internet. The use of Twitter's application programming interface for sending and receiving text messages by other applications often eclipses direct use of Twitter.

### The business case

Twitter is one of the best ways to become a thought leader on a topic or industry. There are entire businesses built around training people to use Twitter most effectively, and specialized applications to enhance the Twitter experience abound. Twitter is an essential platform at this time, both for individuals and for organizations, as it offers significant reach, especially when tied in with LinkedIn and Facebook. Businesses can also pay to be included in the "Who to Follow" feature, an option not unlike buying an ad on Facebook or LinkedIn.

### Similar platforms

Facebook, Plaxo

# Yelp

| | |
|---|---|
| URL | www.yelp.com |
| Company | Yelp, Inc. |
| Headquarters | San Francisco, CA |
| Year introduced | 2004 |
| No. Users | 38 million visitors (August 2010) |
| Demographics | Young adult |
| Category | Location-based social networking |
| Cost | Free to users/paid ads |

## The Story in a Nutshell

Yelp is a social service to help consumers review and find local businesses. Individuals sign on to the fee service and become "Yelpers" helping to build the network of over 11 million local reviews. Yelp is a free service but is monetized by selling ads to local businesses, which are clearly marked as such on the site. Business owners can also create a free account which is a good way to help control how the business is portrayed on the site (users can write about businesses without that business having created an account). Yelp is broadly used, especially in major cities and can be critical in building word-of-mouth referrals. Of course it can be used to amplify complaints too. Like other location-based social sites, users can gain elite recognition through the site. The Yelp Elite Squad is what the company calls the Yelpers who frequently contribute well-written reviews under a real name and photo. These people are given a Yelp Elite badge on their profile, branding them a valued community member.

As a business, once listed, a company can communicate with customers both privately or publicly. The account provides analytics to track how many people view your business page. It is possible to create a mini site with photos, history, and announcements. From

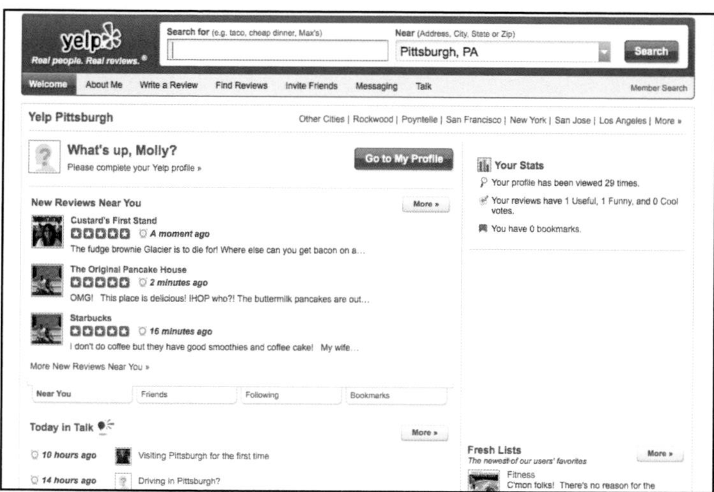


a customer's point of view, if they are seeking "printing services" in a ZIP Code, the site will display a small map with designators as well as a listing with contact information. If the company has been reviewed by customers, the reviews would be indicated. The search needs to be refined since "printers" also would yield a hotel that offers printers for guests. If you seek "marketing" services, any company that is in a marketplace or market square would come up.

## The business case

After exploring the business owner section and services, we became convinced that registering your business on Yelp would be an excellent move and would help users to find your business. This is especially true if you have a brick-and-mortar storefront operation. Posting complaints or compliments about customer service on public social sites is becoming standard operating procedure for a lot of consumers, so keeping abreast of what's said about you in any of these geo-social sites is important. Since the focus of Yelp is to do just that, it is really important to pay attention to it in particular. The help services of Yelp are impressive. Twenty-five million unique visitors were reported for April 2010 by (siteanalytics.compete.com). Certain metro areas have a greater penetration of Yelp listings (the top 30 are listed on yelp.com), so companies in these areas should be most inclined to register and monitor. If nothing else, keep monitoring Yelp, it has a good chance of growing and being a good source to exploit word-of-mouth referrals.

## Similar platforms

Foursquare, Gowalla, Loopt

# YouTube

| URL | www.youtube.com |
|---|---|
| Company | YouTube, LLC (subsidiary of Google, Inc.) |
| Headquarters | San Bruno, CA |
| Year introduced | 2005 |
| No. Users | 48 million |
| Demographics | Diverse |
| Category | Video sharing |
| Cost | Free |

## The Story in a Nutshell

U.S. Internet users watched 30.3 billion videos in April 2010 (comScore.com), with 13.1 billion video (that's 43.2% of all the videos viewed online) views through Google sites of which YouTube accounted for the vast majority. YouTube is simply *the* place people go to watch videos. YouTube was put together by three former PayPal employees in 2005 and was bought by Google a year later. While much of YouTube's content is provided by amateur videographers (with clips going viral to millions of page views), there are also many professional organizations, like TV networks and movie companies, which take advantage of YouTube's huge potential audience through the company's partnership program. YouTube offers many advertising opportunities including in-video ads, which can appear on videos that relate to a particular brand. Businesses can also create YouTube channels, completely branded and customized. There are also promoted videos that work much like Google AdWords, where a company's promoted videos can show up when specific keywords are used in a YouTube search.

YouTube is used by people of all ages and backgrounds, from professional moviemakers to tweeners. Anyone can view YouTube videos without opening an account, but users must be registered in order to upload a

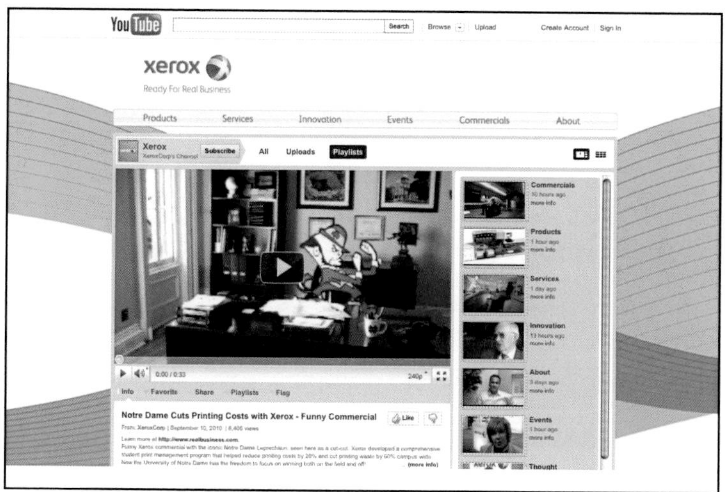


video. Because it's a video site, there are many helpful videos on YouTube for users to learn how to take advantage of all of the options the platform avails.

The list of branding options for marketers is many, including video page banners, video page icons, and branded channels with banners and links. Branded channels can be embedded on other sites so they can be shared with Web pages or blogs.

YouTube Insight, the platform's analytics and reporting tool, enables anyone with a YouTube account to view detailed statistics about the audience for the their uploaded videos. With Insight, you can see how often a video is viewed, by which region in the world, and how popular it is in comparison with other videos being watched.

### The business case

With options for branded channels, ad banners, and analytics through YouTube Insight, YouTube has really developed a full-fledged opportunity for marketers to take advantage of its massive audience. But even if a company doesn't wish to pay for these options, YouTube is a great place to host videos and do your own grassroots promotion through other social media sites. It can be a challenge to put together a meaningful video (and too many printers simply post videos of their plant in operation, which no one really cares to see) but it's well worth the investment.

### Similar platforms

blip,tv, Gawkk, Hulu, Metacafe, VEVO, Vimeo

# 5 Tips for Social Media Travelers

It's pretty easy to set up a profile on most public social media platforms, but you have to do a little digging to take full advantage of the options most offer. We created this section of the book to help those just starting out on their social media engagement journey with some step-by-step tips to make the most out of the social platforms—but even a seasoned social media traveler is likely to find a few useful nuggets they may have been too busy to discover on their own.

We focus here only on the big three social networking platforms: Facebook, LinkedIn, and Twitter, along with a few tips on monitoring and aggregation tools to help you better manage your social engagement efforts.

## LinkedIn

### Create a Unique URL

To help build your personal brand (and it's important to do that, especially if you're in sales or want to grow your reputation as a thought leader) create a **LinkedIn "vanity URL"**—it will be something like www.linkedin.com/in/yourfullname. **This can be used to help optimize your own Google search results.** LinkedIn has a high **Google PageRank,** so a personalized URL

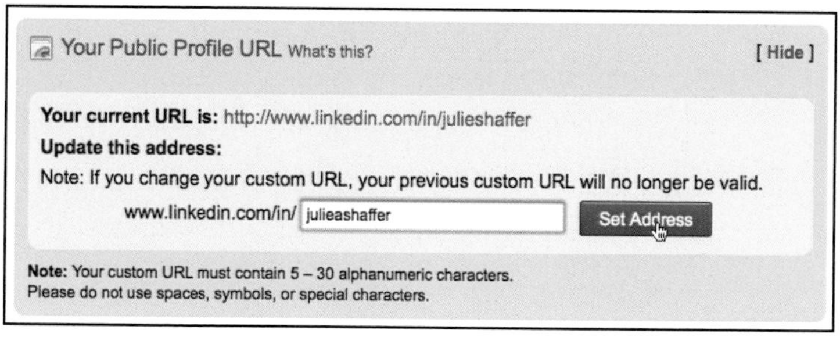

Your Public Profile URL What's this? [ Hide ]

**Your current URL is:** http://www.linkedin.com/in/julieshaffer
**Update this address:**
Note: If you change your custom URL, your previous custom URL will no longer be valid.
www.linkedin.com/in/ julieashaffer Set Address

**Note:** Your custom URL must contain 5 – 30 alphanumeric characters.
Please do not use spaces, symbols, or special characters.

with LinkedIn in the name will help your name come up closer to the top in a Google search. Here's how you do it.

1. Click on "Edit Profile" from the "Profile" dropdown menu (found in the top navigation bar of the home page).

2. Click on "Edit" next to the URL listed on the "Public Profile" line.

3. Click on "Edit" in the "Your Public Profile URL" section at the top of page. This will take you to a page that reveals your current URL and lets you update that address. Most custom URLs begin with www.linkedin.com/in; you can change the part that comes after that using 5–30 alphanumeric characters, no symbols. If you have a well-known nickname or word you'd like to use other than your full name, you can add that here instead (although for LinkedIn we recommend that you stick with your own name, although if you have a common one, it may already be taken and you'll have to settle for an alternative).

4. Click on the "Set Address" button once you have entered your custom URL and you're done. You can change your custom URL after you've set it, but be aware that if you do, your previous custom URL will no longer be valid.

5. Key it into a search engine and test it out! Now add it to your email signature or business card.

### Give recommendations to get them

Having **Recommendations** from your peers or customers on your LinkedIn profile is **a great indicator of the types of relationships you build and even the quality of your work.**

If you've just started using LinkedIn and don't have any recommendations, or even if you've been on for a while and don't have any recent ones, how do you go about getting them? Well, directly asking one of your contacts for a recommendation is something many people do, but it can be kind of awkward for both of you. If you've gotten such a request from someone else,

Make a recommendation

Name: Mary | Garnett | mgarnett@printing.org

Enter a name OR select from your connections list.

Recommend this person as a:

- **Colleague:** You've worked with them at the same company
- **Service Provider:** You've hired them to provide a service for you or your company
- **Business Partner:** You've worked with them, but not as a client or colleague
- **Student:** You were at school when they were there, as a fellow student or teacher

Continue

you know what we mean: it kind of puts you on the spot. A softer way to do it is to **write a recommendation for someone else.** When you write a recommendation, LinkedIn sends that person a note with the text of your recommendation and asks if they want to reciprocate. Most people will be pleased with the fact that you thought to recommend them and will reciprocate.

Think of contacts with whom you've been pleased to work or someone that's done a good job for you on a project (or okay, just someone from whom you'd like to receive a recommendation). Don't be overly flowery or verbose in your recommendation of them; just honestly put down what you see as some of their best qualities or describe the great job they did for you.

The recommendation you write won't be posted automatically on your contact's profile. LinkedIn shows your contact the recommendation you wrote, asking their approval to post it to your profile, and then asks them if they want to reciprocate. Even if they only accept your recommendation without reciprocation, **your name is now a more prominent part of their profile.**

## Importing contacts to your LinkedIn network

To expand your LinkedIn network you either ask someone else to connect with you or you accept someone else's invitation to connect. You can search for people you already know from your own address book to jump in quickly. It's a pretty easy process—here's a quick walk-through.

1. Log in to LinkedIn and click the "Add Connections" link at the top right of the screen.

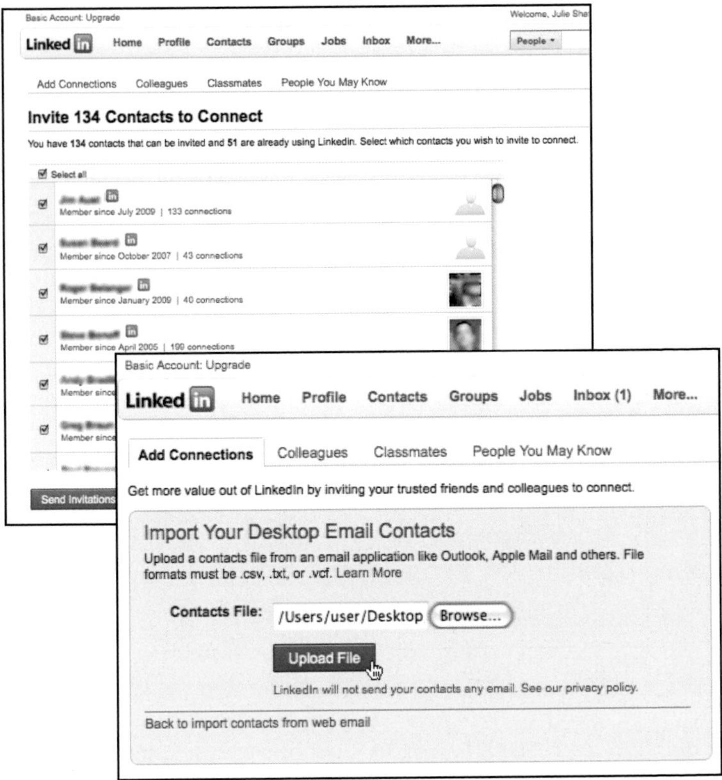


2. You can add your contacts from Web-based email platforms, like Gmail, just by entering your user name and password in the “See Who You Already Know on LinkedIn” section of the next page.

3. If you want to harvest contacts from an enterprise email platform like Outlook, you just have to import a contact list in a. csv, .txt, or .vcf format, which you've previously exported from that application. You can find out how to do that from the help center for each of those applications. (For Entourage, simply click on “Export from the File” menu and select “Contacts to a List” when asked “What do you want to export?” on the next screen.)

4. Once you've imported your contacts, LinkedIn presents you with a list of all of them, indicating which have a profile on LinkedIn. You can choose to select all and

send them all an invitation, but it will be a generic one that says something like "Join My Network on LinkedIn" or "YourName would like to stay in touch on LinkedIn."

While this is a quick way to invite dozens of people in one fell swoop, **it's far more effective to customize the canned invitation message,** especially when you send invitations to people who are not already in your email contacts list. This means you'll be sending invitations one at a time, but it could be worth it to send personalized messages.

## Finding contacts through filters and search

Besides the Add Connections option, LinkedIn offers three more filters for finding connections: Colleagues, Classmates, and People You May Know. **Colleagues** will be anyone who lists the same current or previous place of employment as you in their profile. **Classmates** will have noted that they attended the same school as you, at the same time. **People You May Know** works by looking for common attributes between individuals (e.g., same company, industry, or school) and makes a prediction on likelihood that you might know that person. After you've done a search through either of these filters, LinkedIn lets you create a customized message you can send to invite the entire group at once. If it's a group from a previous employer, you can say

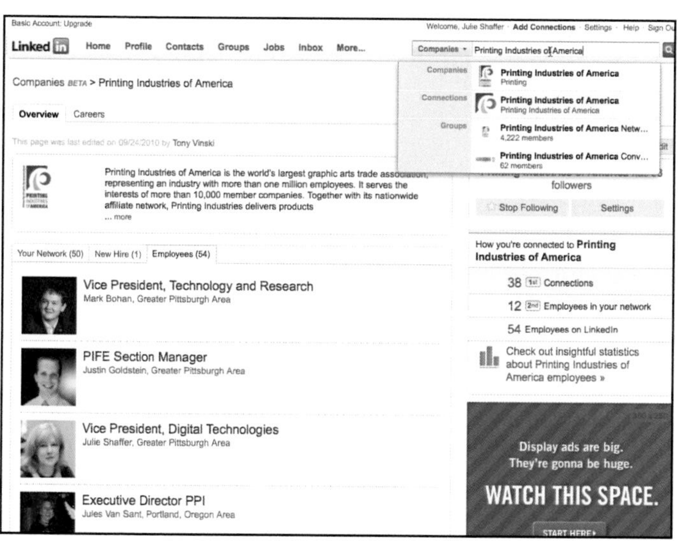

something like "Hey, was thinking about the good-old days at ABC Printing. Let's catch up through LinkedIn!" Still not as nice as a personalized message, but at least it tells the person what you have in common if you haven't been in touch with them in a long time.

You can also find people through the search function that's fixed in the top right corner of any LinkedIn page. Select "People" in the search pull-down menu and enter a name. You'll be presented with a list of LinkedIn profiles, and you can scroll through them to find the person you're looking for. You can also refine your search using filters.

The **Advanced** search option let's you do a search based on the same filters. Beyond the basic filter search for name, current and past company, location, school, title, or keyword, you can search for contacts based on relationship to you (1st, 2nd, or 3rd degree or Group) and industry. If you want to purchase LinkedIn Premier ($25–$100 per month depending on level purchased), you have more advanced search options including LinkedIn group participation, interests, job function, seniority level, and years of experience and whether they work for a *Fortune* 1000 company. Obviously a lot of **this search refinement is good for prospecting employees or for jobs, but it's also a great way to prospect for clients.**

Similarly, you can select Companies as the main search criteria and enter a specific company name. You will be presented a list of employees with LinkedIn profiles broken into three categories: those in your network, those who are new hires, and the entire list of all people who claim to work at the company on their LinkedIn profile. A relatively new LinkedIn feature is the ability to follow a company, which is done simply by searching for a company and clicking the "follow" option on the right side of the page. You can create custom settings for how you want to follow a company and be notified when an employee joins, leaves, or is promoted or when the company updates its profile.

### Using search to find a contact in a vertical

Say I've built a Web portal for a pharmaceutical company to manage the collateral material and labels for some of their brands. Now that I have the experience and infrastructure to

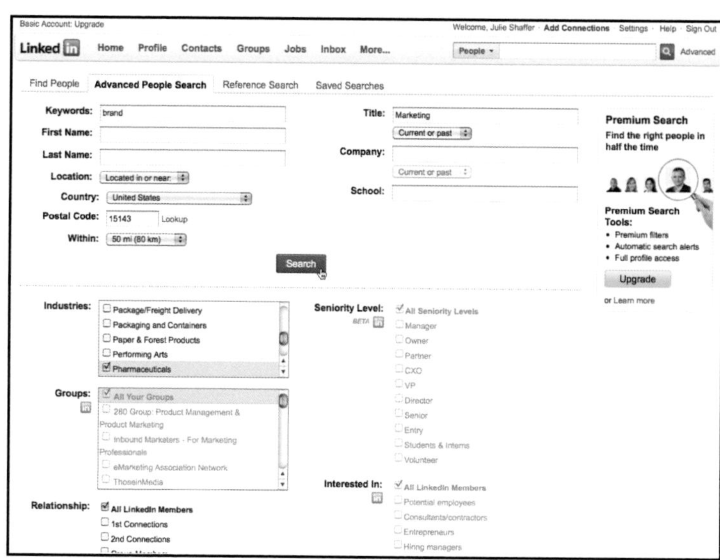


host this kind of portal, I'd like to maximize it by offering a similar portal to another company. But I have no contacts in any other pharmaceutical company, so I want to use LinkedIn to find them. Here is one way I could go about finding a contact, using the Advanced search option (without using any of the "for pay" search options).

1. Select "People" on the search pull-down and click on the "Advanced" link.

2. I'm presented with a page offering a number of search fields. I want to contact people who are in the marketing department, so I enter "marketing" in the Title field.

3. I only want to talk with people within my own vicinity, so I set a distance of 50 miles under the "Within" field, based on my ZIP Code. The distance option goes to 100 miles.

4. I select "Pharmaceutical" within the Industries section and "All LinkedIn Members" from the Relationship section. I could limit my search to only those in my network, but at this point I'd like to see as many potential contacts as possible.

5. I choose to sort by Connections, in the hopes of finding some potential contacts within my network. (The sort option is way down at the bottom of the page.)

6. After clicking "Search" I am served up a list of more than 80 people with marketing in a past or current title.

7. There is one 2nd degree contact at the top of the list, a marketing communication director at a relatively small local company. I find our mutual acquaintance is someone I know well. This is a viable lead.

8. At this point I can ask my mutual contact for an introduction through the Get Introduction option. I could ask this person to be part of my network too, but we think it's generally bad form to make connection requests to complete strangers.

9. A second person in the list is in one of the same LinkedIn groups that I am. This means I can send a direct message to this person and not rely on InMail (which is only an option with the "for pay" Premier service) or an introduction, a big benefit of joining groups.

**Once you start to really master the search tools to glean potential new business contacts, you'll learn how to**

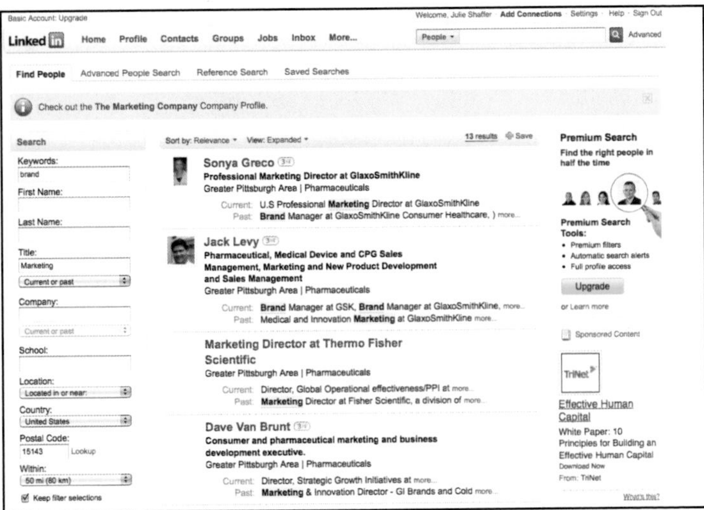

**effectively refine your searches.** In this example, I attempt to narrow the results by adding a keyword to my search criteria. Since the portal product I offer is a brand management tool, I figure it would resonate with people who have had some experience in branding. So I add "brand" to the keyword search, leaving all other criteria the same as my initial search. I came up with a far smaller list of potential contacts, 13, but all of them are marketing experts, and three are brand managers—the perfect audience for my message.



## Export LinkedIn contacts

Your LinkedIn network is a rich database of people who have agreed to stay in contact with you—and unlike other social media platforms, LinkedIn lets you take it with you. **You can export all of your LinkedIn contacts to a file that you can then import into a CRM system, spreadsheet, or address book.** Take advantage of this opportunity to own your LinkedIn contact database and export yours to a place where you can use it outside of the platform. You only get a limited amount of data—first and last name, email address, company, and current job title—but that's enough for, say, an email or PURL campaign.

1. Select "My Connections" from the Contacts pull-down menu.

2. Click the small link at the bottom right of the screen that says "Export Connections."

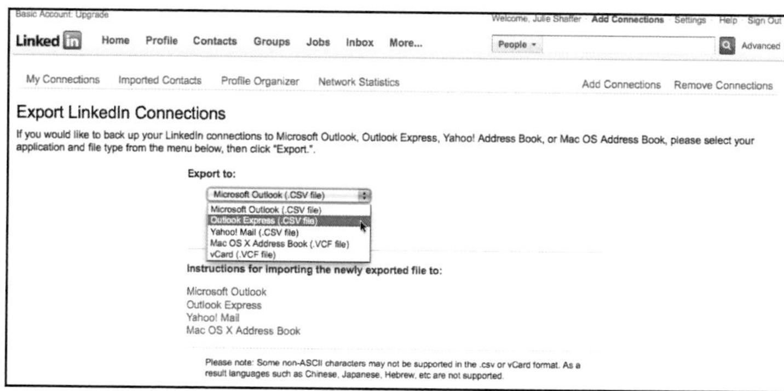

3. Select the format in which you want to export your contacts—.CSV or vcard .VCF—and enter the text from the security image to verify that you're not a spambot and click "Export." LinkedIn even provides help files covering how to import the file into your email client.

4. Now that you've got the data (you can open the .CSV file directly in Excel as a spreadsheet) and place it into your CRM or whatever you're using as your CRM. Now you can include additional information as you gather it or add other types of data, like phone number, how you know the person, whether they are a potential client or peer, and so on.

Now you have a backup of your LinkedIn contact database if nothing else.

Make sure you have noted two email contact addresses in LinkedIn. Many people set up their account using their business email address as the primary contact, and that seems to make sense because this is a business-oriented platform. But consider this: if you only list your business email as your contact address and then you leave the company for whatever reason and the company closes your email account, you'll no longer have access to your LinkedIn account. Redundancy always makes sense, but doubly so when you're talking about your precious contacts database; keep it your own and add a second, personal email address, and you might want to consider making it your primary LinkedIn contact address.

## Ask (and answer) questions on LinkedIn Answers

The **Answers** option in LinkedIn is a great place to interact with people from the entire LinkedIn community, not just your personal network. When you ask a question in Answers, you will by default query all of the people on LinkedIn, unless you opt only to share your question with connections.

You can ask a question for the obvious reason—you could use an answer to a specific problem. But you can also put questions out there to stir up conversation and interact with new people on a topic of your choice. It also gives you the option to directly email 200 of your own contacts with the question so you can literally

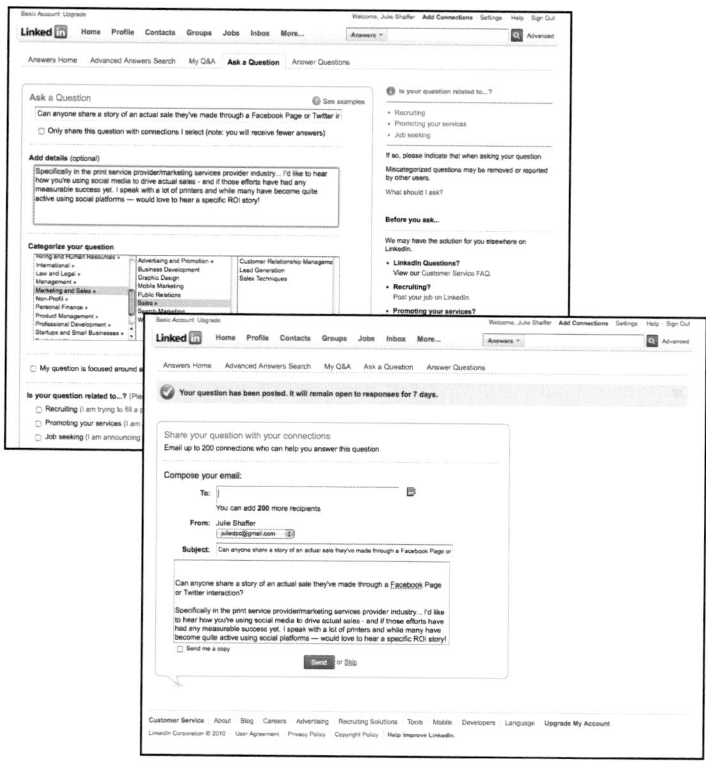


put the question, and your name, in front of them through another venue.

When you ask a question, you will then choose the answer that you feel best answers it. The person who answered the question will then be given a point of expertise in the category of the answer. **That means if you answer other people's questions, you too can build your reputation as a subject matter expert!** All this will be reflected on your profile and is a great way to build rapport with others in the LinkedIn community.

To ask questions:

1. Select "Answers" under the "More…" pull-down menu. *Note:* You can ask up to 10 questions per month.
2. Before you ask a question make sure someone else hasn't asked a very similar question recently. Select the "Advanced Answer" tab and enter a couple of

keywords and, if you wish, a category as well. If your question hasn't already been answered, click the "Ask a Question" tab.

3. Enter a business-related question as simply as possible (you have to do it in 256 characters or fewer). If you want to restrict your question to your own connections, check the "Only share this question with connections I select" option.
4. Flush out your question a bit more in the "Add" details section (you have room for 1,996 characters).
5. Select a category under which you want the question to be organized. If the question relates to a geographic region, choose an area based on country or ZIP Code.
6. If the question is overtly intended to promote a business, you can select that option.
7. Click the "Ask Question" button. You'll be presented with a follow-up screen that gives you the option to email your question directly to 200 of your contacts.

### Syncing your LinkedIn and Twitter accounts

LinkedIn offers some tight ties with Twitter which you can manage through **Twitter Settings.** The Settings page gives you the option to choose to display all tweets on your profile or only tweets in which you've added a **#in** tag (example tweet:

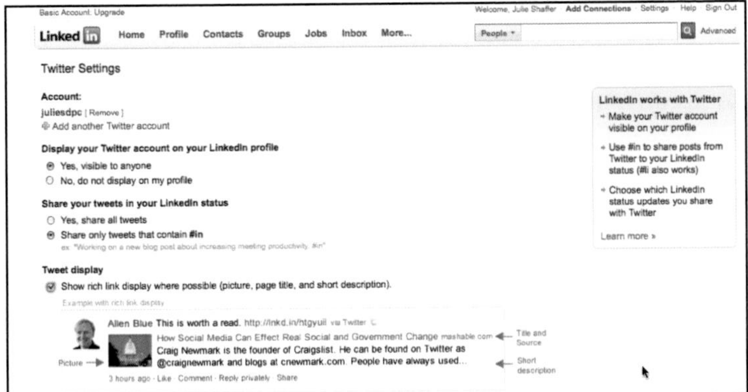

*Looking forward to talking about LinkedIn in my Converge Conference session. #in*).

You'll also find the **Tweets** application under the "More..."' menu (if you don't see it, you may have to add it from the Application Directory, also accessible from the "More..." pull-down). From Tweets you can compose and send Twitter updates without leaving the LinkedIn platform. You can also see all of the people you follow and all of the tweets you've made. Select the "Connections" tab and you'll see all of your LinkedIn contacts that also have a Twitter account. Each contact you are not already following on Twitter has a **"Follow"** button you can click to follow them automatically without leaving LinkedIn.

Should you follow all of your LinkedIn contacts on Twitter as well? Not necessarily, but doing so helps you engage with them on an additional platform and, should they reciprocate and follow you as well, offers you an additional venue through which to engage with them.

## Beef up your LinkedIn profile

The line of copy directly under your name on your LinkedIn Profile is called a **Headline.** Many people have their job title listed here (if nothing else is put into this area, LinkedIn will put your title here by default), but that's a mistake—your title belongs in the **Position** section where you list the details about your job. Your Headline should be just that: a pithy statement about what you have to offer professionally.

So instead of merely listing your job title, put some key phrases about what you do or what you have to offer in the Headline section. This is critical, because when people find you in LinkedIn searches, or when you contribute to Group discussions or the Answers section, the first thing they see is a little box with your name, photo, and your headline. It should tell them more about you than just your current job title. **You should treat your headline like your introduction when networking. Focus on what you can do to help them.**

By the same token, you should take full advantage of the **Summary** section of your profile to tell a more detailed story about yourself. Many people, once again, put their job title here and maybe a sentence or two about their job. **You get 2,000**

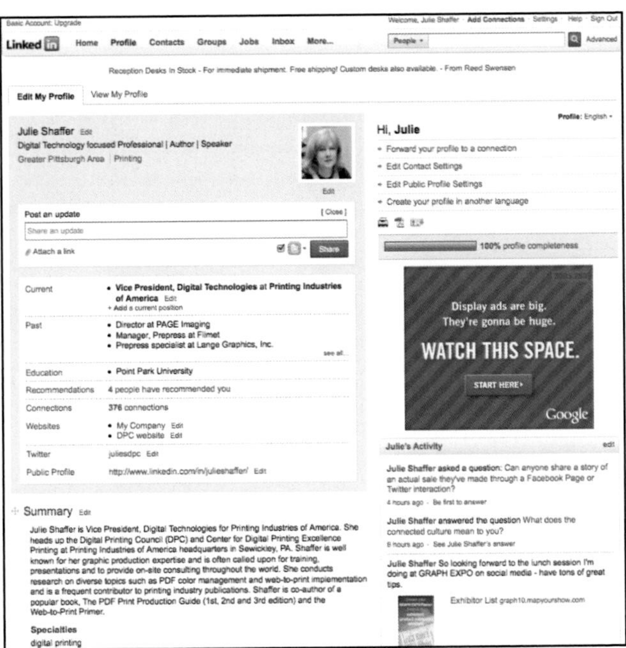


**characters in this Summary area, so use it all to tell a story about what you bring to the table.** You can list articles you've written, speeches you've given, case studies about customers you've helped, and so on.

## Use Applications to extend your reach

Like Facebook and other social networks, LinkedIn offers application support and the option to link to other social platforms. Check out the **Applications Directory** ("Get More Applications") accessible from the "More…" pull-down menu.

If you have a blog and want to further syndicate it through your profile, you can do so using the **Blog Link** application. Blog Link updates your LinkedIn profile with your latest blog posts and, conversely, pulls the posts made by others in your network so you can keep tabs on them all from within LinkedIn. It works with most blogging platforms, including TypePad, Movable Type, Vox, WordPress.com, WordPress.org, Blogger, LiveJournal, and many more.

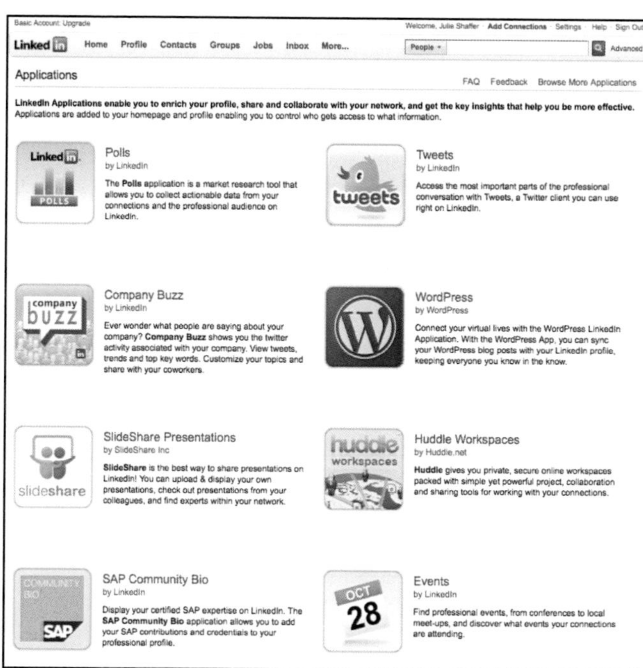


You can also load up the **Polls** application to run opinion polls of your 1st-degree connections (you can pay to poll a larger group).

To let people know the events you'll be attending or notify your network about events you're managing, the **Events** application is the right tool, or let people know where you'll be through the **TripIt** (MyTravel) application.

If you do presentations, you can use the **SlideShare** link to post them on LinkedIn.

**Sharing your blog posts and your slideshows certainly adds to your reputation as a thought leader** and shows the value you contribute to the industry. So take advantage of these applications that enhance how you can use LinkedIn in your business.

## Take part in LinkedIn Groups

Out of all the features on LinkedIn, the **Groups** feature is one of the most powerful for helping you actually engage with others. Leading a group, or actively taking part in a group's discussion, positions you as an expert and it makes you the center of an information topic.

There are more than 700,000 groups on LinkedIn, some, like the **eMarketing Association Network,** boasting well over 100,000 members. But with only a few hundred members, a group can foster very active dialogue, especially on a hot topic in a particular industry. The **Printing Industries of America Networking Group,** for example, is well attended with lively conversations, and it connects our members with the greater graphic communications industry. **The value you will receive out of group engagement is tremendous and it can generate a powerful community that supports its growth.**

While it's tempting to join hundreds of groups, if only to see the long list added to your profile, it's best to keep it down

to a manageable number, say two dozen or less, that cover topics about which you're very knowledgeable (so you can feel comfortable taking part in the conversation there) or about which you want to grow more knowledgeable. When you join a group, LinkedIn shows you a list of all the other group members who are in your network. **This provides you with another point of common interest with others and another opportunity to engage.**

You can manage the setting for each group you join, things like whether and how often you'd like to get email updates about the group discussions, but you have to do this for each group you've joined individually. You'll find the interface when you're on a page for a specific group, from "My Settings" under the "More…" pull-down menu.



## Twitter

Setting up a Twitter account is a straightforward and easy process. Just click the "Sign up" button at Twitter.com, enter your name, a username and password (availability of both are instantly checked—your user name can be your name, your company name, or a term that will be recognizable to your audience), an email address, agree to the terms of service, and create your account.

You'll then be presented with a bare-bones home page. Before you start sending tweets you have to set up your profile and customize your Twitter home page. **You could just leave the generic Twitter clouds in the background, but that doesn't help promote your brand.** The following tips will help you enhance your new Twitter account.

### Making the most of your profile

Choose "Settings" found under the pull-down menu in the upper right corner of your home page and you're presented a screen with your account information and six tabs along the top for areas that you can customize: Account, Password, Mobile, Notices, Profile, Design.

The two areas that you should set up now are your profile and the design of the page. While it might not seem that critical, **it's really essential to create a compelling profile,** as this is what potential followers see, and **people use it to help determine if you are worthy of being followed.** Here are some specific tips on how to set up your profile to make it unique and compelling.

1. You'll want to upload a profile **Picture;** otherwise your tweets will be accompanied with a generic egg-head image (only newbs or people who don't want to be recognized allow that). If this is a personal Twitter page, then by all means use a photo of you for your profile picture. If you will use this Twitter account to follow and connect with business acquaintances, you will want to use either a professional photo or a snapshot that shows you in "business casual" (i.e., not in a Speedo or bikini on the beach!). However, if this is to be a business-centric page, you will want to make this picture something like a logo or other compelling image that favorably represents the organization.

   The profile picture has to be between 48k and 700k in file size in JPEG, PNG, or GIF format. You won't be able to upload anything larger or smaller or in another

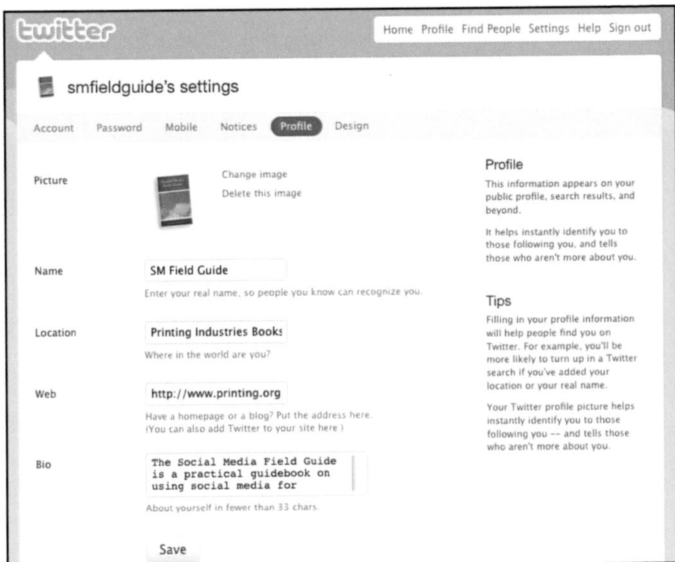

format. Twitter will display the profile image as a perfect square, so if you have a picture that doesn't have an equal height-to-width ratio, it will display a square hunk right out of the middle. So use a picture with the main content in the center, or better yet, crop the image with even height and width dimensions in a photo editing software package and you'll get the precise crop you want when you upload it into your Twitter profile.

2. You can set the **Name** to either your own name or that of the organization. This is different than the username you set up when you created the account. The user name is your official Twitter account identifier (i.e., the Twitter URL for this book is http://twitter.com/#!/smfieldguide with an address of @smfieldguide). The name field in your profile is the name of the person who set up the account, and this is displayed on your profile (in the new version of Twitter, that is—more on that when we get to the Design tab). You can leave this as your actual name or make it the company name instead if you're building a business account not linked to a specific person.

3. If you want to tell the world where you are located, set a physical **Location.** This is beneficial if you're looking for a local audience, and most businesses would want to state the location of its headquarters here. However, there is no reason you have to provide a physical location; in the case of the *Field Guide* page, we put "Printing Industries Bookstore."

4. While it might seem obvious that you'd want to list your company home page under **Web,** consider having your Web developer set up a special landing page just for the people who click through and visit you from Twitter. This has an SEO benefit and will help you determine some of your reach from this social media platform and gives you a chance to further your communication with them. If you have a blog, you might want to set that as the link from your Twitter account as a place to continue your Twitter conversations in a venue where you're not limited to 140 characters per message.

5. Your **Bio** is arguably the most important part of your profile setup. You get 160 characters and should use it judiciously. This, more than anything else, tells potential followers who you are (or who you think you are) and should be more than just a statement like "we're a print/ marketing services provider." It could be your company slogan or tag line or a laundry list of what you offer. Even better is a light-but-information-filled couple of sentences that says something compelling about you. For example, author Paul Castain's (@paulcastain) bio says this: *Author Castain's Sales Playbook Trainer of sales rock stars. Keeper of the whupass. I specialize in sales training, sales leadership & social media!*

   What's the whupass? Why put such a thing in a bio? People may be curious (is it something like "opening a can of…?") and review his full profile, admire the quality of his Tweets, and maybe follow him. Castain has 12,600-plus followers at the time of this writing.

## Customize the design of your Twitter page

Twitter announced a new version of the platform in September 2010, significantly changing the page layout. While the new version offers far more information on a user's page, it took away a good portion of the background real estate that many

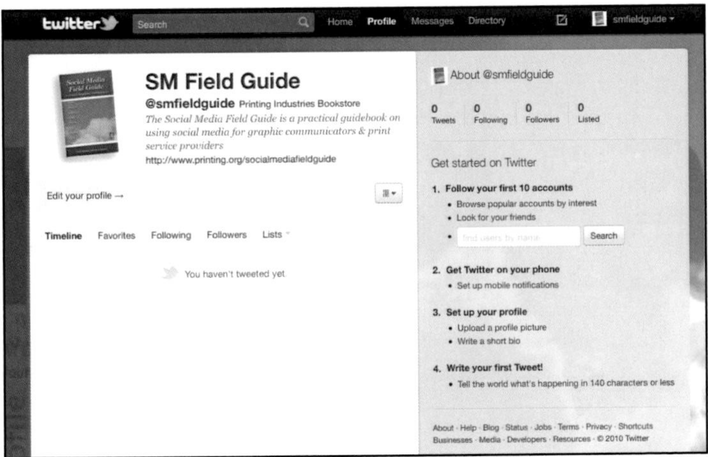

professionals had customized with a branded image. By the time this book is published, it's possible that the new version is all that will be available on Twitter, but as of this writing, you can toggle between the new "preview" version and the original version. **When designing a background for Twitter, it makes sense to design it with the new version in mind.**

While Twitter provides a number of "themes" under the **Design** settings tab, we don't suggest using those. Particularly if you're selling your marketing or creative services, **your Twitter page should show off your creativity as much as possible** within the strict constraints of the platform. If you search on the keywords "Twitter backgrounds" or "Twitter templates" using a search engine, you'll find many sites that offer free or inexpensive canned Twitter backgrounds, and some are quite impressive. But again, it is better to create a unique site that says something about you or your organization's creativity. Still, while you might not want to use a canned template from a resource site like **www.tweetbacks.com,** it is a good idea to download one to get a feel for the "live" area where you can put

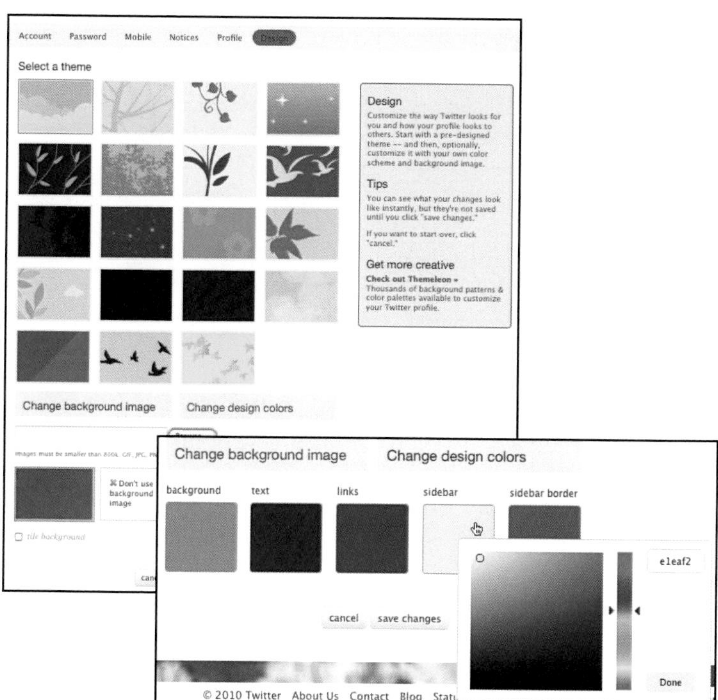

personalized information that won't be obscured by the **Twitter Feed** area.

In the "old" Twitter, there was an area to the left of the Twitter Feed that, when viewed at full screen, offered space to place some special imagery/messaging on the background image. This varied with screen resolution and a user's viewing conditions, but it was about 245 pixels wide. There was space to the right too, but that was less viable for messaging as the upper left corner is the "anchor" for the background image. With the new Twitter layout, this "free" area is much smaller because Twitter is using more real estate on the page for content. That's one reason it's so important to use the bio area so judiciously—you can't "say" much on the background, textwise at least.

**Your Twitter background says a lot about you and your business,** so take the time to come up with a creative design that ties to your other branding efforts. You can create the design in any application from which you can eventually get an image file in PNG, GIF, or JPEG formats. To make sure your background fills the screen for most resolutions, create an image of at least 1600×1024 pixels at 72 dpi. While this may sound like too large an image to be under 800k in size, with JPEG compression in particular, it can be done. Some of the free online templates are available in Photoshop format, while **TweetBacks** offers free templates in PowerPoint format (from which you can save to any of the three acceptable file formats). Keep your most relevant branding/messaging to the upper left corner of the design within roughly 80 pixels from the left edge and not much more than 500 pixels in height. Give it a border of a few pixels at the left and top. It can take a few tries to get the image to mesh just right with the Twitter layout, but it's well worth the effort to have a nice clean design.

Here are the specific steps for setting up your custom Twitter theme:

1. Go to the Design section of the Settings page.
2. Click "Change background image" (under all those canned Twitter themes) and navigate to and upload your background image. Do not click "tile background image" unless that's the technique you're trying to achieve (it's usually ugly, so don't even think about it!).

3. Click the "Change design colors" link. You'll see the canned Twitter theme colors for the background, text, link, sidebar, and sidebar border. If you'd like to change any of these colors, just click on the color patch and you'll be presented with a color picker. Manipulate to the color you like then click "Done."

4. While you can preview them immediately, none of these changes are fixed until you click "save changes" at the bottom of the settings page.



## Finding people on Twitter

A growing number of people add a Twitter handle to their email signatures and business cards (you'll learn how to accomplish this later in this chapter). Enter any known Twitter address in the search bar and you'll find accounts to follow right away. Once you follow a friend, client, or someone with similar interests, you can easily browse the accounts those folks follow (or by whom they are followed) and discover others you wish to follow. This, in our opinion, is really one of the best ways to find others with similar interests.

In the Twitter universe, however, it's perfectly acceptable to follow people you don't know personally as well. The Twitter application offers plenty of ways to help you start connecting with others. When you open a new account, a click on one of the links under the **"Follow your first 10 accounts"** option takes you to the **"Who to Follow"** page. Here you'll find three tabs: "View Suggestions," "Browse Interests," and "Find Friends."

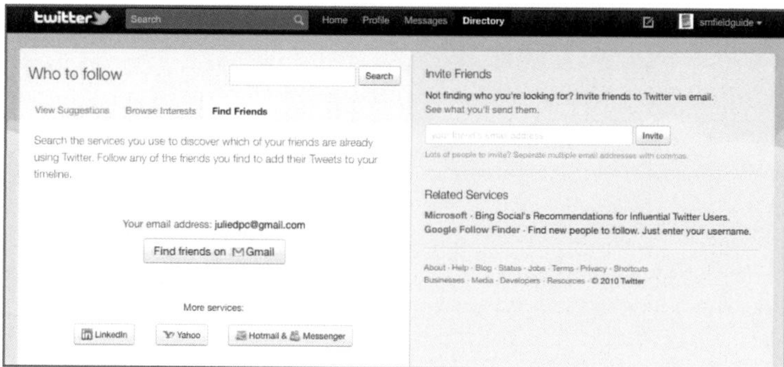

The first two offer suggestions for people with like interests based on an algorithm that looks at your bio information, the people you follow, and the people they follow to make suggestions, but this is really not too helpful when you're entirely new to Twitter, having neither followers nor followees.

The **"Find Friends"** option requires authorizing Twitter to sift through your Web-based email or LinkedIn contacts to find people to follow (the LinkedIn method is described in the LinkedIn tips section of this chapter). There is also a place to key in the email addresses of acquaintances on this page, but that method sends a canned (although editable) message and is really more of an invitation to become a Twitter user. Frankly, it's kind of hokey to send such a message to someone who may already be a seasoned user of the Twitter, so unless you're writing to someone you know for certain is not already a Twitter user, we think it's best avoided.

When you're new to Twitter, it's OK to follow more people than are following you, but be aware that ultimately you should keep your follower-to-following ratio in balance, especially if you want to be viewed as an influencer or resource to others. But **the great thing about following others is that they may just follow you back,** and over time, you'll begin to build your Twitter network!

### Build your Twitter community with third-party tools

Even though Twitter offers a decent search feature **(http://search.twitter.com/)** to help you refine searches by specific criteria (words, hashtags, people, places, dates, and "attitude"), there are third-party applications that offer more refined search options.

**WeFollow** (http://wefollow.com/) lists top Twitter accounts (based on the number of followers each has) by category, with standards like celebrity, social media, entrepreneur, media, politics, and sports. If you want to find people based on a specific tag, you can key it into a search bar, which will suggest known tags that use the characters you're typing, much as Google does, showing you how many accounts relate to the keyword as well. This is a great way to find people in a particular vertical market,

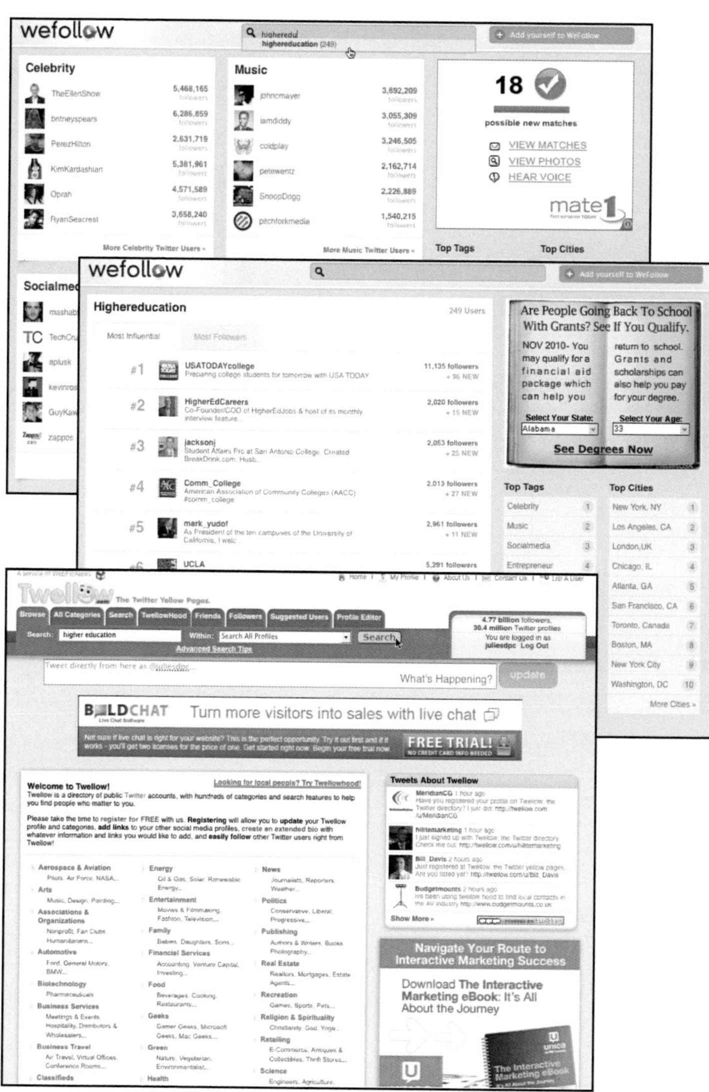


as many would mention it in their profile/bio. You can add your profile to WeFollow too, providing several keywords by which you can be searched.

**Twellow** (www.twellow.com) is the Twitter "yellow pages," claiming to have 4.77 billion followers and more than 30 million Twitter profiles. Here too you can search by keyword or by any of hundreds of preestablished categories. You can link your Twitter account to Twellow and write an expanded bio of 2,000 characters, enhancing what you can say in Twitter. Through the **TwellowHood** option, you can find people in your local region, a handy option for sales representatives.

Those are just two of the Twitter community-building tools on the market. Others include **My Tweeple** (www.mytweeple.com), a relationship management tool aimed at helping users build followers as well as find others to follow. **Twitaholic** (http://twitaholic.com/) simply lists the top 100 Twitter accounts measured by number of followers. **Twitter Friends** (http://twitter-friends.com/) a.k.a. **Tweetmetrics,** is a site that helps you find "relevant" people to follow. Most of these services require that you allow the application to have access to your Twitter account, so be careful and engage in some due diligence before you allow that access—at least do a Web search on the name of any service you're considering using to make sure there aren't known problems or complaints about it.

### Follow Twitter accounts

Like all social media platforms, Twitter is constantly updating and changing. To keep abreast of the latest updates on the Twitter platform, follow the company's links: @feedback, @fledgling, @jointheflock, @safety, @spam, @support, @twi, @

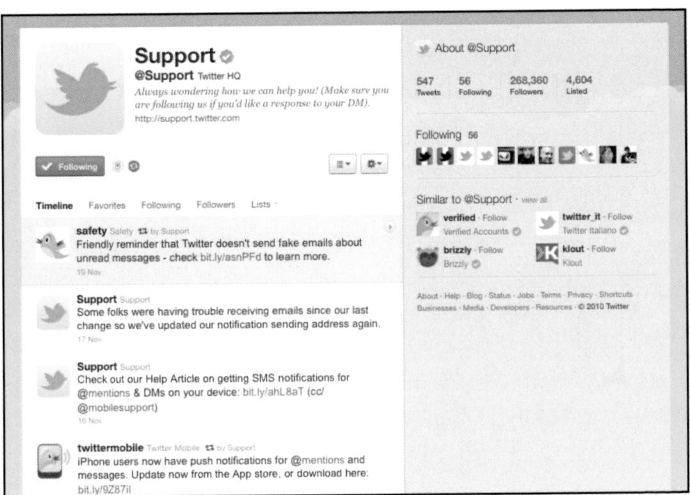

twitter, @twitterapi, @twitterbusiness, @twittermedia, and @twittermobile.

If you're looking for ideas on how to use Twitter in interesting ways, follow **Clever Accounts** (@CleverAccounts), where tweets feature people and organizations doing just that. In one tweet, Clever Accounts recognized **@cookbook,** a site that posts complete recipes in 140 character tweets, like this one: *Salmon Chowder: bbq 2filet3m/side@high. Brwn 2leek&garlc&celery/T oil. Simmr9m+2c h2o&tater/bay. Heat+2c lgtcrm/2T tompaste&dill/s+p; +fish.* You can share your great Twitter story, once you have one, with Clever Accounts, and you'll find they just might feature you in an upcoming message.



## Post more than 140 characters

**Composing meaningful 140 word messages is an art in itself.** Sometimes you have something to say that just can't be said in such a small bite. You can, of course, post a message in several segments, but there are third-party tools that let users post additional content in a Tweet.

**TwitWall** (http://twitwall.com/) is one of these. When you open a TwitWall account, it creates a profile for you that uses your Twitter background, profile picture, and bio. If you want to post a message in more than 140 characters, launch TwitWall and enter your message along with an associated picture or movie if you wish. When you post the message to Twitter, it posts the first part of the message with a link to your TwitWall account. When readers click the link, they are redirected to your TwitWall page, where they can see the full message and any associated files.

**Posterous** (www.posterous.com) provides a way to manage posts to Twitter and most other established social networking accounts from an email account (or Web interface, mobile device, or one of many Twitter clients, like **Tweetie**). Similar to TwitWall, Posterous posts messages on Twitter, using up to 130 characters of the message and using the balance for a link back to the user's Posterous account for the rest of the message. But Posterous is a more powerful site and is **one of a group of tools that can help a user manage many different social accounts in one place.** One can even register a domain through Posterous

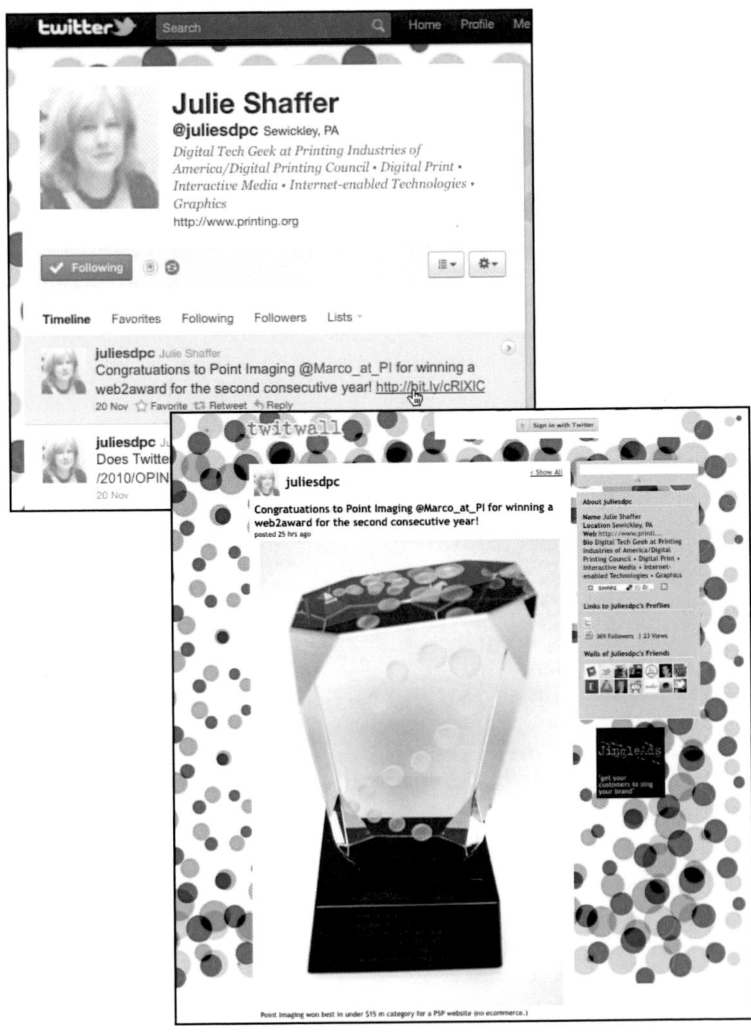


so that your links go to a customized URL, creating a kind of universal social landing page.

## Learning Twitter lingo and etiquette

Like any community, Twitter has its own colloquial language and established way of doing things, and **it behooves you to learn it to more readily join the conversation.** Here are a few key symbols and conventions.

juliesdpc Julie Shaffer
You're a printer & using Twitter, but are you using it effectively? Let's talk about how over lunch #GRAPH_EXPO Tues Oct 5 12:15 pm-1:45 pm
16 Sep

**# (hashtag).** Twitter users place a hashtag (pound symbol) before a word or phrase (tag) in order to add Tweets to a category. While there are no formal rules for hashtags, there are many universally used ones, like **#FollowFriday.** Popular hashtags show up on Twitter searches as trending topics. Anyone can create a hashtag, but be aware that if you add a hashtag to a tweet and you have a public account, anyone who does a search for that hashtag can find your tweet, not just your followers. Hashtags are a great way to build discussion around an event or topic, or to join an existing one; in fact, creating or taking part in a trending topic is the main goal of using a hashtag.

**@.** The @ symbol is a method of calling out to others on Twitter in the form of replies or mentions. If you start a tweet with @username, that message will show up in that user's @ **Mentions** tab. If you're replying directly from someone's tweet by clicking on the curved "Reply" arrow in the update, Twitter will automatically include the @username in your tweet. You can also use the @username in the body of a tweet to give a shoutout or mention to that person, and the tweet will show up in their @Mentions tab.

**Message (formerly known as DM or Direct Message).** Very different from @replies or mentions, a Message is a private correspondence between Twitter users and cannot be viewed by others. Private messages can only be sent to followers, not to anyone who is not following you. They can be sent via your Twitter account on the Web or from a phone or most third-party applications. Note that when a sender or receiver of a private message deletes the message, it disappears from both the sender's and recipient's inboxes.

**RT (Retweet).** Sharing someone else's tweet with your followers is what retweeting is all about. When you use a third-party tool to retweet a post, the tool will usually start the retweet with an "RT" so it's clear the message is a retweet. Many will allow you to add a personal comment to the retweet if the original message is short enough (and you can further shorten the original, but only if you can do so without changing the meaning). If you can, it's a good idea to do so in order to put your personal stamp on a retweeted message, but wholesale posting a message without acknowledging the source is a form of plagiarism, not to mention really uncool in the Twitter world. When you retweet from the **Timeline** in Twitter, the picture and name of the person who posted the original tweet shows up in your Timeline, along with the retweet symbol (two arrows) and your name, indicating that you retweeted that person's comment. Before you retweet anything, verify the link and make sure it's valid or you are wasting your time—and that of your followers.

**Be polite and don't spam on Twitter.** Every Twitter follower is like a gift—they are offering to be your audience. Don't repay them that courtesy by bombarding them with overt sales messages unless that's what your Twitter account is expressly for and your followers know it (i.e., a Dell sales outlet Twitter account is for selling Dell equipment). Try to keep a balance of business and non-business/personal/current events/chatty messages. A decent ratio would be 1 non-business message to every 6–10 industry or business-centric messages. **Social media is social, it is entirely appropriate to mix some personal comments**—as long as they are of the type you'd discuss at a cocktail party or reception with clients—into your Twitter stream.

Thank people for following you or for re-tweeting your messages, but don't use automation tools to automatically send canned messages back to them. A widely used time to thank followers is on Fridays, and often people include the #FollowFriday hashtag in such posts.

### Use a URL shortener to save space

There is no point in wasting any of those precious 140 characters with a URL link—just use a URL shortener to replace long links with much shorter ones. While Twitter now runs messages through a link service (http://t.co) to help prevent malicious activity like phishing attacks, it really doesn't reduce the size of a URL link like third-party applications. Many aggregator tools, like TweetDeck, integrate automated URL shortening tools,

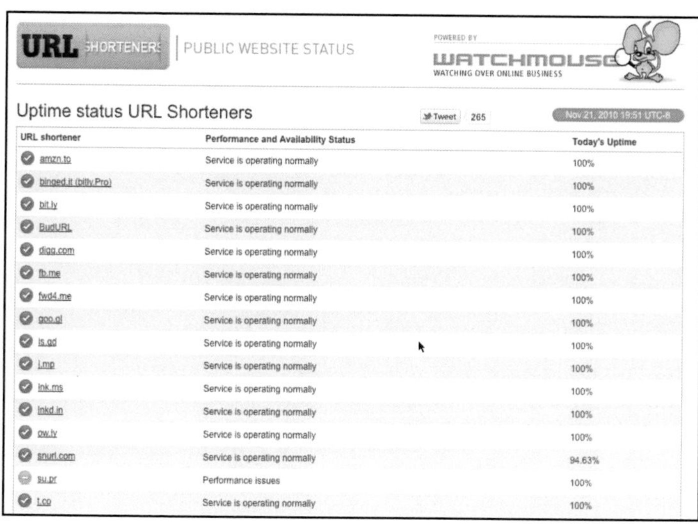


| URL shortener | Performance and Availability Status | Today's Uptime |
|---|---|---|
| amzn.to | Service is operating normally | 100% |
| binged.it (bitly Pro) | Service is operating normally | 100% |
| bit.ly | Service is operating normally | 100% |
| BudURL | Service is operating normally | 100% |
| digg.com | Service is operating normally | 100% |
| fb.me | Service is operating normally | 100% |
| fwd4.me | Service is operating normally | 100% |
| goo.gl | Service is operating normally | 100% |
| is.gd | Service is operating normally | 100% |
| j.mp | Service is operating normally | 100% |
| lnk.ms | Service is operating normally | 100% |
| lnkd.in | Service is operating normally | 100% |
| ow.ly | Service is operating normally | 100% |
| snurl.com | Service is operating normally | 94.63% |
| su.pr | Performance issues | 100% |
| t.co | Service is operating normally | 100% |

but you can also directly use any of dozens of URL shortening applications. Watchdog organization **Watchmouse** built a public site (http://url-shorteners.public-website-status.com/) to help users monitor uptime on these shortener sites. To name just a few, there is **Goo.gl** (offered by Google), **Tinyurl.com, Budurl.com,** and **Bit.ly** (http://bit.ly/). An interesting side note: Bit.ly, like all other trendy domains ending in .ly, is registered through Libya. Another, **vb.ly,** was shut down without warning by the Libyan government during September 2010 for showing an image of the site's co-owner, Violet Blue, wearing a sleeveless blouse, something apparently considered "adult content" under Libyan law. The service was resurrected as **vbly.us** in October 2010.

## What should I tweet about?

Twitter compels you to write a tweet by asking you to answer the question **"What's happening?"** What should you write in that blank box and tweet out to your followers? What do you have to say that will make people find you worth following?

The bottom line answer to that question is, in turn, a series of questions that you have to ask yourself. Why did you open a Twitter account? Who do you want to be perceived as through Twitter? What message do you want to send to the Twitterverse?

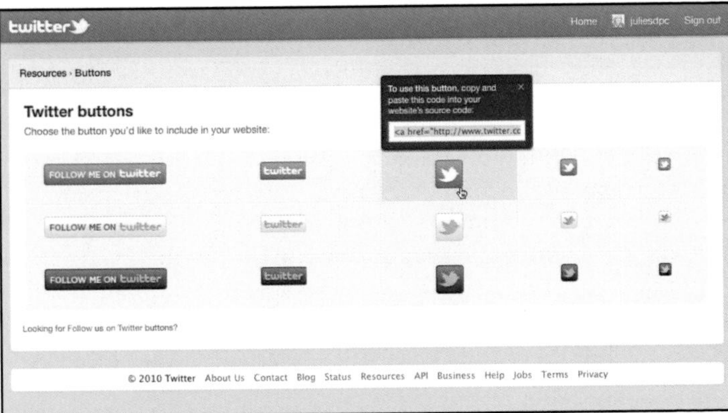


Assuming that you've joined Twitter to use it as a marketing tool to help you grow your business, here are a few ideas:

1. Twitter is a great tool to use as a pointer to your own website or blog. Any time you post something new at either location, let your followers know. And make sure that you have links to your Twitter account on your website and/or blog page. Twitter offers premade follow buttons with the HTML code ready to copy and paste right into your website. Just log into your Twitter account and navigate to this page: http://twitter.com/goodies/buttons. Take a look at the HTML code associated with any button and you'll see your account information is already there! Send it on to your webmaster and you'll be ready to rock.

2. Cite relevant information snippets and factoids that your intended audience may find interesting. Want to share the fact that print remains relevant in today's world? You'll find relevant stories to help prove that point at the Printing Industries of America website (www.printing.org) or through The Print Council's information site www.printinthemix.org.

3. Do you have case studies of successful projects you've done for customers? Make sure you have them posted on your website and provide a link to them through Twitter.

4. Going to a conference or other industry event? Holding an event of your own? Let everyone know! Tweet

about it several times in advance and, in the case of a conference or trade show, be your own journalist and tell your followers what you're learning.

5. Retweet content or links that you think your audience will appreciate, and don't forget to give credit to the originator of the source message!
6. Have you, your production staff, or salespeople gotten any questions that might be of interest to your general audience? Go ahead and tweet out the question and answer (you can do this through a couple of tweets, by pointing to a Q&A section of your website, or by using Posterous or TwitWall to post longer answers). And there's no reason you have to wait to get questions from customers—make up your own questions then provide the answers!
7. Every now and then, share a personal story, opinion, or information about a charity or event that matters to you. Remember, it's social media, and it's OK to throw some purely social comments into your business Twitter account.



## Facebook

Should you use Facebook as a place to interact with just your personal friends and family, or should you use it for business contacts as well? We hear a lot of debate about this question, especially when it comes to one's "personal" Facebook page. Some people maintain two personal accounts, one that is truly personal and one for business contacts, but that breaks the terms and conditions that you agree to when you sign up for a Facebook account (see tip on that subject below).

It's a largely personal decision with a fairly simple solution. If you want to connect with business acquaintances on Facebook but don't want to mix both kinds of friends on your personal account, simply create a **Facebook "Page"** for yourself. Facebook Pages don't work in quite the same way as a personal account, but they serve the goal of maintaining contact on the social platform of choice for half a billion people. However, with a little bit of effort, you can segment your personal and business friends into lists and segment the kinds of things each can see when they look at your Facebook page.

### Read the Facebook terms and conditions

This is the case for Facebook or any other social media platform; know what you're signing up for. With Facebook in particular, some of the terms can seem pretty rigid, and while it's hard to police half a billion accounts, the company does enforce its rules.

Click on the "Terms" link at the bottom of nearly any screen in Facebook and you will see the full text of Facebook's terms and conditions. In the site's own words, here are a few of the conditions to which you're agreeing when you set up a Facebook personal or business page:

- You will not create more than one personal profile.
- You will not use your personal profile for your own commercial gain (such as selling your status update to an advertiser).
- You will not transfer your account (including any page or application you administer) to anyone without first getting our written permission.
- You will not use our copyrights or trademarks (including Facebook, the Facebook and F Logos, FB, Face, Poke, Wall and 32665), or any confusingly similar marks, without our written permission.
- If you collect information from users, you will: obtain their consent, make it clear you (and not Facebook) are the one collecting their information, and post a privacy policy explaining what information you collect and how you will use it.
- You will not offer any contest, giveaway, or sweepstakes ("promotion") on Facebook without our prior written consent.

Note that Facebook has published a separate set of guidelines for promotions, and it's critical to review that document if you intend to run a promotion there. There are limitations on promoting to people under the age of 18, to certain countries, and on certain types of products. Facebook can shut down anyone's personal or business page at any time, so it makes sense to follow the rules to the best of your ability.

### Facebook privacy settings 101

It couldn't be easier to set up a personal Facebook account. Facebook doesn't offer any kind of editor to customize the look of a user's home page (although there are third-party tools to help you do that, more on that later), so there isn't much to do in terms of design. The critical thing is to make sure you fully understand your account settings, and particularly your privacy settings, to maintain your privacy but still make it an effective social networking tool.

Unless you want the entire world to be able to view everything you post on Facebook (and few people would), you want to clamp down the privacy settings, keeping a balance between being invisible and being over-exposed. Facebook adds new options constantly that may impact a user's privacy settings, so it makes sense to periodically check them to make sure they're set to your liking. In the past, Facebook would add a "feature" that affected a user's privacy and the default settings would be to allow "everyone" access to a user's information. Now there seems to be

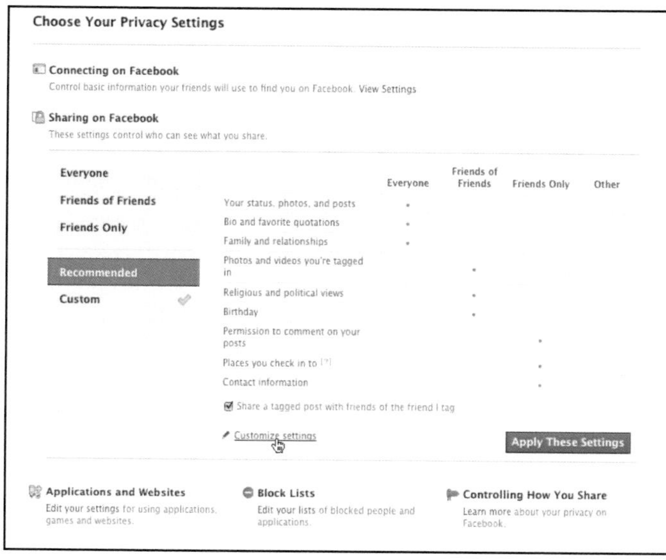

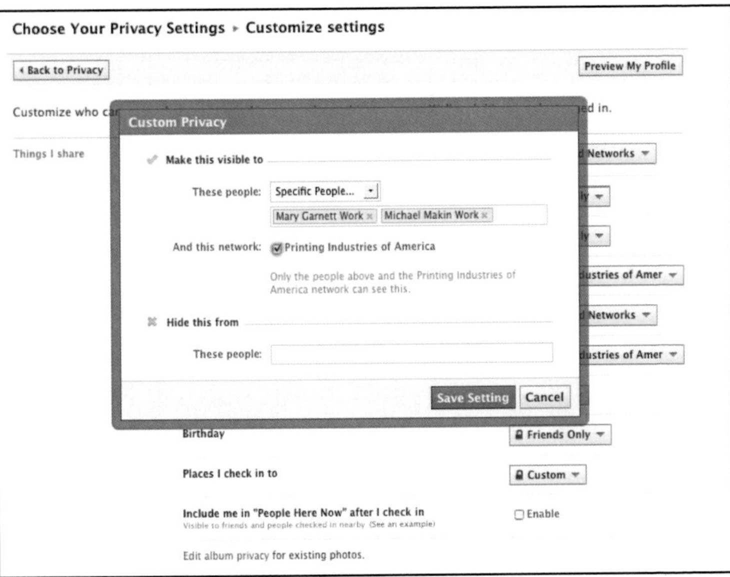


an "opt-in" policy, such that new options are not automatically selected for users, although this is not always the case.

You can access the **Privacy Settings** after logging in either from the Account pull-down menu or from the My Account page, under Privacy. While Facebook offers several pre-configured settings options you should take the time to review the **Customize** settings page in order to fully understand all of the privacy options and set up the optimal settings for your account.

From the Customize settings page, you can set the access for each option to make it accessible to Everyone, Friends only, Friends and Networks (think schools or businesses), Friends of Friends, or Custom. As a general rule, you should allow very few settings to be viewable by "Everyone" on your personal page (a business page is a different story). However, your name, profile picture, gender, networks, and username are always available to everyone—that's a basic Facebook tenet and something you cannot control. Options set to allow access to "Everyone" is part of your public profile, can be seen by anyone who views your account on Facebook, and is accessible to games and other applications. The Custom option lets you further restrict visibility to specific people (from your friends list) or only to yourself.

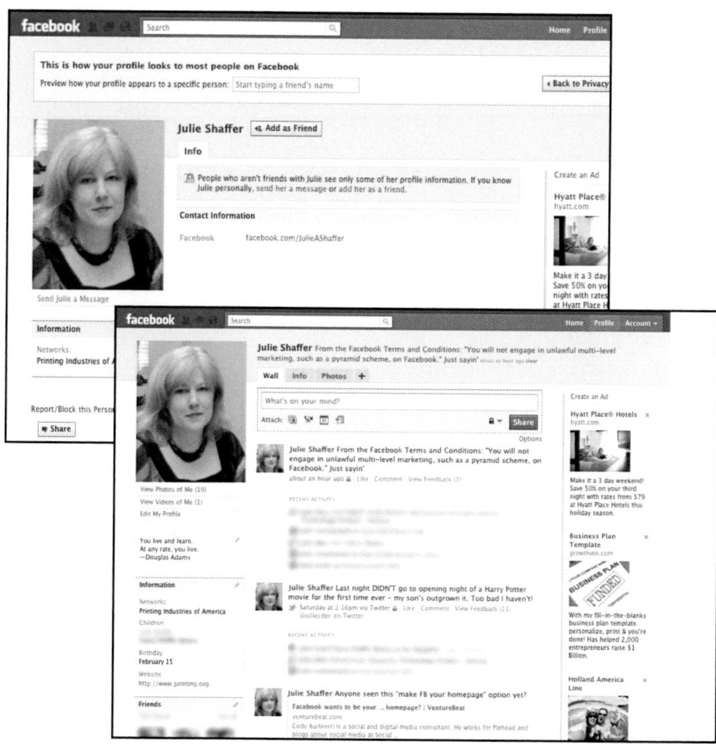


*These screen captures compare Julie's public profile with that seen by her friends on Facebook.*

When you click the "Preview my Profile" button at the top of the Customize privacy settings window, you'll see what your public profile looks like.

## Manage applications and websites privacy settings

It's possibly even more critical to manage how applications, games, and other websites can access your Facebook profile information. At the bottom of the Choose Your Privacy Settings screen, you'll find a link to edit the privacy settings for applications and websites. Every game you access or website you allow to link to your Facebook account is recorded here, and you can manage how those accounts can interface with your data. A critical option here is controlling which of your information is available through your friends. You may be hyper

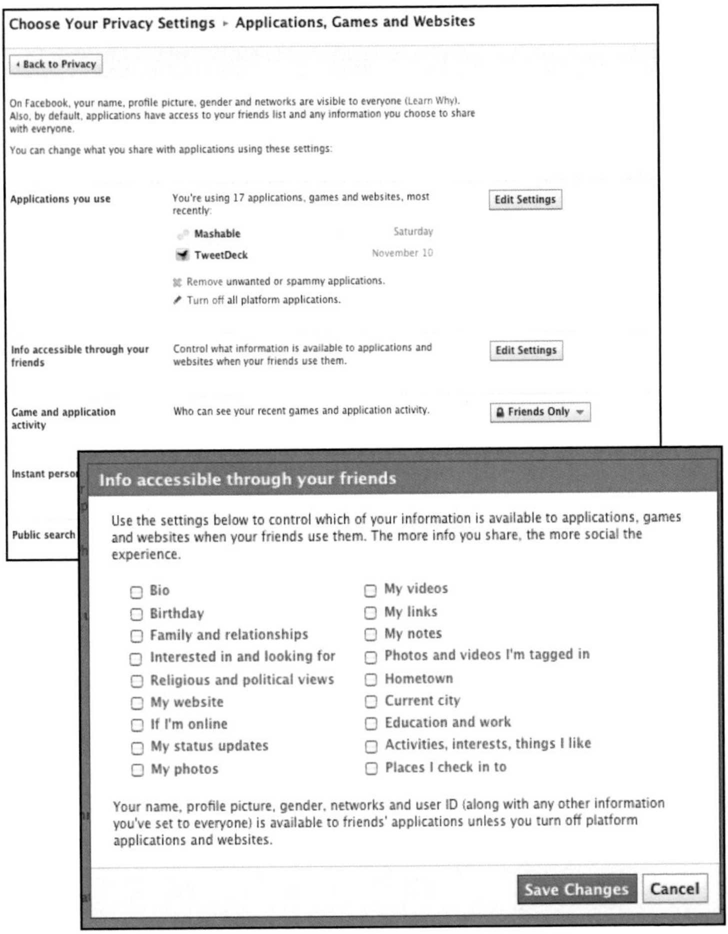

Choose Your Privacy Settings ▸ Applications, Games and Websites

‹ Back to Privacy

On Facebook, your name, profile picture, gender and networks are visible to everyone (Learn Why). Also, by default, applications have access to your friends list and any information you choose to share with everyone.

You can change what you share with applications using these settings:

Applications you use — You're using 17 applications, games and websites, most recently: Mashable (Saturday); TweetDeck (November 10). Remove unwanted or spammy applications. Turn off all platform applications. — Edit Settings

Info accessible through your friends — Control what information is available to applications and websites when your friends use them. — Edit Settings

Game and application activity — Who can see your recent games and application activity. — Friends Only

Instant perso…

Public search

**Info accessible through your friends**

Use the settings below to control which of your information is available to applications, games and websites when your friends use them. The more info you share, the more social the experience.

- Bio
- Birthday
- Family and relationships
- Interested in and looking for
- Religious and political views
- My website
- If I'm online
- My status updates
- My photos
- My videos
- My links
- My notes
- Photos and videos I'm tagged in
- Hometown
- Current city
- Education and work
- Activities, interests, things I like
- Places I check in to

Your name, profile picture, gender, networks and user ID (along with any other information you've set to everyone) is available to friends' applications unless you turn off platform applications and websites.

Save Changes | Cancel

diligent in separating your personal photos and comments from professional friends, but your friends might not be. Your links, videos, photos, activities, and just about anything else can be shared by your friends to their network. If you manage a mixed business/personal page, you might want to consider going into the “Info accessible through your friends” option and restricting most of the information that can be shared (think photos in particular).

You will also want to review the privacy settings for the “Applications you use” and realize that when you give an application access to your data, it is often carte blanche. Ask yourself if it's worth using the game or application to give that company complete access to your personal information. In our opinion, it's viable to grant access to automation tools like TweetDeck, but games … not so much. As a general rule, grant such access judiciously.

Now, if you wish for your Facebook page to be found through a public search, do go ahead and enable the public search option from this screen (it is disabled by default).



## Managing your Facebook Friends

It's possible to maintain a personal Facebook account, including professional friends, and still have some freedom of expression with your personal opinions and beliefs. The best way to do this is to use the list feature within the **Edit Friends** page to categorize your friends into groups. You can set up two to start, calling them something like "professional friends" and "personal friends" (you can also set some people up to be on both lists). Here's what you do:

1. Go to the Edit Friends option under the Account tab on your Facebook page.
2. Click on the "Create a List" button, at the top right of the Friends page.

3. Enter a name in the box at the top of the window. Start with "Professional Friends."

4. Scroll through the displayed list of all your Facebook friends and click on those you want to add to the list.

5. Click the "Create List" button. Now you have a list of your professional friends.

Now use this list in combination with your privacy settings to determine what you want your professional friends to see.

1. Go into the Custom Privacy Settings page.

2. Click on the pull-down menu beside the item to which you wish to restrict access by professional friends and choose the "Custom/edit" option.

3. Choose a group to whom you wish to make this data visible (Friends Only, Friends of Friends, Specific People, or Only Me).

4. Under the "Hide this from" option, start to key in the name you gave the list—in our example that would be "Professional Friends." Facebook should recognize the name after entering just a few characters of the name. Click "Save setting."

5. To test how this worked, click on the "Preview my Profile" tab and key in the name of a professional contact

in the "Preview how your profile appears to a specific person" box. Whatever you restricted in the previous steps should not be visible.

You can restrict who can see your friends list in this manner, but if you don't want to use that global control, you can also determine which of your friends show up in your Friends list on your profile page. You don't do this from the privacy settings, rather you do it from your profile page. Just click that "edit" pencil in the Friends box on the left side panel and type the names of any friend you'd always like to show up in that panel in the box titled "Always show these friends." Similarly, you can control what shows up in all those sidebar boxes, including **Likes, Links, Notes,** and **Information.**



## Get a personalized Facebook URL (username)

When you sign up for Facebook, you'll be assigned a URL (address) that will probably be long and full of gobbledygook characters—not easy to give to others to help them find you. If you have at least twenty-five friends, you can claim a "vanity URL" that will be much shorter: just the Facebook address, a slash, and the username you select. Just go to this address *http://www.facebook.com/username/* and you'll be able to select your customized address.

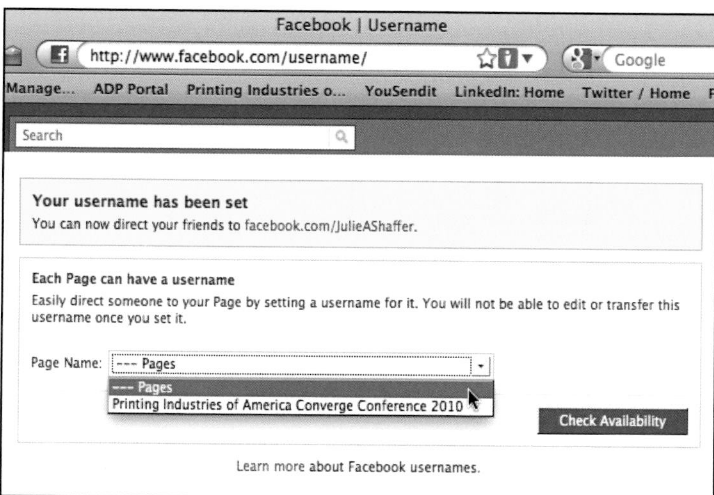

Be aware that with 500 million users, the odds that your name, if it's a common one, is available are not good, but Facebook will suggest alternatives or you can find one on your own for which you're willing to settle. Usernames also must be at least five characters long and can only contain alphanumeric characters (A–Z, 0–9) or a period (dot). Be aware that a period does not count as part of a username, so the trick many people use for email addresses of adding a period between your first and last name to make it unique from someone else with the same name won't work here (i.e., janedoe is considered the same as jane.doe in Facebook). Usernames in Facebook are not case sensitive either.

You can create unique URLs for any Facebook Pages that you manage as well. Certain words are protected and can't be used in a URL, "Facebook" being one of them. And be aware of this: Facebook reserves the right to remove and/or reclaim any username at any time for any reason. Like all public social media platforms, this reminds us that we do not "own" our Facebook Pages, but they exist on another company's platform and we agree to the terms and conditions that company establishes. Which leads to the next tip....

### Creating a Facebook Page (business account)

Once you have set up a personal Facebook account, you can manage any number of separate Facebook "Page" accounts. Many businesses maintain a Facebook Page as the company's presence on the platform, but individuals can have one or more for their own business persona as well. A Facebook Page is different than a personal page in that it is not limited to 5,000 friends, as a personal page is. Instead, people "Like" the page, an action that can happen from an outside website via a button, or directly from the Page itself.

A Facebook Page isn't a separate account, rather it is a different "entity" on the site, administered by a person with an individual account. Once an individual on behalf of an organization sets up a Page, additional administrators can and should be added to the Page. To set up a Facebook Page, simply follow these steps:

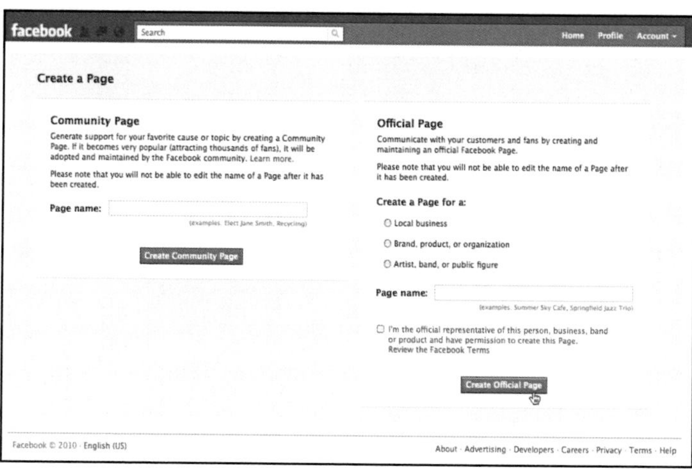


1. Select the "Help Center" under the Account tab and click on the "Pages for Businesses" link under the Ads and Business Solutions section.

2. Click on the "Creating a Page" link, and then the "How Can I Create a Page" link. This will provide you with a link to the Page creation form.

3. Give the Page a name (think carefully about this because you can't change it once it's been set).

4. You have to choose what type of business you are creating a Page for from a list of three: "Local business," "Brand, product or organization," or "Artist, band or public figure." Your choice here determines which built-in applications are made automatically available to you based on relevance. So a band would get video and music-player links pre-installed; an organization would get a message board and links option. You cannot change the type of business you designate when you're setting up the Page, so here, too, think carefully before you choose.

5. Once the page is created, it will not be published until you set it to be. This gives you time to work on customization.

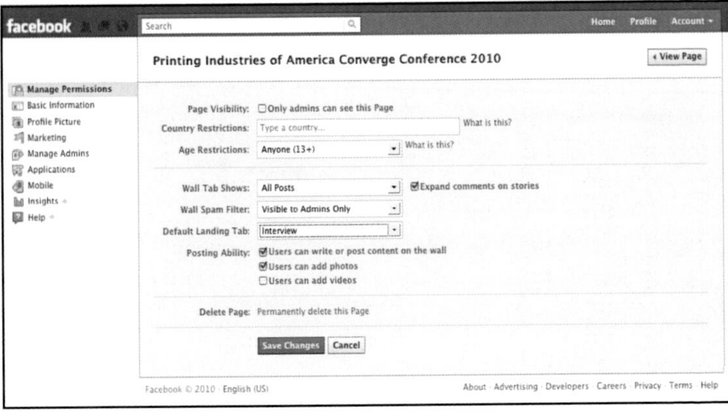


## Customizing a Facebook Page

Click on the "Edit Page" tab to customize the information that appears on the page and add applications. This is a walk-through of each.

**1. Manage Permissions.** This is where you determine what people see on the Page and how they can interact with it. Critical here is setting the "Default Landing Tab" as it determines what your audience sees first. These tabs reflect the applications available to the Page and differ depending upon the type of business you selected on setting up the Page initially. When you add additional applications, they will be added to this list, so you'll come back to this page later if, for example, you wish to set a merchant application as your default landing page.

**2. Basic Information.** Like your personal bio, this is important for letting your audience know what you're all about. This is where you'll set a home webpage, so it is a good SEO opportunity to drive traffic back to your business website.

**3. Profile Picture.** Facebook allows a profile picture 200 pixels wide by 600 pixels high by default. You can vastly customize different tab areas of a business Page through third-party applications, but the "home" page will be defined with this image. Think of it as an ad and be very creative in its design.

4. **Marketing.** You can set up a marketing program to promote your new Page right from Facebook. This area is where you can create an ad that will run in the Facebook sidebar and manage how much you are willing to spend on it (you pay per clicks). But that's the only "for pay" marketing tool here. "Add a Like Box to your Website" takes you to Facebook's social plug-in page, where you can create not only Like buttons, but all sorts of links, including comments, live stream, or a **Facepile** (a display of profile pictures of people who "like" a Page). There is a simple interface that lets you set up the button or box and get the corresponding HTML code, which you'll provide to your webmaster to incorporate into your website. You can also compose and send an email message to everyone who "Likes" your Page—an instant, clean "mailing" list!



5. **Manage Admins.** This is where you set other Facebook users as administrators of this Page. The only requirement is that the person has a personal Facebook account. When a person is added as an administrator of

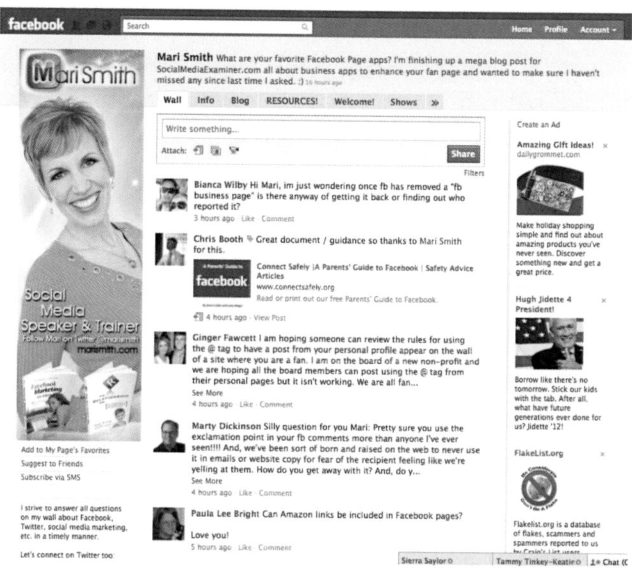


*Mari Smith, a Facebook training guru, maintains an active Facebook Page and uses her profile image to let people know not only what she looks like, but also as a sales tool for her business.*

a Page, they will gain access to this Page via the Manage Pages link under the Account menu on their personal page.

6. **Applications.** Depending on your choice of the three options for type of business the Page was being created for—"Local business," "Brand, product or organization," or "Artist, band or public figure"—you'll see different options under the Added Applications list. Applications are generally accessed through the tabs on a Facebook Page, and you can remove or add applications/tabs at any time. Applications are really the power behind successful Pages, as this is the area where you can customize and create powerful interaction with your audience. If you wish to sell printed products via Facebook, as Mimeo.com has done with its Fotobooks application, you can create an interface here. If you want to gather and display survey information, install and deploy the Polls application. You can browse for hundreds of available applications.

7. **Mobile.** If you need to administer your Page from a mobile device, set up the links to it through this interface.

8. **Insights.** Need analytics to measure the effectiveness of a Facebook Page? You will find them here on the Insights page. At a glance you'll see the number of monthly active users you've got, daily new likes, and total likes for your Page. The data is reported by a few demographics too, including age, gender, and country of the audience. You can export this information in a CSV format to bring into a spreadsheet for analysis and reporting.

9. **Help.** This last link gathers all the Page-related help files in one place.

### Changing the layout of a Facebook Page

Facebook doesn't offer a simple editor to customize Pages, so many of them look much the same. Scripters that know HTML can use the **Facebook Markup Language (FBML)** applications to do some editing, but let's face it, most business

users aren't coding experts. So many tools have come to market to help people customize the look and feel of their Facebook Page.

A tool that came to market in mid-2010 is **Pagemodo** (www.pagemodo.com), offering a very easy-to-use template-driven interface to create custom welcome pages. Pagemodo was used to create a customized Page for both President Barack Obama and Lady Gaga! **Tabsite** (www.facebooktabsite.com) is one of the few products that lets users customize personal Facebook pages as well as business Pages. **Tabfusion** (www.tabfusion.com) offers tabs with links to specific other social media platforms, like Flickr, YouTube and Twitter. **Miproapps** offers true WYSIWYG Facebook Page (tab) design, while others, like **Static520** (www.static520.com) require installation of the static FBML app to the Page you want to customize.

### Manage (or remove) Facebook advertisements

Facebook Ads are sometimes paired with social actions (as in "Liking" a page). This means that your friend's name can be served up to you in a Facebook ad for something, or yours can be included in an ad presented to one of your friends. You can prevent this by going to the "Facebook Ads" tab on the "My

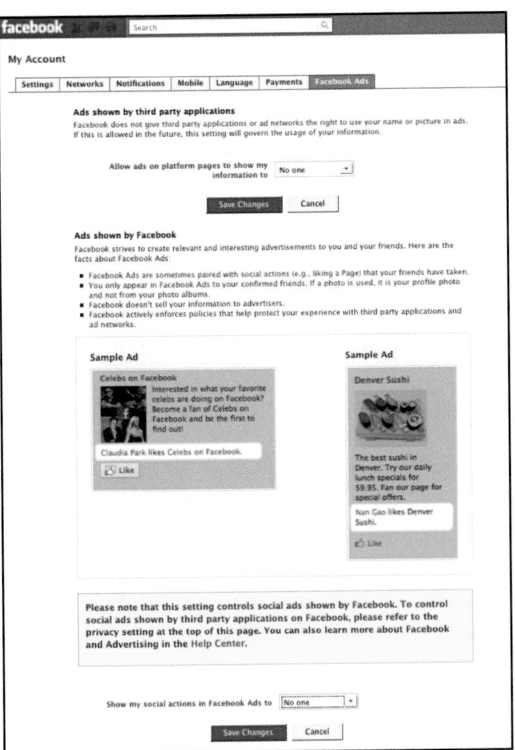


Account" page, scrolling all the way to the bottom, and changing the "Show my social actions in Facebook Ads to" option to "No one."

There are a number of Add-ons for Firefox that promise to remove ads from your view in Facebook. **AdBye – For Facebook** is available through the Mozilla Add-ons site (https://addons.mozilla.org) has good user ratings as a viable way to remove ads from Facebook, at least when viewed through a Firefox browser. There are several others, most of which are shareware (the authors asks a small donation for use of the product, but it's not, strictly speaking, required). There are always risks when using shareware, but if you find the ads so annoying that you're willing to take them, give this site a visit.

## What's Next?

Now that you're set up in all of the big three social media platforms, let everyone you communicate with on a daily basis know about it. One of the best ways to do that is to add links to your social accounts from within your email signature.

## Add social media icons

Most business people still use email for the bulk of their correspondence, so including links to your social networking accounts as part of your signature line is almost as important as listing your phone number. The process for putting links into your signature may differ somewhat depending upon which email service you're using, but most make it pretty easy to include a hyperlink in your signature (the one exception being Entourage, the Mac Outlook client). You can use a social media icon graphic for the link, or just a line of text. We're not fond of adding graphic attachments to every email, which is what happens when you add an icon to your signature, but many feel the visual link is worth it. Here's a general look at how to set up email signature links in Microsoft Outlook.

1. If you plan to use social media icons for your links, you have to acquire them. There are plenty available online, most are public domain. Twitter, Facebook, and most other social sites offer them somewhere in their help center, but there are also packages available

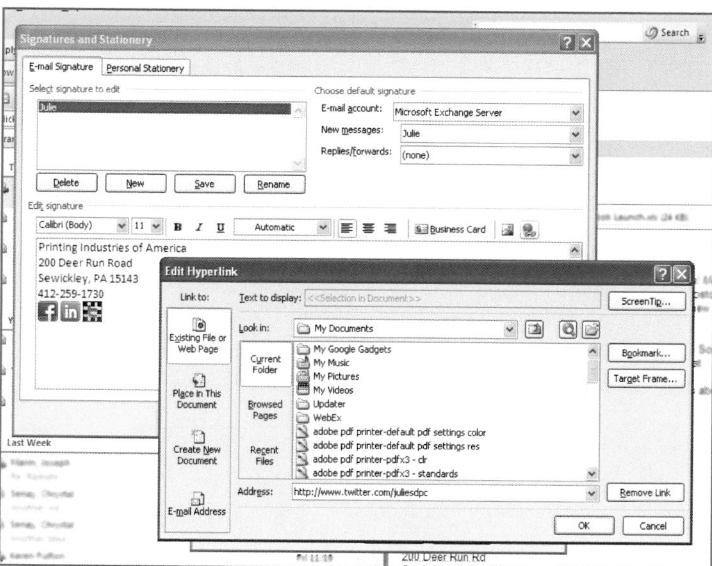

from central clearinghouse sites that include batches of icons for the most common social platforms. Two of these include **Icon Dock** (http://icondock.com) and **Iconspedia** (www.iconspedia.com/).

It's important to keep icon graphics as small as possible, as they add clutter and file size to emails. Most of the canned packages let you choose from an assortment of sizes. You'll want to use image links of no more than 24 pixels wide for email attachments. If you want to change the size of a graphic, you can use a photo imaging application or an online tool, like the free image manipulation site **Picnik** (www.picnik.com).

2. Now you need to capture the hyperlinks themselves. Just navigate via browser to each of your social media sites, log in, and then copy your full public link. This is not necessarily the address that shows up in the URL navigator in your browser. For example, when you're on your home page in Facebook, the URL will be the Facebook home page, and when copied and pasted into a browser, it will go to the Facebook home page, not yours. The URL that displays when you're on your profile page is the one that will lead to your profile or use your "vanity URL" if you've claimed one (look for how to do that in the Facebook tips section). Look for your name/handle in the URL. Test this by copying the URL, logging out of the site, and pasting the address into the URL locator on your browser. If it takes you to your public profile you've got it right. Copy your hyperlinks into a text editor, like Word, to hold until you're ready to use them.
3. Open Outlook and navigate to the signature editing screen following this path: Tools > Options > Mail Format > Signatures. Under the Email Signature tab you'll see your current signature. Click in this signature at the location where you wish to put your hyperlink.
4. If you're adding icons, click on the "Picture" button (looks like sun and mountains) and navigate to the icon graphics you've collected. Click on the first one you want to show up in your signature and click "insert." It will show up with a selection window around it in your

signature. Click off of the graphic and you'll see how it will show up in your signature. If you're happy, add a space beside it and click the "Picture" button to add any additional graphics you'd like to include and insert each of them.

5. Now go back and click on the first icon in your signature to select it and click the "Hyperlink" button (looks like a chain). Here you can either key in your hyperlink or copy and paste it from your text document. Do this for each icon.

6. You can also add the text version of your hyperlinks directly into the signature without (or beside) the icons. Just put the cursor in the signature area where you wish the link to appear, click the "Hyperlink" button, enter the link, and click "OK." You'll see the link show up immediately in the signature. Click "OK" to close the window and you're done.

This process can be done with some variation with nearly all email clients (save Mac Entourage).

# 6 Social Media Road Trip



## Introduction

Most of us have experienced a "spur-of-the-moment" road trip on our own or vicariously through others. One type of spontaneous road trip is the one where you have little to do and little to lose, so the road trip is a fun diversion. You do little map reconnaissance, you explore the scenery along the route, and wrong turns or "no vacancy" signs are minor inconveniences since you have all the time in the world.

As you mature in your life and your schedule fills, unplanned and unstructured road trips are limited because time and resources are too valuable, so you research trusted resources, talk to experienced travelers, and read reviews where you can.

The social media road trip is of the latter type: in the social media journey for your company, you must do the research; talk to experienced sources; and read and seek out reviews of the pitfalls, wrong turns, and false starts others have had along the way.

Reading this book has been part of your research and review process, and this chapter will provide you with two types of resources: interviews with industry people willing to share their

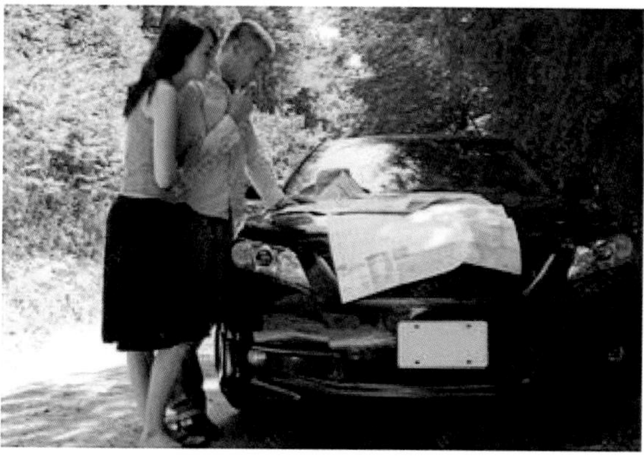

experiences, and first-person accounts from experienced trekkers along the social media trail. So let's begin with a few interviews that may give you some insight into what industry people are doing so you can learn from their experiences.

## Part A—Interviews

### Interview #1
### Good things happen when you learn to listen

**Renee M. Berger, Creative Director**
**Western States Envelope & Label**
Renee.Berger@westernstatesenvelope.com
www.westernstatesenvelope.com/

**Note:** In the beginning of this book, this story was used as a sterling example of where social media monitoring could lead you. In Western States Envelope & Label's case, it led to a new product, but there is value in the entire story, not just the example mentioned earlier.

Renee Berger is an energetic enthusiast for social media tools. Western States Envelope & Label, a wholesale printer to the trade, has more than 28,000 individual customers and 37 outside sales force with more than 625 employees. The sheer volume of customers made the efforts in social media worth her time. Berger and another employee, intern Eric Kidman, manage all of their social media initiatives among other job responsibilities. Berger mentioned that she has tremendous senior management support for the resources needed.

#### Social Media Tools in Use

Western is actively involved in Twitter, Facebook, LinkedIn, YouTube, and Flickr among others. When asked about whether any new business has resulted, Berger responded that it is difficult to pinpoint new business but the differences in inquiries, customer questions, rankings, and listings are all positive. Statistically, Western has seen a rise in the number of page views on their website, and Google Analytics supports the increase in company rankings and placement. Originally, Berger was excited about the potential of social media tools but also a bit skeptical too. Now her doubts are replaced with energy and interest in all the potential.

## Top Ten List for Social Media Value

Berger reviewed a top ten list of reasons she believed social media tools are valuable:

The use of social media tools has:

1. Defined and grown their defined market
2. Increased their brand awareness
3. Increased prequalified leads
4. Reduced cost per lead
5. Established credibility in the marketplace
6. Increased page rankings and site traffic

7. Provided a vehicle to listen to customers and identify trends
8. Increased sales cycle by providing a quicker turnaround for quotes.
9. Provided a mechanism for monitoring of the competition
10. Allowed the sidestepping of ad blindness (Renee described this as another vehicle to market to customers and become a trusted partner, source, and friend and to be the "go to" company for clients.)

## Social Media Feedback Creates a New Revenue Stream

Berger also mentioned an interesting event that occurred with a customer due to the increase in communication. While participating in printjunkie.net, Berger heard a customer identify a problem resulting from the heat of a laser printer causing a letter to stick to the window material in a window envelope. That led her and her company to ask other customers on LinkedIn to confirm additional experiences with the problem. The feedback led to the development of a specific new product. Working with key personnel, Western Envelope investigated the potential and the company invented a new product called the Digi-Clear™ envelope—a new side-seam window envelope with a laser-compatible window material.

This envelope has started a new revenue stream for the company and answers the needs of customers who used high-temperature lasers for printing envelopes. This new type of high-temperature window envelope was uncovered by participating in social media. According to Steve Brocker, vice president of Sales and Marketing for Western States, the new offering began a revenue stream not only for Western but also for the printers who use the envelope with their customers, thereby increasing the printer's bottom line. It doesn't get any better than that!

*Western States Envelope & Label has been an envelope leader since 1908 by forever reinventing themselves to keep pace with customers' growing demands. They invest in the latest equipment, employ innovative design approaches, and have exceptional in-house engineering capabilities.*

## Interview #2
## Communicate through the customer's medium

**Brian Wolfenden, Director of Marketing Communications**
**Presstek, Inc.**
bwolfenden@presstek.com
http://www.presstek.com

### Social Media Tools in Use

Mark Levin, while employed at Presstek, indicated that Presstek is using Facebook, Twitter, and LinkedIn and have been using social media tools as part of an overall marketing campaign with email blasts, direct mail, ads, and more. He believed that social media tools had a certain element of generational use. "If you want to reach a boomer, you are more likely to use email or phone; as the next generation of customers emerge,

we are finding that Twitter, Facebook, and LinkedIn are good communication sources."

Presstek is using the three tools as part of an integrated marketing approach. As an example, an open house may be tweeted with a link to the Web page with details; in the future a tweet may mention a "Tuesday special" and lead people to their site with opportunities for discounts. All social media efforts are part of their marketing responsibilities. While Levin could not relate and define new business results, he did believe it was all important to their overall marketing position.

Brian Wolfenden, director of Marketing Communications, mentioned the most common applications of social media have been to announce events via press releases and Web posting and then tweet about the event and post the event on Facebook. Following the event, they post images on Facebook and tweet a link to drive people to the Facebook page. They might also issue a press release on the website and tweet about the release to drive people to the site. Other tweets might share a story in a trade publication or a CTP specialist job opportunity.

### Discretion Needed in Social Media Messages

Levin noted some caution for employees of any publicly held company where sensitive information may be inadvertently communicated on a social media platform. He mentioned the sensitive client relationship also. As an example, when a piece of equipment is sold, an announcement of the sale or the placement location of the equipment must be done with the customer's agreement; otherwise, the information may cause confidential information to violate the sale terms. An inadvertent slip by an exuberant employee who mentions the sale of a press with the customer's name and location may lead to untold breaches of the relationship or issues related to staffing in the customer's company. Even an innocent comment about the financial health of the company, interpreted as a reason to purchase or sell shares, can be questioned in terms of insider information.

"All employees must be educated and informed as to the boundaries in using social media in business," Levin said.
At Presstek, selected technical employees monitor blogs and discussion boards for information, questions, or comments that may be needed related to the equipment. Presstek also monitors

several of their large customers' interactions with social media in order to keep up with issues important to those clients.

### Message to Readers

Levin says: "Social media—it's real and of value; people should adapt to this new experience to communicate. In order to continue to sell to different generations, we must adapt to the way customers choose to interact. In general social media is of great value and overall communication tool to be used in combination with other marketing tactics."

*Presstek has been an innovator with a mission to change the way offset printing is produced. Presstek solutions are designed to make it easier for printers to meet the increasing customer demand for high-quality, faster turnaround printing with improved profit margins and provider of environmentally responsible DI® digital offset presses and computer-to-plate (CTP) solutions.*

## Interview #3
## Twitter works—when you learn how to use it to your advantage

**Scott Dubois, Vice President Cross-Media Services**
**Reynolds DeWalt**
sdubois@reynoldsdewalt.com
www.reynoldsdewalt.com

### Social Media Tools in Use

In a recent conversation, Scott Dubois mentioned that Reynolds DeWalt is using Facebook, Twitter, and LinkedIn. He reviewed his thoughts on each tool.

**Facebook.** Dubois mentioned he was considering abandoning Facebook. "Facebook is right for a consumer brand but in our business we don't appeal to consumers. The high-level customer executives we deal with aren't going to Facebook especially to find professional service. They don't congregate in Facebook. Vistaprint-type companies are good in Facebook since consumers use Facebook—it is a printing model where B-to-C encourages fanatics about the products."

**Twitter.** Twitter is good according to Dubois. Twitter enables updates to social media profiles—it is the engine that drives

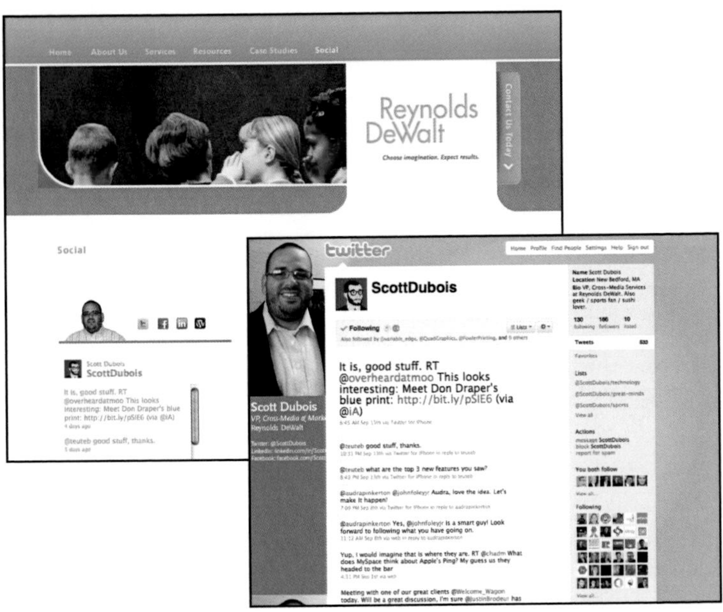


it all. "Twitter enables you to be a thought leader." Lists are wonderful when they're centered around a subject (e.g., marketing, automation). You want to be in that stream. Readers need to remember that social media is not free advertising—a big mistake people make, said Dubois. He did not think the messages should be campaign-focused either, for the most part. He believed that messages should be about finding something interesting and publishing to the world with the author's own "take" on the information. As an example, he found a mobile device article about Apple vs. Flash; he posted it and made a comment on the points of view. He did that for a column in *Newsweek* as well and shared it with the group the following week. Twitter helps keep a running commentary going. He mentioned that he has a personal account as well as a Reynolds DeWalt account so they can cross over with information.

He gave additional examples of conversations on Twitter; for instance, he converses with people such as John Foley (InterlinkONE Inc.), and he talks about his irritations and customer service in regard to Southwest Airlines and business travel. Dubois indicated that most topics were related to business and the rest of a miscellaneous nature.

### Amplifies Relationships

Dubois believed that social media amplified current relationships, and it helps as he becomes familiar with his followers who are customers. Customers care about what he's saying. In this world of customer management publishing, there are three things that happen in social media:

1. Someone finds your company.
2. Then they find you on LinkedIn.
3. Then they join a Twitter conversation.

Dubois used social media as well as public speaking as a business development process and to build himself and Reynolds DeWalt as an authority. Dubois works at being a thought leader or subject matter expert, and social media tools are vehicles for these efforts. Customers will look for a personality or the company through social media.

### Profiling Customers in Social Media?

Dubois said "absolutely yes" All account reps follow LinkedIn and tweet and retweet with clients. They also use iGoogle and RSS feeds for custom news alerts. Additionally, Reynolds DeWalt uses alerts for customers so that any time a customer is in the news, Reynolds DeWalt will post links to the story.

Reynolds DeWalt does not see other social media sites as mainstream or major players, but they are big into customer management and use **Salesforce.com,** which has a custom field for tracking Facebook, LinkedIn, and Twitter feeds right in there. They monitor social media on the organizational level as well as the individual level. Reynolds DeWalt does not issue a written social media policy for employees.

### Search Engine Optimization

Reynolds DeWalt has performance benchmarks for its website and ensures that all required H1 H2 tags and unique descriptors meet the threshold. But for Reynolds DeWalt, SEO is not the most important thing on the radar.

*Reynolds DeWalt is a leader in integrated cross-media marketing programs. In-house capabilities span design, development, programming, execution, and media production.*

**Interview #4**
**A new way for customer relationships—blogs**

**Karyn "KJ" Johnson, Director of Marketing & PR**
**Heritage Solutions**
kjohnson@heritagesolutionsok.com
www.heritagesolutionsok.com

Karyn "KJ" Johnson is the director of Marketing at Heritage Solutions in Oklahoma. She joined the company less than a year ago and has already established her social media wings with both customers and staff at the company. KJ covered two areas in our conversation that are relevant to our *Social Media Field Guide.*

**Search Engine Optimization.** One of KJ's first tasks was to work on increasing the listing of Heritage Solutions when a Google search was made. She checked with a recommended social media business advisor and implemented the suggestions.

As a result, the rankings on the pages increased after following the suggestions.

**Blogs.** KJ began a blog shortly after arriving at Heritage. She freely admits that she studied up on blogging to learn tips to ensure success. Her blog goal is basically to communicate with her customers (#1 goal). In the process, her blog views and links out to other sites have increased traffic to the website (#2 goal) and have further increased her company's rankings on a Google search (#3 goal). When asked if these goals have increased sales, her response was quick and to the point: "Yes, we have made our customers aware of some of the terrific projects completed for other customers." This new awareness has increased requests from current customers.

After only a few months, she has nearly 6,500 views of the blog. The tone of the blog is more informational and friendly with less emphasis on education. Keeping the tone of the writing more on the friendly side helps entice customers to work with the company. Her posted pictures are also fun and informational. KJ adds notes about customer activities, their projects, and their results. All of this is approved by the customers in advance of posting the information on the blog. A quick look at her blog shows a very nice organization and referral basis for items posted on the blog such as business cards, fulfillment, promotional products, variable data, etc. Pictures of clients, employees, and finished products add interest and excitement. Check out this very good blog from a printer aka solutions provider: www.heritagesolutionsOK.blogspot.com.

*Heritage Solutions specializes in cross-media publishing in order to meet the challenges faced by our customers. They offer a wide array of solutions in printing, publishing, and distribution.*

## Part B—First-Person Accounts from Social Media Travelers

### Traveler #1
### First steps in social media

**Chip Chebuhar, Regional Vice President of Sales**
**Corporate Press, Inc.**
cchebuhar@corporatepress.com
www.corporatepress.com

#### Social Media First Steps

Social media at Corporate Press is a new initiative that we are excited about. Our efforts are being headed up by Michael Marcian, our vice president of Marketing. We recently launched a new website, complete with "live chat" features, and have begun the process of building a presence on Facebook. Results are still to be determined, but more importantly we are gaining firsthand experience which allows us to better serve our clients

with total marketing solutions. No efforts with blogs at this point. I think our social media efforts are going to go a long way toward enhancing our relationships with both current clients and new prospects.

### Message to Printers: Get Started!

Get started! Start small, update regularly, learn as you go—and enjoy the experience. Too many organizations wait until they have it "perfect"—and by then they have missed the opportunity.

## Traveler #2
## Beware: There's good and bad—But get involved!

**Jason Ellis, Vice President Business Development**
**The E.F. Group and Accu-Print**
jason@accu-print.com
www.accu-print.com; www.theefgroup.com

### Social Media Tools in Use

We are very involved in as much social media as we can. I have a Twitter account with over 150 followers that I am active in. We have a page for Accu-Print on Facebook as well, but I still don't think Facebook is a place for businesses; it's more of a personal space. I personally don't want a business trying to talk to me in my personal space. Twitter is a good place for people to recognize you as a leader. If you share good information with people and are involved in the community then people will turn to you for answers. We have been unsuccessful getting anyone to respond to coupons or giveaways on Twitter. I don't find any use in blogs nor do I read any.

### Social Media Tools Evolving and Disappearing

I also feel that in the social media space there will be another Facebook or something of this matter down the road. As everyone told us to jump into MySpace, which is now obsolete, I also feel this will happen with Facebook as the numbers now show usage is dropping.

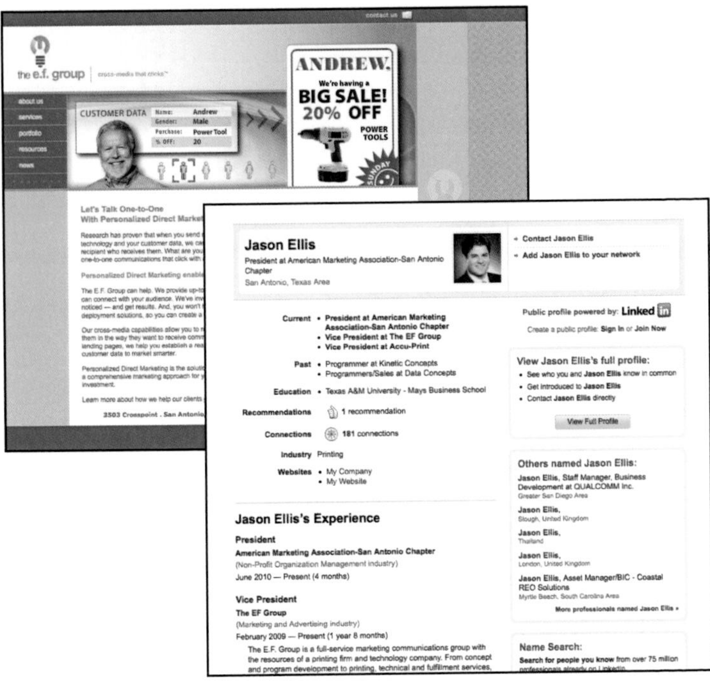


### Hard to Measure

I haven't seen any good numbers on business from social media. It's hard to put dollars to any of it unless someone is answering an ad, coupon, or giveaway on social media ... and none of them have worked. I think most people that follow are just interested in marketing trends and what you are doing rather than waiting for a free business card offer.

### Message to Printers: Use It as Part of Marketing Tactics

It's just another form of media to have your name in front of people, like postcards, e-blasts, Web analytics, SEO, and anything that puts your name out there. Social media can do this for you, but I wouldn't invest too much money into doing it as there are a lot better forms of marketing out there.

## Traveler #3
## Social media—Get smart, get trained!

**Larry Miles, Sales Manager**
**McClung Companies**
larrym@mcclungco.com
www.mcclungco.com

### Early in Social Media Game—So Far, So Good

As a company we are currently using Facebook and Twitter. Additionally we have a company profile on LinkedIn and will soon have our own YouTube channel. We have had a relatively smooth experience as we begin our efforts in the social media space. We have two main objectives: first to demonstrate that our company has a competent understanding of social media and how to implement it into an overall marketing strategy, and second (or simultaneously) to connect with our customers on another level. It is really too early to accurately measure our results against the metrics we've designated. We've connected

with 51 people on Facebook (51 "Likes") and have 17 followers on Facebook. So far no "lows," and the "highs" are that we feel like we're making a successful debut into the social media space.

We do have a company blog. We currently update it two to three times a week with educational information repurposed from our newsletters. We will supplement this information with a weekly posting from a member of our staff in the very near future, as well as use it as a platform to highlight our customers' achievements.

**Improving Customer Contacts**

We have not yet gotten any business directly from our social media efforts. So far the greatest benefits we've received from our social media efforts have been in the form of longer, more involved conversations between our account executives and our customers. Social media is a great point of discussion, especially if you can address it competently with your customers.

**Message to Printers: Get Smart, Get Trained**

Don't waste time trying to figure it out on your own. Go get trained by someone who is competent in the social media space, has demonstrated that competency, and can give you a path to develop your own plan. Before you talk to your customers about it, be sure that your sales representatives know what they're talking about.

## Traveler #4
## Many social media resources, many rewards

**Mary Gay Marchese, Public Relations**
**Markzware**
pr@markzware.com
www.markzware.com

**Social Media Tools in Use**

We are primarily using Twitter, LinkedIn, Facebook, and YouTube. But we have a presence on Posterous, FriendFeed, Screencast and Blip.tv. We have four Twitter accounts in different languages in addition to our main Twitter account.

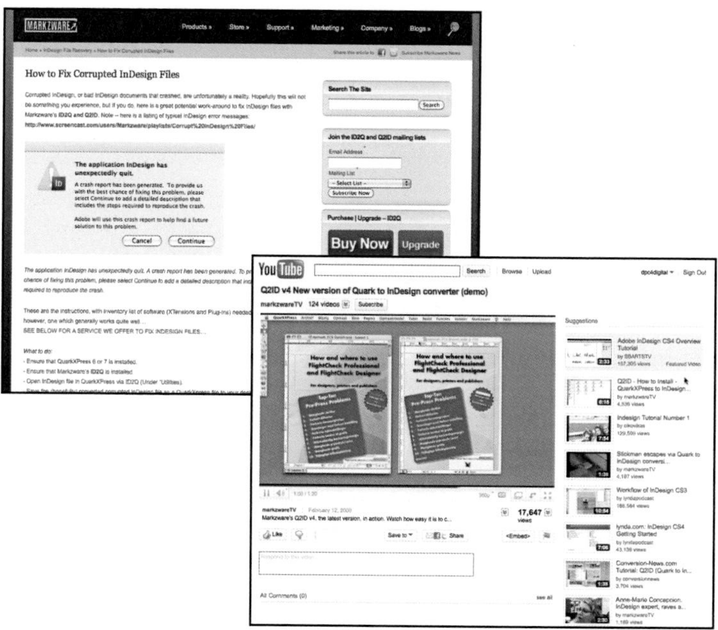


## A Litmus Test to Continue a Resource

In addition to the tools listed above, we also use a MySpace page and numerous others (many video sharing sites). However, there is a litmus test that is simply two things:

- Do we see incoming referral links from activity we have pushed via the site?
- Is the social media platform worth the effort? (Do we at least get a buzz via dealing with it?)

If these things do not occur, it will fall to the very low priority list, due to duties and workflow.

In general our social media activities have been very good. When I see the views on some of our YouTube videos (more than 14,000 views on one in particular) and the number of Markzware mentions on Twitter, it makes all of the hard work worthwhile.

It does take work and effort to really get a presence on these platforms. You have to be a community member and offer helpful information. Naturally, some marketing is accepted, but you cannot cross the line; otherwise, other members will call you out.

### Blogs Are a Priority

Our first priority is our blog, where we try to offer important industry info for graphic designers, publishers, and prepress operators, not just info on Markzware FlightCheck, preflighting, file conversion, or recovery of bad InDesign jobs. Our priority of social media tool use is: (1) Markzware blog, (2)Twitter, (3) LinkedIn, (4)YouTube, (5) Facebook.

Facebook does not have nearly the number of subscribers as our blog, Twitter, LinkedIn, or YouTube. Nor do we see as much click-through from that "Fan Page," at least as of yet. Now, we could and will push this, but Facebook "Fan Pages" do not allow much linkage to other social networking sites; thus, it is less of a priority for now (I am sure they will change this).

The blog is like our main portal for content. Textually it is the main place we will enter it. YouTube is the main channel for videos—it is not the best quality, but has the most viewers and thus you get the most views via YouTube.

Twitter also feeds LinkedIn and our blog feeds many tweets to Twitter (via RSS). Thus Twitter is really key, along with our blog and YouTube. We also use Twitter to engage customers and potential customers almost daily. With alerts, we can see when others want to convert InDesign to Quark and offer ID2Q in a reply tweet, for example. This is a great way to interact with others, and at the same time all of your "followers" can also see what is going on.

LinkedIn has seen great growth with the advent of Groups and the news and discussion one can submit and comment on. This is a *very* professional place and we are working on building our personal networks, as well as the Markzware Group on LinkedIn.

### Blogs Key to Generating Business

We do a lot with our main blog (http://markzware.com/category/blogs/) but also have numerous other micro blogs on WordPress and Posterous which are more focused. The idea with http://markzware.com/category/blogs/ is to be as informative as possible. It is important to keep a flow of posts going out, but also they must be relevant. We focus a lot on customer testimonials but also talk a lot about general market issues and developments, such as a recent iPod post which generated a lot of hits.

Our blog is really key for one service we offer: fixing bad Adobe InDesign files. Actually, this is a really nice story, for we used not only YouTube to show how we are doing this task of recovery (here: http://www.youtube.com/watch?v=QNncZIR6Jx0), but then we also posted several items around how we offer this service and what customers need to do to request a bad .indd file to be fixed. We offer this *only* on our blog and YouTube and have a steady business of bad Adobe CS InDesign jobs to fix every day!

As you know, many will use Google when they need something. If your InDesign file goes bad on you, you do a quick search, and we show up generally on top. It is that easy. All accomplished via social networking and blogging.

**New Business Results of Social Media Use**

Besides the fixing bad files service, we get customers in via Twitter, YouTube, and LinkedIn. Often we can see direct sales through our Affiliate program via links in Twitter, blogs, YouTube, and other forums on the Internet. Not to mention we engage many on Twitter and see a lot of positive responses that must be also generating sales, although that is harder to gauge.

**Message to Printers: Social Media Is Here to Stay**

It is just another form of good, old-fashioned networking; however, if you position your accounts and presence correctly, it will work twenty-four hours a day, seven days a week, year after year. Engage the communities and enjoy it. There is one thing for sure: there are *many* graphic designers, creatives, and print buyers out there on Twitter and other social networks. Stay focused and build up your community. It seems like an impossible task at first, but before you know it, you will have many followers or subscribers to your blog.

One tip for a printer is the following: Apart from your main blog, YouTube account, and Twitter page, perhaps try to focus in on a niche that you specialize in and make separate accounts and blogs for this. You can of course link back to your main accounts, but for SEO (search engine optimization) it may be good to also have, for example, a blog just about "door hanger printing." Then post only about issues around that and keep it really focused on door hanger printing. You'll be surprised what links or other articles you'll find to write about on the deepest niche markets!

### Traveler #5
### Build it; they will come—eventually!

**Scott Edwards, Web Manager**
**Unigraphics Limited**
scotte@unigraphics.mb.ca
www.imagineitprintit.ca

#### Social Media Tools in Use

I am currently using Facebook, Twitter, and LinkedIn; read several blogs and use the popurls® news aggregator to find interesting and relevant articles; and use the HootSuite tool to manage my accounts across the three platforms. I am the primary social media user in the company and have taught a few others some uses and continue to push for more usage by all.

**Facebook:** I have set up a Fan Page for our online Web store, imagineitprintit.ca. We currently have just over two hundred fans. I use the platform to give news and updates to customers as well as run some promotions and contests. I encourage users to contact us via our Facebook Fan Page with any questions or customer service issues. So far, it is hard to get users to participate in the conversations. I find I post but get very little reaction. I feel that will change as our user base grows and people start using our website. I don't do much on the "personal" side of Facebook. My own profile is kept separate from work for the most part, other than sharing the odd post from the Fan Page, like contests. I have set up other Fan Pages for specific products that have their own "brand." I have not yet developed any of those pages yet, though, just reserved the names.

**Twitter:** I have two accounts on Twitter: my personal one, linked to our website, and the official imagineitprintit.ca account. My personal account is more for sharing articles I find interesting and talking to people, giving us a human face. I have been using tools like Monitter to look for live keywords which I can then respond to quickly. I often offer tips, advice, and help or

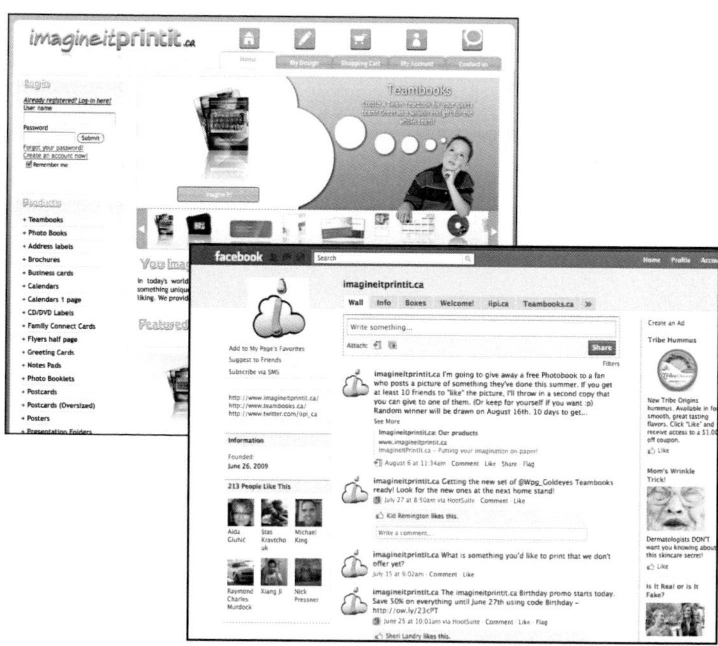


refer people to our website on Twitter. We do want to use it for contests and customer service in the future as well. The toughest part about Twitter is to know when to join the conversation; also, there are not a lot of people talking about some of my keywords. It is sometimes tough to find the right word to look for.

**LinkedIn:** I have created my professional profile on the site. I use it to see what connections I have and use them if I need to. I add to my network whenever someone I work with also has a LinkedIn profile. I also use it to seek expertise if I have a question or to give answers to others looking for them. I have had some members of our sales team sign up to offer advice and answers as well in order to establish themselves as experts in the printing and book fields.

### Blogging Not as Easy as It Sounds

I have one created for our website but don't update it often enough. I find it hard to be the only one trying to generate new content. Finding interesting things to talk about every few days does not come easy. We also started on a blog on our Hignell Book Printing site, but again, the content is difficult to keep generating. I find it hard to get others on board and have them write articles.

I have used other people's blogs, though. I will approach writers who have an audience who may be interested in our products and ask for a review or mention and give coupon codes to their readers. I have offered others free products to use as a giveaway on their blogs. This use of blogs is very new to me, and I haven't had any results to comment on yet, mostly waiting on responses at this point.

### Waiting on Conversions

All of this hasn't produced much conversion yet. It is starting, though. My goal at first was to just lay the foundation of our online community and work on it as we grow. I think these are all great tools, it is just a matter of letting people know you are here.

### Message to Printers: Build It and They Will Come—Eventually!

Social media is something every company should be looking into. It is where your customers are and will be. It is not easy to start getting into it, though, especially if you don't have a large, established fan base already. Don't get discouraged if the results don't show up right away. It will take time and patience, creativity, and honesty to build a strong presence in the social media world.

## Traveler #6
## Balance and consistency needed

**Vanessa Hilton Tripp, Operations Manager**
**Diversified Companies, LLC**
vtripp@divcompanies.com
www.divcompanies.com

### Social Media Tools in Use

We are currently using Facebook. I created our page last year and currently administer the page. We have a little over a hundred fans without really trying. We have had some minor interactions. We have had two current clients write great reviews and hope to get some more once our page is more active. I would like to do more with Facebook because I think it is one of the most valuable free marketing tools, but I just don't seem to have the time or creativity to figure out what to post.

We don't have any blogs to date, but we would like to. Our blogs would focus more on daily life at our offices, entertaining the readers, and building relationships with our clients who subscribe so we aren't just another faceless vendor.

### Better Customer Relations

No new customers yet as a result of these actions, but we are enhancing relationships with current clients. I have used Facebook to advertise client workshops we have hosted and gotten one or two registrants. I also have gotten a few quote requests or orders on the days that I posted stuff. I believe that is because when a client sees our name pop up on their news feed, we are in the front of their mind for the next time a project arises.

### Message to Printers: Balance and Consistency Needed

I think social media tools can be effective if used properly. The biggest advice I have is to be consistent in what you do. If you post every day, post every day—not once every few weeks! But also, don't over-post or else you will begin to be looked over as

people get tired of seeing info that doesn't apply to them. Find the balance that works for your company and its target audience.

# A Social Media and Five Vertical Investigations

## Introduction

The following report is an example of how to compare information related to the vertical's use of social media. The template presented may be used by individual companies whose predominant customers are represented in a vertical. The following document contains five selected verticals of the many that are available. The five selected for this report are: health care, pharmaceuticals, franchises, insurance, and financial services. See note below for information related to other verticals.

How to use this report

1. Identify the top vertical/s of your customer base.
2. Match your vertical with one of the five selected in this appendix or note if your vertical is contained in the larger report noted.
3. Review interested verticals and enlarge the outline with additional information you believe you need for your use.
4. Add this new found information into your knowledge base for your customers to help determine your social media effort as part of your business plan and/or marketing campaign for your company.

**Note:** Other verticals are available in the full report titled, "Social Media Investigations of Top Verticals."

The verticals represented in the full report are: health care, pharmaceuticals, franchises, higher education, travel & tourism (hotels), gambling, restaurants, financial services, utilities, insurance, motor vehicles, retail stores, small business, associations, telecommunications, publications, and gaming and toys.

## 1. Health Care

### Primary Associations

*American Hospital Association*
*www.aha.org*

The American Hospital Association (AHA) is a national organization that represents hospitals, health care networks, and their patients and communities. There are 5,000 hospitals, health care systems, networks, other providers of care, and 37,000 individual members of AHA. The AHA has provided education, representation, and advocacy activities since 1898.

*American Medical Association*
*www.ama-assn.org*

The American Medical Association (AMA) promotes the art and science of medicine and the betterment of public health. The AMA helps unite physicians nationwide to work on both professional and public health issues. Founded in 1847, the AMA is now the largest medical association in America.

*Consumer Healthcare Products Association*
*www.chpa-info.org*

Founded in 1881, the Consumer Healthcare Products Association (CHPA) represents the leading manufacturers and distributors of nonprescription, over-the-counter (OTC) medicines and nutritional supplements. The CHPA is committed to promoting the vital role of OTC medicines in America's health care system through science, education, and advocacy.

*National Association for Healthcare Quality*
*www.nahq.org*

The National Association for Healthcare Quality works with health care quality professionals from every specialty by providing vital research, education, networking, certification, and professional practice resources.

*National Association of Managed Care Physicians*
*www.namcp.org*

The National Association of Managed Care Physicians (NAMCP) enhances the ability of practicing physicians and other health care professionals through accredited continuing medical programs, research, and communication, to succeed in managed care environments and integrated delivery systems. The NAMCP is run by physicians for physicians in the managed health care industry.

**Top Players- HMO**

*Kaiser Permanente*
*www.kaiserpermanente.org*
*recipe.kaiser-permanente.org/*

Kaiser Permanente uses RSS Feeds, podcasts, and blogs to communicate about current events related to the health care industry and the latest news regarding research studies. A blog written by Dr. Preston Maring shares information about healthy recipes, eating, and other healthy living topics. The blog is updated often with tips on how to use seasonal fruits and vegetables in healthy dishes and recipes. They also utilize Twitter, Facebook, and YouTube.

- Facebook: Kaiser Permanente Thrive; 9,000 plus Likes; Activity level: infrequent (several posts/month)
- Twitter: KPNewscenter; 450+ following, 3500+ followers; Activity level: frequent (several posts weekly)

*United Health Group*
*www.unitedhealthcaregroup.com*

The United Health Group uses RSS feeds to deliver the latest healthcare news to subscribers. They have also developed an application for the iPhone which allows users to find doctors by specialty and proximity through the use of GPS.

*Aetna*
*www.aetna.com*

Aetna has created a mobile Web application which allows users to search for doctors, dentists, and facilities. Users are also able to buy insurance; view their ID cards, claims, and personal health records; and check drug prices through the use of their cell phone.

*Health Care Services Corporation*
*www.hcsc.com*

Health Care Services Corporation uses RSS feeds to provide up-to-date news concerning the health care industry, they can also be followed on Twitter.

*Blue Cross Blue Shield*
*www.bcbs.com*

Blue Cross Blue Shield uses RSS feeds and Facebook in order to provide up-to-date news, health care tips, and advertise to consumers. They also offer "Blue TV" and "Blue Radio," which are videos and sound clips from health care experts discussing issues that impact health care in America.

Those are the top HMO websites that have the most evolved social media efforts. Other health and medical insurance organizations have well-developed websites and are engaging in new ways. Cigna, for example offers audio podcasts on health and wellness issues. Some of the other players in this space include:

*CIGNA*
*www.cigna.com*

*Well Point Health Networks*
*www.wellpoint.com*

*PacifiCare Health Systems*
*www.Pacificare.com*

*Humana*
*www.humana.com*

*Coventry Healthcare*
*www.coventryhealthcare.com*

## 2. Pharmaceuticals

### Primary Associations

*Academy of Managed Care Pharmacy*
*www.amcp.org*

The Academy of Managed Care Pharmacy (AMCP) empowers its members to serve society by using sound medication management principles and strategies to improve health care. They provide education and advocacy for their members. The AMCP can be followed on Facebook, LinkedIn and on Twitter.

- Twitter: amcporg, 230+ followers; Activity level: infrequent (several posts/month)

*American Association of Pharmaceutical Scientists*
*www.aaps.org*

The American Association of Pharmaceutical Scientists (AAPS) is a professional, scientific society with more than 12,000 members from academia, industry, government, and other research institutes worldwide. They provide a forum for the exchange of knowledge among scientists to enhance their contributions to public health. The AAPS can be followed on Facebook, LinkedIn and they also use student video contests to raise awareness for the pharmaceutical sciences.

- Facebook: American Association of Pharmaceutical Scientists, 900+ Likes; Activity level: infrequent (several posts/month)

*American Pharmacists Association*
*www.aphanet.org*

The American Pharmacists Association (APhA) is the largest association of pharmacists in the United States, consisting of 60,000 practicing pharmacists, pharmaceutical scientists, students, and pharmacy technicians. Most of today's specialty pharmacy organizations can trace their roots to APhA and the many sections and interest groups it has served. The APhA uses an eCommunity, Twitter, LinkedIn, Facebook, and RSS feeds to keep their members informed of the latest articles and issues pertaining to pharmacy.

*Drug Information Association*
*www.diahome.org*

The Drug Information Association (DIA) has more than 18,000 members worldwide involved in discovery, development, regulation, surveillance, or marketing of biopharmaceutical products. The DIA provides forums to exchange information and discuss current issues, customized education, and they build and maintain relationships with and among individuals and organizations that drive and share DIA values. They have created their own social network designed to improve collaboration, maximize networking opportunities, and enhance learning potential.

*Pharmaceutical Research and Manufacturers of America*
*www.phrma.org*

The Pharmaceutical Research and Manufacturers of America (PhRMA) represents pharmaceutical and biotechnology companies. PhRMA's mission is to conduct effective advocacy for public policies that encourage discovery of important new medicines for patients by pharmaceutical and biotechnology companies. They use Facebook, Twitter, LinkedIn, and Digg to communicate with their members.

**Top Players**

*Pfizer Inc.*
*www.pfizer.com*

Pfizer utilizes webcasts of conferences, Twitter, and RSS feeds to communicate with their customers.

*Johnson and Johnson Inc.*
*www.jnj.com*

Johnson and Johnson is a founding partner of text4baby. Text4baby provides expecting and new mothers with text messages containing age-appropriate information for her child on topics such as immunization, nutrition, seasonal flu, and oral health.

*GlaxoSmithKline PLC*
*www.gsk.com*
*http://www.morethanmedicine.us.gsk.com/blog/*

GlaxoSmithKline (GSK) is using a blog to communicate with customers. They discuss current news, chronic diseases, health care reform, and news about what GSK as a company. A series of blog entries featured personal stories and the advances made in the fight against cervical cancer. They are utilizing Twitter, Facebook, and Digg as they develop their extensive social media campaign.

- Facebook: GlaxoSmithKline; 2,900+ Likes; Activity level: related posts frequent (several posts weekly)
- Twitter: GSKUS; 130+ following, 5,800+ followers; Activity level: infrequent (several posts/month)

*Novartis AG*
*www.novartis.com*

Novartis has developed Vaxtrak, an iPhone application that tracks vaccinations and immunizations that users have had and may need. Novartis also uses audiocasts, webcasts, and Twitter to keep consumers notified of current events and news.

- Twitter: 8400+ following; Activity level: infrequent (several posts/month)

The following companies use RSS feeds and webcasts primarily for their investors:

- *Astra Zeneca PLC*
  *www.astrazeneca.com*
- *Abbott Laboratories*
  *www.abbott.com*
- *Merck & Co. Inc.*
  *www.merck.com*
- *Wyeth*
  *www.wyeth.com*
- *Eli Lilly and Company*
  *www.lilly.com*

- *Bristol-Myers Squibb Co.*
  *www.bms.com*

## 3. Franchises

### Associations

*International Franchise Association*
*www.franchise.org*

The International Franchise Association is a membership organization of franchisors, franchisees, and suppliers. They educate their members on all facets of creating or buying a franchise. They notify their members of upcoming meetings, seminars, and the latest news regarding franchises through Twitter and Facebook.

*The American Franchisee Association*
*www.franchisee.org*

The American Franchisee Association is a trade association of franchisees and dealers. They work to improve the industry of franchising, while protecting its members' economic investments in their businesses. They are strong advocates for franchisee legal issues in Washington, DC.

*The Center for Total Quality Franchising*
*www.aafd.org*

The Center for Total Quality Franchising represents the rights and interests of franchisees and independent dealers throughout the United States. They promote negotiated franchise relationships within the franchising community and identify, develop, and implement programs, products, and services to build economic strength and bargaining power for their members.

*Franchise Business Support Network*
*www.franchiseealliance.com*

The Franchise Business Network is an online network for people interested in starting franchises. They provide news and articles pertaining to buying, selling, and operating franchises. The Franchise Business Network also maintains an online radio blog hosted by the CEO and founder.

*New England Franchise Association*
*www.nefranchise.org*

The New England Franchise Association (NEFA) brings franchise executives, franchisees, and vendors together to share ideas for success. The NEFA creates these relationships through hosting informative speakers, sharing best practices, and providing networking opportunities. The NEFA utilizes a blog to communicate with their members; the blog consists of articles written about current topics in the franchise industry.

**Top Players**

*Subway*
*www.subway.com*
www.facebook.com/home.php?sk=lf#!/Subway365

The Subway chain has ranked at the top of Entrepreneur Magazine's Franchise 500 rankings for 15 of the past 21 years. Although their most famous ad campaign included the story of Jared Fogle's weight loss, they also use Facebook. Their Facebook page is used to raise awareness of new sandwiches, special deals, and contests. The ability to constantly update Facebook allows Subway to feature deals that may only last one day or a week or offer a limited-time sandwich.

- Facebook: Subway, 3.8 million+ Likes; Activity level: infrequent (several posts/month)

*McDonald's*
*www.mcdonalds.com*

McDonald's uses Facebook primarily for advertising purposes; they have specific pages for their McNuggets, Dollar Menu, and McCafé. McDonald's also has a following on Twitter, where they can advertise special deals and customers can voice their opinion on their menu items.

- Facebook: McDonald's, 6 million+ Likes; Activity level: frequent (several posts weekly)

*7-Eleven Inc.*
*www.7-eleven.com*

The 7-Eleven convenience store chain is currently using Facebook to advertise new products, charitable partnerships, and contests for customers. Customers are also able to voice comments and concerns regarding their experiences at 7-Eleven on the Facebook page.

- Facebook: 7-Eleven, 980,000+ Likes; Activity level: very frequent (several posts daily)

*Supercuts*
*www.supercuts.com*

Supercuts uses Facebook and Twitter to advertise new products, special discounts, and discuss customers' concerns. Customers are even able to post pictures of haircuts that they have been disappointed with.

*H&R Block*
*www.hrblock.com*

H&R Block uses Facebook and YouTube to distribute tax help videos and articles. They also utilize Facebook as a customer service forum.

*Dunkin' Donuts*
*www.dunkindonuts.com*

Dunkin' Donuts uses Facebook for advertising and also has a discussion forum. The forum focuses on topics such as where to locate new stores, customer service issues, and favorite donut choices.

In some cases individual franchisees will create a Facebook page to alert local Facebook members about their business. Often franchises will offer different sales based on the region, making personalized Facebook pages an effective marketing tool. Here are a few more franchise-oriented sites:

- *Hampton Inn/Hampton Inn & Suites*
  *www.hamptoninn1.hilton.com*
- *Jani-King*
  *www.janiking.com*
- *Servpro*
  *www.servpro.com*

- *Ampm Mini Market*
  *www.ampm.com*

## 4. Insurance

An extensive 27-page report by CMO Council is now available: *What's Critical in the Vertical—Insurance.* This free PDF is available at http://www.cmocouncil.org/resources/form-critical-vertical.asp.

### Associations

*American Insurance Association*
*www.aiadc.com*

The American Insurance Association is the leading property-casualty insurance trade organization, representing 300 insurers. Their members include personal and commercial auto insurance, workers' compensation, homeowner's insurance, medical malpractice coverage, and product liability insurance.

*Professional Insurance Marketing Association*
*www.pima-assn.org*

The Professional Insurance Marketing Association (PIMA) serves as a forum for the leading Agents/TPAs/Brokers and Companies involved in the direct marketing of group insurance and related products. PIMA provides a networking community of decision-makers and deal-makers, quality educational programming, and legislative and regulatory updates.

*National Association of Mutual Insurance Companies*
*www.namic.org*

The National Association of Mutual Insurance Companies (NAMIC) is the largest, most diverse national insurance trade association in the U.S. The NAMIC strengthens and supports its members and the property/casualty insurance industry by providing effective and high-value advocacy, member services, and public policy development.

- Twitter: namicnews, 100+ following, 400+ followers; Activity level: dormant (site is there but nobody's maintaining)

*Property Casualty Insurers Association of America*
*www.pciaa.net*

The Property Casualty Insurers Association of America (PCI) provides a forum for discussion and debate, information on current trends in the industry, networking opportunities, and advocacy to its members. Members of PCI range from publicly held national companies to single-state and specialty writers.

- Facebook: 170+ Likes; Activity level: frequent (several posts weekly)
- Twitter: 800+ following, 1,400+ followers; Activity level: infrequent (several posts/month)

**Top Players**

*Esurance*
*www.esurance.com*

Esurance has an extensive media center on esurance.com. The media center includes video and sound clips of their animated television commercials along with a blog discussing safe driving tips, ways to cut spending, and even a section about music sponsored by esurance. Esurance now allows customers to track their claims online, viewing pictures of repairs being done to the vehicle and asking the repair technicians questions online.

- Facebook: Esurance, 1,400+ Likes; Activity level: frequent (several posts weekly)
- Twitter: esurance,220 following, 1,340 followers, Activity level: very frequent (several posts daily)

*Geico*
*www.geico.com*

Geico communicates to its customers through the use of a blog with categories such as sales and service, claims, and auto damage. Geico also has a large media library of their popular commercials, including sound clips that can be downloaded as ringtones. They send out many news releases on their Facebook and Twitter pages. Geico maintains several Facebook Pages, some based on characters from their popular television ads. So there's a page for the Geico Gecko with 140,000 Likes and another for the Geico caveman with over 10,000 (we prefer little green guys with a British accent over big hairy ones, apparently).

- Facebook, GEICO, 87,000+ Likes; Activity level: infrequent (several posts/month)
- Twitter: GEICO, 1,200+ following, 2300+ followers; Activity level: very frequent (several posts daily)

*Allstate*
*www.allstate.com*

Allstate has created the Good Hands Community, an online forum containing discussions and blogs about automobiles, personal finance, and making a difference in your community. Allstate also has a blog titled *Vehicle Vibes;* it is about educating drivers about bad habits such as text messaging while driving, tips on traveling with pets, and vehicle recalls. They can also be followed on Facebook and Twitter.

- Facebook: Allstate Insurance, 23,000+ Likes; Activity level: frequent (several posts weekly)
- Twitter: allstate, 3,900+ following, 6700+ followers; Activity level: very frequent (several posts daily)

## 5. Financial Services

### Associations

*American Bankers Association*
*www.aba.com*

The American Bankers Association (ABA) represents the entire banking industry. The ABA provides banks with resources to meet the challenges of managing compliance risk with regulatory expertise, advocacy, commercial banking information, market research, education, and training.

*Consumer Bankers Association*
*www.cbanet.org*

The Consumer Bankers Association (CBA) represents retail banking such as auto financing, home equity lending, card products, education loans, deposits, and delivery. The CBA provides leadership, education, research, and federal representation on retail banking issues. The CBA can be followed on Twitter and Facebook.

- Facebook: Consumer Bankers Association, 100 Likes; Activity level: infrequent (several posts/month)
- Twitter: CBAConnect, 90+ following, 320+ followers; Activity level: frequent (several posts weekly)

*American Financial Services Association*
*www.afsaonline.org*

The American Financial Services Association (AFSA) is the national trade association for the consumer credit industry. The AFSA provides advocacy in the federal government, legal affairs, public affairs, and education for executives in the industry. They have also created an affiliate, AFSA Education Foundation, with the mission of educating consumers about responsible money management and understanding the credit card process.

*International Financial Services Association*
*www.ifsaonline.org*

The International Financial Service Association (IFSA) provides advocacy, education, and community building opportunities for financial services institutions and suppliers from around the world. The IFSA is the leading forum for analysis, discussion, and action among international financial professionals and industry suppliers on a wide range of topics affecting transaction banking.

*The Community Financial Services Association of America*
*www.cfsa.net*

The mission of The Community Financial Services Association of America (CFSA) is to promote legislation and regulation that protect consumers, while preserving their access to short-term credit options. The CFSA also supports and encourages responsible industry packages. Members of the CFSA make up more than half of the twenty-four thousand payday advance locations nationally.

**Top Players**

*Wells Fargo*
*www.wellsfargo.com*

Wells Fargo has five different blogs listed on their website. They deal with the history of the company to a blog about budgeting spending. A typical blog may be centered on college students and how they spend or how credit cards can affect their credit scores. blog.wellsfargo.com Wells Fargo uses Twitter to answer customers' questions regarding checking, savings, and online banking.

- Twitter: Ask_WellsFargo, 6,000+ following, 5,900 followers; Activity level: very frequent (several posts daily)

*Deutsche Bank*
*www.db.com*

The Deutsche Bank has created a social media presence with the use of Twitter, YouTube, Facebook, Flickr, and RSS feeds and podcasts. The Deutsche Bank uses these outlets to release news stories, press releases, and research findings.

- Twitter: Deutsche_News, TW 470+ following, 3,100+ followers; Activity level: very frequent (several posts daily)

*Discover*
*www.discovercard.com*

Discover uses Facebook and Twitter to stay in touch with their customers. Questions and comments can be posted to these sites and a representative will respond to them personally. The outlets also provide Discover an opportunity to advertise special promotions, news, and personal finance tips.

- Facebook: Discover, 23,000+ Likes; Activity level: very frequent (several posts daily)

- Twitter: Discover, 1,400+ following, 12,000 followers; Activity level: very frequent (several posts daily)

# B Resources for Further Exploration

## Blogs Featuring Social Media Experts

### Chris Brogan (www.chrisbrogan.com)

Chris Brogan has harnessed social media to propel himself into the limelight as a social media marketing expert. He's a fairly prolific blogger and Twitterer, was co-author of *Trust Agents,* and has just written a new book, *Social Media 101*. He runs New Marketing Labs, a new media company, that works primarily with large *Fortune* 100 to 500 companies to design and implement digital marketing strategies. He's also a public speaker for hire. Some of his posts include topics like "50 ideas on using Twitter for business" and "Framing your social media efforts."

### Mari Smith (www.marismith.com)

Mari Smith calls herself a Relationship Marketing Specialist and works with businesses to help them "figure out how to monetize all these new social media tools." Mari focuses heavily on Facebook and her posts are often very technical. She's one of the best how-to resources for improving the look of your Facebook Page. She directly answers questions posted to the wall of her Facebook Page: www.facebook.com/marismith.

### Chris Garrett (www.chrisg.com)

A professional blogger, Chris Garrett is author of five books, including *ProBlogger: Secrets for Blogging Your Way to a Six-Figure Income*. Since he makes his living blogging and writing about blogging, if you're interested in doing more in that area, this is a blog you'll want to consider following. He talks about the art of blogging with practical writing advice such as this post "Defeating Procrastination: Analysis Paralysis."

**Scott Monty (www.scottmonty.com)**

Scott Monty is the Global Digital & Multimedia Communications manager for Ford Motor Company (i.e., he's the social media guy). He must also be very good at search engine optimization, because his blog "The Social Media Marketing Blog" comes up second out of 61 million hits in a Google search on the phrase "social media marketing companies." In addition to his blog, in which he reveals his social media insights, Monty maintains a presence on twenty-three different social media sites. He has links to all on his blog site.

**Technorati (www.technorati.com)**

This "search engine for blogs" indexes over 112 million blogs and 250 million tagged pieces of social media. Blog authors tag their content and Technorati uses those tags to categorize search results on the site. During July 2010, a search for blogs relating to "social media" on Technorati.com yielded 6192 results. The top three of those: Mashable, ReadWriteWeb and The Next Web. Technorati allows for search by general topic (like Sports, Technology and Business,) by tag, people or by popularity (Top 100.) In beta is a new option Technorati List, a PR and outreach platform that lets organizations and blogger blatantly pitch a product or service. For now, this service is free.

## Books

- *Engage: The Complete Guide for Brands and Businesses* by Brian Solis
- *The New Rules of Marketing and PR* 2nd edition by David Meerman Scott
- *Social Media Marketing for Dummies* by Shiv Singh
- *Socialnomics: How Social Media Transforms the Way We Live and Do Business* by Eric Qualcom
- *Inbound Marketing: Get Found Using Google, Social Media, and Blogs* by Brian Halligan and Dharmesh Shah
- *Trust Agents: Using the Web to Build Influence, Improve*

*Reputation, and Earn Trust* by Chris Brogan and Julien Smith

- *The New Community Rules: Marketing on the Social Web* by Tamar Weinberg
- *The Cluetrain Manifesto: The End of Business as Usual* by Christopher Locke, Rick Levine, Doc Searls, and David Weinberger
- *Groundswell: Winning in a World Transformed by Social Technologies* by Charlene Li and Josh Bernoff
- *Marketing to the Social Web: How Digital Customer Communities Build Your Business* by Larry Weber
- *Emergence: The Connected Lives of Ants, Brains, Cities, and Software* by Steven Johnson
- *Collective Intelligence: Mankind's Emerging World in Cyberspace* by Pierre Levy
- *Linked: How Everything Is Connected to Everything Else and What It Means for Business, Sciences, and Everyday Life* by Albert-Laszlo Barabasi
- *The Long Tail: Why the Future of Business Is Selling Less of More* by Chris Anderson

## Research Organizations and Websites

### Social Media Examiner
**www.socialmediaexaminer.com**

This "free online magazine" was ranked as one of the world's top 100 business blogs within months of its October 2009 launch. Founded by Michael Stelzner, best known for his WhitePaperSource.com, a clearinghouse for all things related to white paper advertising, the Examiner features in-depth how-to articles and video links from well-known social media practitioners, in-depth case studies, interviews, research reports, and opinion pieces. Stelzner also offers an annual online conference, The Social Media Summit, featuring WebEx-style seminar delivery, with online access to all session videos, transcripts, and slideshows for a year.

**Mashable**
**www.mashable.com**

An "online guide to social media" and one of the top 10 blogs in the world, Mashable features breaking news on Web-centric happenings, products, reviews, detailed how-to articles, marketing tips, and viral videos. More than 2.7 million people follow Mashable on four major social platforms, Twitter, Buzz, Facebook, and RSS feed. The site features a "mashup" of information beyond social media, including entertainment, development and design, business, mobile, Web-centric technology, Apple, and tech jobs. Mashable has gotten into the conference scene with a summer tour that rolled through five major cities in 2010, featuring appearances by Mashable staff and contributors. That would include Pete Cashmore, who founded Mashable in 2005 at the age of nineteen. He's one of the new breed of under-thirty CEOs who have developed a rock-star-like persona, and his personal appearances draw throngs of groupies. We've arrived at the time in history where geeky is actually considered sexy.

**The Pew Research Center's Internet & American Life Project**
**www.pewinternet.org**

The Pew Internet & American Life Project is one of seven projects that make up the Pew Research Center, a nonpartisan, nonprofit "fact tank" that provides information on the issues, attitudes and trends shaping America and the world. The Internet Project produces well-researched reports exploring the impact of the internet on our daily life, education, health care, and civic and political lives. All of the surveys are freely available on the website, and, as time goes on, a historical picture of how the Internet is changing our lives is emerging. The Pew Internet Project produces some of the best demographic information on American citizens' online activities. RSS feeds are available "for serious Pew junkies only."

**All Facebook**
**www.allfacebook.com**

All Facebook is "the unofficial Facebook resource." It's a website that acts as a clearinghouse for any news or information about Facebook. Aside from news, the site features statistics on Facebook apps, listing the top applications, developers, and fastest-growing and worst applications for the day, week, or month. This is also where you'll find details about the leading Facebook Pages, which can be sorted by category, with the number of Fans (Likes) and daily/weekly growth rate of each. We'd like to say that this categorical sorting mechanism is a good way to check up on the Facebook Pages for various vertical, but when we checked for the top Pages (based on number of Fans) in the Medical Service category, the top Page listed was "Not being on fire." Not too helpful. The Facebook Page Leaderboard is a bit more helpful, showing trending Pages and topics. To start out, just make sure yours is not showing up on the "Worst Pages" listing.

**Experian Hitwise**
**www.hitwise.com**

Hitwise developed proprietary software that Internet Service Providers (ISPs) use to analyze website logs on their network. The sample size is huge (25 million people worldwide, including 10 million in the U.S.). The supposedly anonymous data (the site hosts an audit report by PricewaterhouseCoopers on the company's methodology) is aggregated and provided to Hitwise, where it's combined with data from opt-in partners, and the result is a suite of industry standard metrics relating to the viewing of websites including page requests, visits, average visit length, search terms, and behavior. The top websites, social networking sites, retail sites, and search engines are posted to the site's Data Center each week. This is a great way to see trending moves from one social site to another and where and how people search for data. Since early spring 2010, Facebook has supplanted Google as the top website worldwide. Specific verticals are featured periodically for a deeper dive on how industry-specific Web and social sites stack up.

**TechCrunch**
**www.techcrunch.com**

TechCruch has grown from a simple blog about technology into a network of tech-focused sites. Among them is Crunchbase (www.crunchbase.com) a free database of technology companies, people, and even investors that anyone can edit. Because it's a wiki, you can't know if the data is accurate, but like any socially maintained site, inaccuracies are often self-correcting, as other contributors will seek to set the record straight. There is also CrunchGear, focusing on gadgets; MobileCrunch; TechCrunchIT; and The Gillmor Gang, a site that features content provided by social media (cringe!) gurus. This is a great suite of sites to review via RSS feed to keep tabs on technology and Web-focused news

**Search Engine Land**
**http://searchengineland.com**

Search Engine Optimization (SEO) is often one of the goals of social media engagement, especially for a company with an e-commerce site. Search Engine Land is a news and information site covering search engine marketing, searching issues, and the search engine industry. The site is published by Third Door Media, which also produces the Search Marketing Expo conference series and the Search Marketing Now webcast events. The site offers several newsletters and RSS feeds on SEO-related topics and several topic-related columns, including one on analytics and measurement, conversion science, granular how-to tips and social media.

# C Social Media RFP Template

## Introduction

The purpose of this section is to give a brief overview of the company issuing the request for proposal (RFP) and the social media project or desired work relationship between the company and the vendor.

### 1. Company Overview

<Company ABC's History>

<Company ABC's business objectives>

<Reasons why Company ABC intends to participate in social media>

### 2. Overview of Project

<Objectives of the project>

<Explanation of type of vendor relationship desired, i.e., Project-based, Agency of Record, etc>

### 3. Overview of Audiences and Stakeholders

<List primary audiences for the company, i.e. demographics, psychographics, etc>

<List primary information needs of each audience group>

### 4. Primary contact

<List Company ABC's primary contact for questions related to process and RFI document>

## Guidelines for Proposal Preparation

1. Issuance of this document to a list of potential Vendors by <Day> <Month> 20XX
2. Questions from potential Vendors to be received by <Day> <Month> 20XX (please specify which format – phone call, email, fax)
3. Responses from issuer to be sent by <Day> <Month> 20XX
4. On the basis of the replies to the RFP document, a short list of potential Vendors will be selected and this group will be asked to present demonstrations of their capabilities and vision for the project. These meetings will be completed by <Month> XXth, 20XX
5. Awarding of the contract to selected Vendor by <Month> XXth, 20XX
6. Work to commence by <Day> <Month> 20XX

## Vendor Questions and Qualifications

### COMPANY DETAILS

1. Vendor Company Name
2. Parent Company (if applicable)
3. Ownership structure
4. Years in operation
5. Mailing address (Head Office)
6. Other office locations
7. Main telephone
8. Fax number
9. Web URL
10. Vendor blog URL
11. Primary Vendor contact (name, title, phone and email address)

12. Total number of Vendor employees
13. Number of Vendor employees whose primary function is social media
14. Top five social media clients by revenue percentage and length of relationship
15. Current clients (social media work only)
16. Percentage of total revenue that is social-media related
17. Please list three references for social media work including; Company name, primary client name, contact details and brief explanation of services provided
18. List of accounts lost or resigned in the last two years
19. Please list any potential conflicts with existing Vendor client base and this RFP
20. Senior social media staff bios
21. Links to senior social media staff profiles on social sites (i.e. LinkedIn, Twitter, Facebook...)
22. Please provide a complete list of relevant social media platform and technology partners, with URLs
23. If a partner, outside contractor or anyone not currently employed with the company has prepared any part of this response, please list details

**GENERAL**

1. Please list all social media services provided to clients
2. Do you have any proprietary tools or products related to social media?
3. Please list any experience you have with integrating social, paid and/or earned media
4. Please identify your most common type of clients, with examples: marketing, communications, IT, human resources, internal deployment of Enterprise 2.0 programs, other
5. Please list and provide links to primary social media

communication channels for your company (i.e. Company blog, Twitter account, Facebook group, blogs authored by principals, etc.)

**STRATEGY**

1. Please outline your social media strategy process
2. Which stakeholder groups do you typically include in a strategy engagement?
3. Describe the final deliverable of a strategy engagement
4. What is your approach to risk management in social media?
5. How do you incorporate existing applications, websites, microsites and newsletter programs into your overall social media strategy?
6. How do you ensure compliance with client legal requirements?
7. Please describe your approach to integrating across client marketing, customer service and corporate communications departments? Please provide an example of your work in this area
8. How do you approach adapting a traditional brand into a two-way dialogue?
9. Please provide a case study of your strategy work that resulted in a social media initiative and the business results achieved

**REPUTATION MANAGEMENT / SOCIAL MEDIA MONITORING**

1. What is your brand/reputation monitoring process (i.e. proprietary tools used, methodology, etc)?
2. What is your opinion on automated sentiment analysis?
3. What technology do you use to assist in online monitoring?

4. How long (on average) between a potential issue being posted online and being flagged to the client?
5. What volume of mentions has your organization handled in the past (e.g. 2,500 mentions per week)?
6. What is your quality assurance process to ensure that the large volumes of data gathered in the monitoring process are handled efficiently and representative of the overall online conversation?
7. Please detail your methodology for handling online crises
8. What services do you provide in support of online crisis management?
9. Please describe the structure of your crisis management team, including bios and relevant experience
10. How do you assess which mentions require immediate responses and which do not?
11. Please outline your general approach to sourcing and responding to comments
12. Please provide a case study detailing your work for the purposes of managing reputation or online crisis management, including outcomes and lessons learned
13. Please include a sample of your monitoring report format and/or a link to appropriate dashboards (specifics should be removed)

### METRICS AND MEASUREMENT

1. What methodology do you use for measuring the success of your social media programs for clients? Please provide specific examples based on past work.
2. Have you developed any proprietary metrics? How have you applied these for clients?
3. How have you defined R.O.I. from a social media perspective in the past?

4. How do you take data points generated from various social media channels and measurement tools and combine to give an objective/comprehensive view?
5. What is your approach to server analytics and community analytics for program measurement?
6. Do you have the capability to measure cost per lead or cost per acquisition? Please provide an example of a project on which you have done so.
7. What platforms are you unable to measure accurately, or able to provide only limited measurements from?
8. Please provide a sample of a measurement document or final report (specifics should be removed).
9. What percentage of the budget do you recommend be dedicated to metrics and measurement?

**EDUCATION**

1. Do you offer social media training services for clients?
2. What format does your training take (i.e. workshops, presentations, walkthroughs, webinars/online learning)
3. What internal processes do you have in place to ensure that your staff are kept current on social media innovations and best practices?
4. How do you measure progress and evaluate training effectiveness?
5. Please provide sample curriculum/outline
6. Please provide testimonials or feedback from training participants

**SOCIAL MEDIA CHANNELS**

1. What are your design, creative and community management capabilities?
2. What percentage of staff are dedicated to building and

deploying social media solutions versus management and consulting?

3. Please describe your experience with the following platforms and tactics:

    - YouTube or similar video sharing sites
    - Blogs
    - Content Management System (CMS) and Customer Relationship Management (CRM)
    - E-mail Newsletter Campaigns
    - Facebook Groups or Pages
    - Facebook Apps
    - Other social networks and social networking tools
    - Mobile application development
    - Twitter or other forms of microblogging
    - News sharing sites (i.e. Digg, Reddit, etc.)
    - Virtual Worlds
    - Augmented reality
    - Photo sharing (i.e. Flickr)
    - Other content sharing sites (i.e. Scribd, Slideshare, Delicious, etc.)
    - Social Media press releases (SMPRs)
    - Crowdsourcing or Wikis
    - Forums
    - Real world events organized via social media (e.g. Tweetups)
    - Ratings/Customer service sites (i.e. Yelp, ePinions, etc.)
    - Podcasting

4. Please provide examples of social media channel development work completed within the last two years

## COMMUNITY AND INFLUENCER OUTREACH (SOCIAL PR)

1. What is your process for identifying influencers within various social media channels?
2. How do you determine and define "influence"?
3. What is your outreach process for communicating with identified online influencers?
4. What is your point-of-view on the December 1, 2009 FTC Guides for Advertisers and their impact on your influencer outreach programs for clients? How have you put this into action?
5. What tools and approaches do you use for Influencer Relationship Management? (third-party, proprietary, etc.)
6. How have you integrated Influencer Outreach with traditional communications and/or marketing campaigns?
7. How do you approach seeding conversations within stakeholder groups?
8. What is your exit strategy with influencers once the initiative is completed?
9. How do you ensure authenticity and transparency when conducting outreach on behalf of a client?
10. Please provide a case study of an online community outreach project.

## CLIENT SERVICES & PROJECT MANAGEMENT

1. How is a typical client engagement with your firm structured?
2. How do you structure your account teams?
3. Please outline your internal communication structure. If your account staff is separate from your project management staff, please detail how these teams work together.
4. If you are selected to provide social media services for [Company ABC], who will be assigned to our business (please provide names, titles and short biographical notes).

5. What percentage of senior staff involvement is structured in to your projects? What role do they play?
6. What is your rate card?
7. How are your projects priced? — Using an hourly rate? blended agency rate?
8. What change management practices does your agency employ?
9. What reports will be provided to [Company ABC] in order to communicate project milestones and overall project health?
10. What is your process for gathering business requirements?
11. What is your process for client reviews or acceptance testing?

*From Social Media Group, socialmediagroup.com.*

# References

## Introduction References

About.com. *Web Trends: The Web 2.0 Glossary.* http://webtrends.about.com/od/web20/a/web20-glossary_2.htm.

Jantsch, John. *Duct Tape Marketing: The World's Most Practical Small Business Marketing Guide.* Nashville: Thomas Nelson Inc., 2007.

Safko, Lon. *The Social Media Bible: Tactical Tools & Strategies for Business Success,* Second Edition. Hoboken: John Wiley & Sons, Inc., 2010.

Wikipedia. http://en.wikipedia.org/wiki/Social_media.

## Chapter 1 References

Burson-Marsteller. *The Global Social Media Check-up 2010.* http://www.burson-marsteller.com/innovation_and_insights/blogs_and_podcasts/BM_Blog/Lists/Posts/Post.aspx?ID=160 accessed 14 September 2010.

Bloomberg Business Week. "Newspaper Ad Spending Drops Least in 4 Years Amid Web's Strength" by Amy Thomson citing Newspaper Association of America. 7 September 2010. http://www.businessweek.com/news/2010-09-07/newspaper-ad-spending-drops-least-in-4-years-amid-web-s-strength.html

Center for Digital Future. University of Southern California USC Annenberg School. 2010 USC Annenberg Digital Future Study, http://www.digitalcenter.org/pdf/2010_digital_future_final_release.pdf.

CMOSurvey.org. "Highlights and Insights August 2010: Social Media Spending Remains High." *The CMO Survey Results.* Fuqua School of Business, Duke University and American

Marketing Association. http://faculty.fuqua.duke.edu/cmosurvey/survey_results/ accessed 8 November 2010.

comScore. *Social Networking Ranks as Fastest-Growing Mobile Content Category.* http://www.comscore.com/Press_Events/Press_Releases/2010/6/Social_Networking_Ranks_as_Fastest-Growing_Mobile_Content_Category accessed 8 November 2010.

Gigatweet. Counter. 6 November 2010. http://gigatweeter.com/counter

Harvard Business Publishing. "E-Book Devices Expected to Reach 10 Million U.S. Homes," *Harvard Business Review: The Daily Stat* (referencing Forrester Research). http://web.hbr.org/email/archive/dailystat.php?date=090810 accessed 14 September 2010.

Internet World Stats. *Internet World Stats: Usage and Population Statistics.* "Internet Usage Statistics—The Internet Big Picture: World Internet Users and Population Stats." www.Internetworldstats.com/stats.htm accessed 14 September 2010.

ITU Academy. *ITU expects 5 billion mobile subscribers in 2010.* 19 February 2010. http://academy.itu.int/index.php/news/item/89-itu-expects-5-billion-mobile-subscribers-in-2010 accessed 14 September 2010.

Mashable.com. "YouTube Surpasses Two Billion Vide Views Daily." Ben Parr. http://mashable.com/2010/5/17/you-tube-2-billion-views/ accessed 14 September 2010.

mobiThinking. *Global mobile statistics 2010: all quality mobile marketing research, mobile Web stats, subscribers, ad revenue, usage, trends….* {citing Strategy Analytics) http://mobithinking.mobi/mobile-marketing-tools/latest-mobile-stats?dm_switcher=true, accessed 8 November 2010.

*The Nielsen Company. What Americans Do Online: Social Media and Games Dominate Activity.* http://blog.nielsen.com/nielsenwire/online_mobile/what-americans-do-online-social-media-and-games-dominate-activity/ accessed 14 September 2010.

PaidContent.org. "Newspaper Fas-Fax: E-Edition Circulation Up 40 Percent." Staci D. Kramer. *paidContent.org: The Economics of Digital Content (citing Audit Bureau of Circulation).* http//

paidcontent.org/article/419-newspaper-FasFax-e-edition-circulation-up-40-percent/ accessed 14 September 2010.

Pew Internet & American Life Project. *Change in internet access by age group, 2000-2009. Feb 3, 2010. http://www.pewinternet.org/Infographics/2010/Internet-acess-by-age-group-over-time.aspx* accessed 14 September 2010.

———. *Demographics of Internet Users.* http://pewinternet.org/Trend-Data/Whos-Online.aspx accessed 14 September 2010.

———. *The Future of Social Relations,* Janna Anderson and Lee Rainie. http://www.pewinternet.org/Reports/2010/The-future-of-social-relations.aspx accessed 14 September 2010.

———. *Millennials Will Make Online Sharing in Networks a Lifelong Habit,* Janna Anderson and Lee Rainie. 9 July 2010. http://pewinternet.org/Reports/2010/Future-of-millennials/MainFindings.aspx accessed 14 September 2010.

———. *Social Media and Young Adults,* by Amanda Lenhart, Kristen Purcell, Aaron Smith, Kathryn Zickuhr. February 3, 2010. http://pewInternet.org/Reports/2010/Social-Media-and-Young-Adults.aspx.

———. *Understanding the Participatory News Consumer: How Internet and Cell Phone Users Have Turned News into a Social Experience,* Kristen Purcell, Lee Rainie, Amy Mitchell, Tom Rosenstiel, and Kenny Olmstead. March 2010. http://pewinternet.org/Reports/2010/Online-News/Summary-of-Findings.aspx accessed 14 September 2010.

PublishersWeekly.com. "June e-Book Sales up 119%," PW Staff. 20 August 2010. www.publishersweekly.com/pw/by-topic/digital/content-and-e-books/article/44217-june-e-book-sales-up-119-.html accessed 14 September 2010.

Stelzner, Michael A. *2010 Social Media Marketing Industry Report: How Marketers Are Using Social Media to Grow Their Businesses.* April 19, 2010. http://www.socialmediaexaminer.com/social-media-marketing-industry-report-2010/ accessed 14 September 2010.

Technorati.com. *Technorati Blog Directory.* http://technorati.com/blogs/directory/ accessed 14 September 2010.

———. *Technorati Top 100.* http://technorati.com/blogs/top100/ accessed 14 September 2010.

Wired.com. "The Web Is Dead. Long Live the Internet." Chris Anderson and Michael Wolff. 17 August 2010. http://www.wired.com/magazine/2010/08/ff_webrip/all/1 accessed 14 September 2010.

## Chapter 2 References

Advertising Age. "What's Your Brand's Social ID? Lost Amid the Tweets, Posts, Streams and Feeds Is Your Brand's Identity." Chris Perry. http://adage.com/digitalnext/article?article_id=145795 accessed 14 September 2010.

Andruss, Paula. "Making the Most of a Relationship." *Deliver Magazine:* 6 (3) July 2010. delivermagazine.com. http://www.scribd.com/doc/34939485/Deliver-Magazine-Volume-6-Issue-3-July-2010.

Burson-Marsteller. *The Global Social Media Check-up 2010.* http://www.burson-marsteller.com/innovation_and_insights/blogs_and_podcasts/BM_Blog/Lists/Posts/Post.aspx?ID=160 accessed 14 September 2010.

Fast Company. "Does Corporate Reputation Matter?" by Austin Carr citing Harris Interactive. 9 April 2010. http://www.fastcompany.com/1612020/does-corporate-image-matter

Garyvaynerchuk.com. http://garyvaynerchuk.com/.

Gleeson, Ed. *Print Market Update Third Quarter 2009.* Sewickley, PA: Printing Industries of America.

Li, Charlene and Josh Bernoff. *Groundswell: Winning in a World Transformed by Social Technologies.* Boston: Forrester Research, Inc., 2008.

MarketingSherpa. *Top 7 B2B Case Studies for 2010. http://www.hubspot.com/marketingsherpa-top-7-B2B-Case-Studies-for-2010/.*

Mashable.com. "Old Spice Sales Double With YouTube Campaign." Samuel Axon (referencing Nielsen data). http://

Mashable.com/2010/07/27/old-spice-sales/ accessed 14 September 2010.

Morgan Stanley. *The Mobile Internet Report Setup.* 15 December 2009. http://www.morganstanley.com/institutional/techresearch/pdfs/2SETUP_12142009_RI.pdf accessed 14 September 2010.

*The Nielsen Company. What Americans Do Online: Social Media and Games Dominate Activity.* http://blog.nielsen.com/nielsenwire/online_mobile/what-americans-do-online-social-media-and-games-dominate-activity/ accessed 14 September 2010.

NielsenWire. "Nielsen Reports March 2010 U.S. Search Rankings." 28 April 2010. http://blog.nielsen.com/nielsenwire/online_mobile/nielsen-reports-march-2010-u-s-search-rankings

## Chapter 3 References

Aberdeen Group. *The ROI on Social Media Marketing: Why It Pays to Listen to Online Conversation* by Jeff Zabin, October 2009.

Advertising Age. *You're Using Social Media. But Just Who Is Overseeing It All?* by Kunur Patel 22 February 2010. http://adage.com/digital/article?article_id=142221 accessed 9 November 2010.

Adweek. "Ford: Moving On: Ford's one of the hottest brands on the road. So how does it plan on staying there?" by Jean Halliday. 23 May 2010. http://www.adweek.com/aw/content_display/news/agency/e3i3088c639a8acf60c38472702091c07d4.

Arsenault, Jocelyn. "Social Media ROI: Things You Might Want To Track" on JocelynArsenault.com. 15 April 2010. http://www.jocelynarsenault.com/social-media-roi-things-you-might-want-to-track accessed 9 November 2010.

Automotive Digital Marketing. "Automotive Social Media Marketing Examples and Case Studies" by Ralph Paglia. 30 October 2010. http://www.automotivedigitalmarketing.com/profiles/blogs/automotive-social-media-3.

CMO.com. *The CMO's Guide To The Social Media Landscape.* http://www.cmo.com/social-media/cmos-guide-social-media-landscape

CMO Council. *Protection from Brand Infection: Marketing's Fight Against Fakes, Fraud and Infringements.* http://www.cmocouncil.org/programs/current/protection.asp accessed 9 November 2010.

Econsultancy. *Value of Social Media Report.* February 2010. http://econsultancy.com/us/reports/value-of-social-media-report

Ford Motor Company. *2009 Annual Report.*

Forrester Research, Inc. *What's The Social Technographics Profile Of Your Customers?* http://www.forrester.com/empowered/tool_consumer.html accessed 9 November 2010.

———. *Introducing Peer Influence Analysis: 500 billion peer impressions per year,* by Josh Bernoff, 26 April 2010. http://forrester.typepad.com/groundswell/2010/04/introducing-peer-influence-analysis.html accessed 9 November 2010.

Kawasaki, Guy. "How to Use Twitter as a Marketing Weapon." *Holy Kaw!* 22 February 2010. http://holykaw.alltop.com/twitter-as-a-weapon-demo-script accessed 9 November 2010.

Kirkpatrick, David. *The Facebook Effect: The Inside Story of the Company That Is Connecting the World.* New York: Simon & Schuster, 2010.

MarketingCharts.com. "Top 10 Visited Social-Networking Websites & Forums, September 2010," citing Hitwise. http://www.marketingcharts.com/?s=September+2010&submit=»&paged=5 accessed 9 November 2010.

Marketing Vox. *8 Tips for Hiring a Social Media Expert.* http://www.marketingvox.com/8-tips-for-hiring-a-social-media-expert-046003/ accessed 9 November 2010.

Pew Internet & American Life Project. *Reputation Management and Social Media* by Mary Madden, Aaron Smith, 26 May 2010 http://pewinternet.org/Reports/2010/Reputation-Management/Part-1/Searching-for-ourselves-online.aspx accessed 9 November 2010.

Savell, Lawrence Esq. "Minimizing the Legal Risks of Using Online Social Networks." Law.com. 28 June 2010. http://www.law.com/jsp/article.jsp?id=1202462946165 accessed 9 November 2010.

Scott, David Meerman. The New Rules of Marketing and PR: How to Use News Releases, Blogs, Podcasting, Viral Marketing and Online Media to Reach Buyers Directly. Hoboken: John Wiley & Sons, Inc., 2007.

Social Commerce Today. *PowerReviews 2010 Social Shopping Study | Top Line Results* by Paul Marsden. 14 May 2010. http://socialcommercetoday.com/2010-social-shopping-study-top-line-results/ accessed 9 November 2010.

Social Media Group. Social Media Proposal (RFP) Template. http://socialmediagroup.com/social-media-rfp-template/ accessed 9 November 2010.

Soshable | Social Media Blog. *Social Media Strategy: Hire, Outsource, or DIY?* by JD Rucker on 19 June 2009. http://soshable.com/social-media-hire-outsource/ accessed 9 November 2011.

Stelzner, Michael A. *2010 Social Media Marketing Industry Report: How Marketers Are Using Social Media to Grow Their Businesses.* April 2010.

## Chapter 4 References

Borders, Brett. "A Brief History Of Social Media" on *Social Media Rockstar,* 2 June 2009. http://socialmediarockstar.com/history-of-social-media accessed 9 November 2010.

Econsultancy. Social shopping could get costly for retailers by Meghan Keane 2 June 2010, citing Omniture. http://econsultancy.com/us/blog/6014-social-shopping-could-get-costly-for-retailers accessed 9 November 2010.

Hitwise. "Top 20 Social Networking Sites." *Top 20 Sites & Engines.* http://www.hitwise.com/us/datacenter/main/dashboard-10133.html accessed 9 November 2010.

Mashable.com. MySpace: No Longer King of Entertainment by Ben Parr, citing Hitwise. http://mashable.com/2009/07/15/myspace-entertainment/ accessed 9 November 2010.

PostRank. "Google Buzz: A Robot Party!" by Ilya Grigorik on *PostRank Blog*. http://blog.postrank.com/2010/04/google-buzz-a-robot-party/ accessed 9 November 2010.

Search Engine Land. "YouTube Hits All-Time Highs In May, ComScore Says" by Matt McGee 25 June 2010. http://searchengineland.com/youtube-hits-alltime-highs-in-may-comscore-45158 accessed November 2010.

Tech Crunch. Facebook Closing In On 500 Million Visitors A Month (ComScore) by Erick Schonfeld, 21 April 2010. http://techcrunch.com/2010/04/21/facebook-500-million-visitors-comscore/ accessed 9 November 2010.

TopTenReviews. "Flickr." http://photo-sharing-services-review.toptenreviews.com/flickr-review-pg2.html accessed 9 November 2010.

# E Glossary of Terms

**Adobe Flash** Adobe Flash (formerly Macromedia Flash) is a multimedia platform used to add video, animation and interactivity to Web pages. Due in part to the lack of support for Flash in Apple iOS (operating system for iPhone and iPad), more developers are using HTML5 to build interactive pages as well. Apple dropped the Flash restriction for iOS apps late in 2010.

**aggregator** A program or application that collects news stories, blog posts, and other frequently updated content and displays them in one place for easier viewing by the viewer or subscriber. These programs check for new content from specific sites on a regular basis, constantly updating the feed with the latest updates. Also referred to as a feed reader, RSS reader, or web feed.

**Ajax** Ajax (short for asynchronous JavaScript and XML) is an assemblage of complementary web development tools used to create interactive web applications. It's not a technology itself, but a group of technologies. Ajax, enables Web applications to retrieve data from a server in the background without interfering with the display and behavior of the current page. Ajax employs a combination of HTML and CSS to mark up and style information.

**alerts** A search engine setup that allows you to schedule an automatic, regular search for specific words or phrases, with the results sent to you by email on a set schedule (i.e., daily) or provided in an RSS feed. For instance, businesses use alerts to be notified when the company, an employee, or a product is mentioned somewhere on the Internet.

**API** Application Programming Interface (API) is system software that allows computer programmers to create interface features or, in a network, determine how the various features will be used.

**archive** A collection of previous posts (blog entries, press releases, news, etc.) that are considered closed but are still available for viewing and sometimes continued commenting. Usually organized by month or year.

**astroturfing** Referring to the brand name AstroTurf for artificial grass carpeting, this term refers to campaigns that appear to be natural, "grassroots" activities generating a buzz but in fact have been carefully choreographed to promote a particular product, service, or stance.

**asynchronous** In general usage, the adjective asynchronous means events or objects that aren't coordinated in time. In the technology sense, however, it has several additional meanings. In the telecommunications world, an asynchronous signal is one that is sent from one network to another at a different clock rate than another signal. In a computer programming environment, an asynchronous operation is one that runs independent of any other operation.

**augmented reality** Augmented reality (AR) is a view of the physical real world which has been enhanced or augmented by computer-generated imagery. Augmented reality is often used to offer a layer of information over the top of a real world view, such as through the lense of a camera on a mobile device, typically in real time.

**avatar** An image used to represent a user (or to exist as his or her alter ego) in online venues; this can be simply the username, a picture or photograph (icon), or even a 3-D figure in gaming venues.

**blog** Derived from the phrase "web log," a blog can be considered an "online journal" or a running commentary from an individual. A blog may stand alone as its own site or be incorporated into a larger website and usually has a specific topic of interest or theme as its foundation. Blog entries often include photos, video, and links to other resources in addition to written entries. When used as a verb, "to blog" or "blogging" refers to the act of writing the content for or updating the blog.

**blogosphere** A broad term meant to encompass the world of blogs and their relatedness to one another, that is, a community of blogs and bloggers. Hyperlinks are often used on key words and phrases that connect from one blog entry to another, allowing one to follow a "conversation" on a topic from one blog to another.

**blogroll** A list of related or favorite blogs recommended by a blogger, usually appearing in a sidebar of his or her own blog.

**Bluetooth** Bluetooth is an open wireless technology standard for exchanging data over short distances from either fixed or mobile devices, using short length radio waves. Bluetooth creates personal area networks (PANs) and offers a high level of security.

**bookmarking** Referring to the act of marking a page in a physical book for easy reference, bookmarking is a function that allows you to "save" a Web page or site for easy access later. A bookmark can be added either through your Web browser or a social bookmarking site (like delicious.com), which also allows you to add tags to your saved pages, allowing others to access them, too.

**bots** Also known as Web bots, Internet bots, spiders, crawlers, and robots, bots are computer programs that are designed to perform automated, repetitive tasks quickly (or more quickly than a human can). Bots can be used for data gathering, web analysis, and to provide automated responses or for less sociable purposes such as spreading spam, searching for hacking weaknesses, or data mining surveillance.

**broken link** A link that no longer takes you to the intended location, either because the page has been deleted, moved, or renamed or because the site's server is down, and returns an error page. Also referred to as a "dead link" or "dangling link."

**chat** Commonly known as "instant messaging," this is an online communication method that happens by typing messages to one person or a group using tools such as instant messengers. These online conversations develop in real time as messages are viewed immediately by the recipient, who can respond instantly.

**clickjacking** As the name implies, this program highjacks a user's computer by taking him or her to an unintended website, leading him or her to innocently enter personal information, and even downloading software such as viruses and spyware.

**client-server** A network architecture in which software operations are split between server tasks and client tasks. A client sends requests to a server, according to whichever protocol is in use, asks for information or an action, and the server responds. This can be compared to a peer-to-peer architecture where each node has equivalent responsibilities.

**CMS** Content management involves processes to organize, categorize, and structure information resources so they can be stored, published, and reused in multiple ways. A content management system (CMS) can collect, manage, and publish content, storing the content either as components or whole documents, while maintaining the "connections" between components.

**comments** Blogs and other online postings (such as articles or editorials) allow the reader to append his or her own thoughts and remarks on the piece, or to other users' comments, via a "Comments" field beneath the original post.

**community building** The act of creating a sense of shared experience through a blog, site, or other online venue by promoting conversations on common interests, goals, and experience among the members or participants."

**confused deputy** This is a nice way of saying "hacked." It's a computer program that is tricked by some other party into misusing its authority.

**content** Any material that makes up the body or subject matter of a site or page, which includes words (original posts and comment streams), pictures, videos, and more.

**cookie** Information sent by a server to a Web browser, essentially telling it "who you are," which is then sent back to that browser each time it is accessed. Cookies help identify a returning user, can remember your login for you, and even create customized pages for them, based on search habits, settings, preferences, etc. Also referred to as Web cookie, Web browser cookie, browser cookie, and HTTP cookie.

**CRM** Short for "customer relationship management," CRM is a system to collect, share, and manage data related to customers for customer service, marketing, and sales purposes. It can be a sales and marketing strategy but is most often used to describe a computer program or service. Social media platforms like LinkedIn can help augment a CRM system, allowing users to download information gathered on the platform into an organizations CRM solution.

**crowdsourcing** Derived by combining the terms "crowd" and "outsourcing," this describes the process of submitting a task to a your audience (an online group or community) and asking for their assistance instead of using a paid employee or contractor. This allows you to take advantage of the wide breadth of knowledge, experience, and expertise of your community and at no cost.

**CSS** An abbreviated reference to Cascading Style Sheets. CSS is a way to control the style of Web pages (written in HTML, XML, or XHTML) in a manner that ensures consistency from page to page. This refers to the design, or look and feel, of each page, rather than the content.

**cyberspace** The alternative world inhabited by frequent users of the Internet and commercial online services. The term was popularized by novelist William Gibson in his book *Neuromancer.*

**DAM** Digital asset management, or DAM, is the process of storing, retrieving, and distributing digital assets (files), such as logos, photos, marketing collateral, documents, and multimedia files in a centralized and systematically organized system, allowing for quick and efficient storage, retrieval, and reuse of the digital files that are essential to all businesses.

**dashboard** Like the instrument panel in a car, this is a page at the front of a site (for instance, a blog) that allows its owner to see data related to use and control and update content.

**DNS** The Domain name service (DNS) is an Internet program that provides a seamless translation of the alphabetical website or email addresses that people use into the corresponding numerical Internet protocol (IP) addresses that computers use during information transfer. The actual computer that handles this is called the domain name server.

**Drupal** Drupal (pronounced /_dru_p_l/) is a free, open source content management system (CMS) written in PHP and distributed under the GNU General Public License.Drupal is used to support many types of Web sites, especially community-oriented sites and blogs.

**Easter egg** Programmers often hide a secret photo, sound or video clip, or game somewhere in movies, DVDs, CDs, computer programs, Web pages, and video games; the trick is to find them.

Sometimes they appear if you just wait long enough or look in the right place; other times a particular keystroke sequence or combination is required to activate the virtual Easter egg.

**ECM** Enterprise content management (ECM) is a document management system that allow the management of an enterprise level organization's information. An ECM system is comprised of the tools, technologies, strategies, and methodologies used to capture, manage, store, preserve, and deliver content and documents related to an organization and its processes.

**email** Short for "electronic mail," these digital messages are sent and stored by way of an email server.

**emoticon** A combination of typographic characters that replicate a facial expression, used to illustrate the mood or tone of a writer's statement. Common examples include :) [happy], :( [sad], :D [grinning], :-/ [perplexed], :-O [surprised], and :P [sticking out tongue].

**Facebook Connect** A program interface that allows a Facebook user to log in to or connect with third-party cites using their Facebook identity, rather than creating new accounts. Connect offers what Facebook calls "dynamic security" to ensure safety of user's data.

**facilitator** Also known as a moderator or administrator, this role involves a person who watches over an online community to monitor content and interactions, facilitate conversation, set rules and guidelines for involvement, or ban troublemakers.

**fair use** Condition under which limited portions of copyrighted material can be used or reproduced without formal permission (but with citation of original source and author or rightsholder). This pertains to very particular circumstances of use, such as teaching, criticism or commentary, news reporting, and research. If fair use is disputed, the courts will determine adherence to the policy based on how the material was used, the nature of the original work, the weight of the selection used in comparison to the body of the work as a whole, and any impact reuse has on the market or audience of the original work.

**fake blog (Flog)** A marketing tactic used by organizations to promote a product or service by creating what appears to be a legitimate third-party blog but is really controlled as a company promotional vehicle. It is considered a deceitful practice and often backfires on the company when consumers realize they've been tricked.

**FBML** Facebook Markup Language ("FBML") is a variant-evolved subset of HTML with some elements removed. It allows Facebook Application developers to customise the "look and feel" of their applications, to a limited extent.

**Federated Identity Management (FIM)** is a system or arrangement in which multiple enterprises/platforms allow users to access their networks with the same identification information. Using such a system is sometimes called identity federation. This is often used in social networking platforms when a subscriber can sign into one with the ID they use on another.

**FeedBurner** FeedBurner is a web feed management provider that provides custom RSS feeds and management tools to bloggers, podcasters, and other web-based content publishers. The service helps both end users get viable content and content creators to distribute it.

**Firefox** Mozilla Firefox is a free and open source web browser descended from the Mozilla Application Suite and managed by Mozilla Corporation. Firefox is the second most used browser used today, behind Internet Explorer and is favored, along with Safari by Mac users in particular. Others include. Google Chrome and Opera.

**firewall** The layer of security that protects internal computer networks from outside intrusions, particularly from the Internet.

**flame war** Heated discussion generated in the comments thread on a post or in an online discussion group. While the negative conversation can be a simple result of people arguing over opposing viewpoints, flame wars are often purposely incited by a user just to annoy or incite other users. Often, a flame war will hijack the discussion and carry it completely off topic and kills the useful discussion.

**folksonomy** A spontaneous, collaborative method of categorizing content; online users annotate information with "tags" or descriptive terms that place it in a category and make it searchable for other users. Also known as collaborative tagging, social tagging, social indexing, and social classification.

**forum** An online space for discussion on specific topics. Forums usually revolve around a special interest and members or users are available to discuss issues and answer questions based on personal knowledge or experience.

**friends** In the online world, friends are your connections and contacts in a particular program, community, or application. Friends are established by linking to one another's profiles; some sites require you to approve, confirm, or accept a friend request, thus allowing access to your information, while others may permit you to "follow" or be "followed" without establishing a mutual connection.

**FTP** Short for file transfer protocol, this is the tool used to retrieve information in the form of electronic files from any number of computer systems linked via the TCP/IP protocol. In effect, users transfer copies of information found on remote computers either directly to their own computers or to a service provider's network and then to their own computers.

**geotagging** The process of adding location-based metadata to a video, photo, or other item online. Latitude and longitude information make the data useful on mobile and GPS devices but can also be used to send location-based news or ads to someone who is logged in online.

**Google Chrome** Google Chrome is a web browser developed by Google that uses the WebKit layout engine and application framework. Chrome is the third most widely used browser, behind Internet Explorer and Mozilla Firebox.

**Graph API (Facebook)** The Graph API is the core of Facebook Platform, enabling developers to read and write data to Facebook. It provides a simple and consistent view of the social graph, uniformly representing objects (e.g., people, photos, events, and pages) and the connections between them (e.g., friendships, likes, and photo tags).

**griefer** Largely related to the world of online gaming, a griefer is a person whose sole intention is to disrupt the game by purposely behaving in antisocial ways.

**groups** In the online world, a group is essentially a community of likeminded individuals; members share common interests, activities, or experience and join together for discussion, connection, and networking. You must join the group to be a member; some groups must approve your request to join before allowing you access.

**hashtag** Popularized in Twitter, a hashtag is any term or string of words (no spaces) preceded by the hash mark (or number, or pound) sign (#). Adding the hash mark before the word creates a link that will take you to all other uses of that particular hashtag term. In essence the hashtag becomes a subject category for all related tweets.

**hat tip** A blogger will often append a post with the abbreviation "h/t" or the words "hat tip to" in order to acknowledge that a reader or associate brought the item to his or her attention. It is a public thank you, or "tip of the hat," for the lead.

**hit** (1) A hit is any request for a file download related to a Web page view. While often mistaken as the number of visitors or page views, it does not directly reflect traffic or activity on a one-to-one basis. A Web page may include a number of files in its construction, for example two photos and two buttons. Accessing this page causes five files to be retrieved, so it results in five hits. (2) Also refers to the number of results returned based on your keyword search in a search engine; having twenty results returned is referred to as getting twenty hits.

**HTML** HTML (HyperText Markup Language), is the predominant markup language used to create web pages. It provides a means to build structured documents by denoting structural semantics for text such as headings, paragraphs, lists, links, quotes, and other items.

**HTML5** HTML5 is the next major revision of HTML. . HTML5 aims to reduce the need for proprietary plug-in-based rich internet application (RIA) technologies such as Adobe Flash and Microsoft Silverlight. The HTML5 has been designed to be backward compatible with common parsing of older versions of HTML. It is being used more frequently to replace Adobe Flash, which until late 2010 was prohibited from applications running on the Apple iOS used on iPhones and iPads.

**HTTP** Hypertext Transfer Protocol (HTTP) is a request-response standard typical of client-server computing. In HTTP, web browsers or spiders typically act as clients, while an application running on the computer hosting the web site acts as a server.

**hyperlink** A word or words in online material that is highlighted in such a way (usually underlined and in blue text) to indicate that it contains an embedded link that will take you to another page, document, or section of a page or document when clicked.

**hypertext** The word or words containing a link to help you navigate to another page, document, or section of a page or document. {OR: The nonlinear format used to create electronic documents with links between related elements

**Internet Explorer (IE)** Windows Internet Explorer (formerly Microsoft Internet Explorer; abbreviated to MSIE or, more commonly, IE), is a series of graphical web browsers developed by Microsoft and included as part of the Microsoft Windows line of operating systems starting in 1995. Its usage share now sits at approximately 50% to 60% and is slowly trending downward especially in the face of new mobile browsers.

**IMAP** The Internet Message Access Protocol (IMAP) is one of the two most prevalent Internet standard protocols for e-mail retrieval, the other being the Post Office Protocol (POP).

**instant messaging (IM)** An online communication method that happens by typing messages to one person or a group using tools such as instant messengers. These online conversations develop in real time as messages are viewed immediately by the recipient, who can respond instantly. Also known as online chats.

**Internet** The "official" name for an international network of computer networks linked to provide and share information and resources about a seemingly limitless number of topics. The Internet, as we know it today, grew out of an effort formulated by the United States government in the late 1960s to protect the important data stored on its computers and to ensure the continued electronic transport of this data in the event of a nuclear war.

**Internet Protocol IP** The Internet Protocol (IP) is used for communicating data across a packet-switched internetwork using the Internet Protocol Suite, also referred to as TCP/IP. It is the dominant protocol of the Internet today.

**Internet protocol (IP) address** The 32-bit binary number that identifies the exact location of a computer on the Internet or a network running TCP/IP.

**ISO** The International Standards Organization (ISO) is an organization that establishes and coordinates uniform, internationally accepted standards.

**JAVA** A programming language that enables developers to write small applications including animation and other advanced features that can be downloaded and run very quickly with most Internet browsers.

**JPEG** Joint Photographic Experts Group (JPEG) is a lossy compression scheme based that is a de facto standard for photographs on the Internet. JPEG allows the user to control the compression ratio and reproduction quality at the point of compression, which may involve sacrificing image quality for file size.

**keyword** A word or group of words used to initiate a search on a particular subject in a search engine.

**link bait** A method by which a blogger or website attempts to generate more traffic or links to his or her site by "baiting" readers with content that is useful, entertaining, or sensational enough to catch someone's eye and compel them to share a link back to it.

**link farming** Websites that try to increase their ranking in search engines by linking to one site and requesting a reciprocal link in return; the website itself often just lists hundreds of links to other websites with no content and often no subject shared by the sites.

**link rot** Link rot, or linkrot, describes the inevitability of links in websites and publications to become inactive over the course of time; this happens because the original article may be moved to a different location or be removed entirely. A small website can prevent link rot by actively checking for broken links each month, but there are also computer applications which can check for broken links.

**listening** In online terms, this refers to keeping watch for when you or your company is mentioned on the Internet, via searches or setting alerts, or monitoring posts to see what topics are popular.

**login** Your username and password combination that identify you give you access to your computer or accounts.

**lurker** Someone who observes or monitors a forum or community but does not participate through comments, discussion, or other interaction. Despite its sinister name, a lurker does not necessarily have bad intentions but may simply choose to remain behind the scenes because he or she is just keeping up to date on a topic or lacks confidence to share an opinion.

**malware** Malicious software, or "malware" encompasses programs like viruses, worms, spyware, and keyloggers, basically any program or code designed to intrude on your system to damage or hijack your computer or collect personal information.

**mashup** A digital mashup is taking a combination of existing files, movies, images, music, etcetera, and creating a derivative product from it. In terms of web development, a mashup is a web page or application that combines data from two or more external sources to create a new service.

**meme** The concept that an idea or process can become "viral," that is, spread quickly among a group of people, compelling them to act in response to it and make it their own. Some common Internet memes are quizzes and blog post topics, while in daily life, chain letters, urban legends, and even buzzwords fit this category. For instance, someone writes a blog post about their five favorite concerts, someone else sees that and writes their own blog post on the topic, and so on.

**metadata** A common definition is that metadata is "data about data" or that it documents the content of a piece of data. Some common examples of metadata are the file name, size, and location of a computer file; the title, author, and ISBN of a book. Online, metadata helps material be searched and show up in search results.

**microblogging** While a typical blog post can be as long or as short as the author wants, microblogging has size limits related to the post. Twitter is a clear example of the microblog format, limiting posts to a maximum of 140 characters or a link to an image or video.

**MIME** Multipurpose Internet mail extensions, or MIME, is the Internet standard defining how graphics and other multimedia files are transferred via email and through Web browsers.

**MMS** Multimedia Messaging Service, or MMS, is a standard way to send messages that include multimedia content to and from mobile phones. It extends the core SMS (Short Message Service) capability which only allowed exchange of text messages up to 160 characters in length.

**MP3** MPEG-1 Audio Layer 3, more commonly referred to as MP3, is a patented digital audio encoding format using a form of lossy data compression. It was designed to greatly reduce the size of audio files while remaining faithful to the original sound (although audiophiles will note that "lossy" means something was lost.

**multimedia** Combining more than one means of providing information—text, audio, animation, and full-motion video—for use as a teaching tool, in a presentation, or for entertainment purposes.

**netiquette** Refers to what is considered to be acceptable behavior on the Internet, in email and messaging, as well as interaction on discussion boards, chat rooms, groups, and communities. For example, it's considered impolite to type in all caps, which is interpreted as yelling.

**network mapping** Network mapping is the study of the physical connections of a network; likewise Internet mapping is a study of the physical connections that make up the Internet. The Internet is so massive, connected by such a great number of physical servers that mapping it can be an onerous task.

**newsreader** See *aggregator*.

**OAuth** allows users to share information and content between sites without sharing a password and while limiting the information that can be accessed from one to another.

**OMA** The Open Mobile Alliance (OMA) is a standards body which develops open standards for the mobile phone industry.

OMA maintains browsing specifications, among other things, for mobile devices.

**online** The state of a computer being connected to and communicating with another electronic device for the purpose of distributing or retrieving information.

**online community** A group or network of people who share common interests and join together on the Internet to discuss, read, or participate in activities related to that shared interest. Also known as a virtual community.

**open profile** The concept that a user's profile from one networking site can also be shared with other sites to which the member belongs, so that an update to information on one site will automatically populate the user's other authorized sites.

**open source** In terms of software development, open source refers to the open availability of source code, allowing others to freely develop other products based upon it. a non-profit group, the Open Source Initiative, acts as a standards body and maintains the open source definition for the good of the community.

**OpenID** OpenID is a shared identity service that enables users of multiple OpenID-enabled Web sites to sign in under one single profile, or single user identity. It's a free and open standard allowing people, particularly those using social media platforms, to control the amount of personal information they provide.

**Opera** Opera is a web browser and Internet suite developed by Opera Software. It's one of the top five browsers in use today. Like any browser, it handles common Web-related tasks, such as Web site interaction, upload and download of files, and social platform access. Opera is offered free of charge for personal computers and mobile phones.

**peer-to-peer** Peer-to-peer refers to direct interaction between two people in a network. In that network, each peer will be connected to other peers, opening the opportunity for further sharing and learning. A peer-to-peer network is one that allows users to access shared devices without going through a server (in contrast to client-server networks.)

**permalink** Standing for "permanent link" this is a URL that directs people to the single article or other post on a website, rather than a webpage that might have multiple items on it. Because this link is tied to a specific item, the address should never be changed so the article is always accessible, hence the sense of "permanent."

**phishing** Scams delivered through email messages and pop-up ads that attempt to trick users into revealing personal information, such as credit card information or passwords, that can be used to commit fraud and steal their identity. Such emails often appear to come from a trusted company that the individual does business with, such as a bank or online auction service, and try to get the information by indicating an account will close if the information is not supplied.

**photosharing** Online tools and sites that allow you to upload and manage your digital pictures via online resources, which in turn make it possible to share your photos with others.

**podcast** A podcast (or non-streamed webcast) is a series of digital media files (either audio or video) that are released episodically and often downloaded through web syndication. The word usurped webcast in common vernacular, due to rising popularity of the iPod and the innovation of web feeds.

**podcatcher** A software program that enables users to subscribe to podcasts and automatically download new programs from RSS or XML feeds.

**poke** A Poke button appears on Facebook users' profiles. Another user can press Poke to attract the attention of the user, an action that can be interpreted as a simple "hi" or a flirtation, though Facebook indicates that it was created without a specific purpose in mind.

**POP** Post Office Protocol (POP) is an application-layer Internet standard protocol used by local e-mail clients to retrieve e-mail from a remote server over a TCP/IP connection. POP and IMAP (Internet Message Access Protocol) are the two most prevalent Internet standard protocols for e-mail retrieval.

**post** Coming from the concept that you "post" an update to your blog, a post is any online message, which also indicates the user and the date and time of the post.

**private message** A message sent outside of a live, public stream of posts; also known as a direct message, or DM.

**profile** Information you choose to share about yourself when opening an account on a social networking site; this could include personal information such as birthday, a picture, interests, and a short bio, often including tags that will help others find you.

**registration** Setting up an account on website, especially one with restricted access, requires selection of a username, password, and possibly other information before utilizing the functionality of a site. Virtually all social media sits require registration of users before they can fully use the service.

**RIA** Rich Internet Applications (RIAs) are web applications that have many of the characteristics of desktop applications, typically delivered either by way of a site-specific browser, via a browser plug-in, or independently via sandboxes or virtual machines.[1] Adobe Flash, Java and Microsoft Silverlight are currently the three top frameworks, with penetration rates around 95%, 80% and 45% respectively.

**RSS** RSS (said to stand for several phrases, most commonly Really Simple Syndication) is a family of web feed formats used to publish frequently updated works (such as blog entries, news headlines, audio, and video)in a standardized format

**SaaS** Software as a service (SaaS, typically pronounced "sass") is software that is deployed over the internet. With SaaS, a provider licenses an application to customers as a service on demand, through a subscription or a "pay-as-you-go" model. SaaS is also called "software on demand" and sometimes "hosted," although this is something of a misnomer.

**Safari** Safari is a graphical web browser developed by Apple and included as part of the Mac OS X operating system. Safari is also the native browser for the iPhone OS As of 2010, Safari was one of the top five browsers used worldwide.

**search engine** A program used on the World Wide Web that searches for specific words and returns a list of sites where they are found to the user.

**Semantic Web** The Semantic Web is an evolving development of the World Wide Web in which the meaning or semantics of information found on the Web is defined, such that machines can process it. It comes from Sir Tim Berners-

Lee's (World Wide Web Consortium director) vision of the Web as a universal medium for data, information, and knowledge exchange.

**SEO** The process of taking steps to improve an organization, product or person's ranking in organic (read:, unpaid) browser search results. Headings, titles, keywords, meta tags, articles, links, tags, social media profiles, reviews and more can all be used in such a way to move an address, site or name higher in search engine rankings

**SGML** The Standard Generalized Markup Language (ISO 8879:1986 SGML) is an ISO-standard technology for defining generalized markup languages for documents.

**Silverlight** Microsoft Silverlight is a web application framework that provides functionalities similar to, and competing with, those in Adobe Flash, integrating multimedia, graphics, animations and interactivity into a single runtime environment.

**SMIL** SMIL or the Synchronized Multimedia Integration Language, is a W3C recommended XML markup language for describing multimedia presentations. It defines markup for timing, layout, animations, visual transitions, and media embedding.

**SMS** Short Message Service (SMS) is a communication service component of the GSM mobile communication system, using standardized communications protocols that allow the exchange of short text messages (160 characters) between mobile phone devices. SMS text messaging is the most widely used data application in the world to date.

**SMTP** Simple Mail Transfer Protocol (SMTP) is an Internet standard for electronic mail (email) transmission across Internet Protocol (IP) networks. While email servers and other mail transfer agents use SMTP to send and receive mail messages, user-level client mail applications typically only use SMTP for sending messages to a mail server for relaying.

**social bookmarking** Social bookmarking is a form of social media that allows users to share, organize, search, tag and manage bookmarks of Web resources. This is not file sharing, where actual files are transferred, rather it's a sharing of pointers to resources of interest to the user. Social bookmarking sites provide metadata (information about the bookmarked sites) so that users do not have to download or even visit the bookmarked site in order to gather information about it. Tags are an example of this.

**social media marketing** Using social media outlets to interact with and communicate with customers, improve customer relations and support, monitor reputation, and share information.

**social network** A social structure made of individuals or organizations) sometimes called "nodes," which are tied (connected) by one or more specific types of interdependency, such as friendship, kinship, common interest, financial exchange, dislike, relationships of beliefs, knowledge, business relationship, and even location. A social network has come to have a more specific meaning, referring to the platforms on which these groups congregate online, whether they be public, like Facebook, or private via an enterprise management system.

**social relation** a social relation or social interaction refers to a relationship between two (i.e. a dyad), three (i.e. a triad) or more individuals (e.g. a social group). Social relations, derived from individual agency, form the basis of the social structure. To this extent social relations are always the basic object of analysis for social scientists.

**social web** The Social Web is often used to describe how people socialize or interact with each other throughout the World Wide Web. Individual are brought together through a variety of shared interests on platforms that are public and open to all persons (over a certain age) or exclusive to members-only organizations.

**software architecture** The software architecture of a program or computing system is the structure or structures of the system, made up of software components, the externally visible properties of those components, and the relationships between them.

**software framework** In the computer programming world, a framework, is an abstraction wherein common code that provides generic functionality can be specialized or overwritten by user code providing specific functionality. Frameworks are a special case of software libraries in that they are reusable pieces of code wrapped in a well-defined Application programming interface (API), yet they contain certain distinguishing features that separate them from normal libraries.

**spam** Spam is the use of electronic messaging systems (including most broadcast media, digital delivery systems) to send unsolicited bulk messages indiscriminately. While the most widely recognized form of spam is e-mail spam, the term is applied to similar abuses in other media, particularly in one-to-many social networks, like Twitter.

**spyware** Spyware is a type of malware that is installed on computers and collects little bits of information at a time about users without their knowledge. The presence of spyware is typically hidden from the user, and can be difficult to detect. Typically, spyware is secretly installed on the user's personal computer. Sometimes, however, spywares such as keyloggers are installed by the owner of a shared, corporate, or public computer on purpose in order to secretly monitor other users.

**status update** A Facebook feature, "status updates" or "status" allows users to post messages for their friends to read. Friends can respond with their own comments and/or press the "Like" button to show that they enjoyed reading it. A user's most recent status update appears at the top of their profile, and is also noted in the "Recently updated" section of a user's friend list.

**streaming** Refers to a sequence of data elements made available over time. An analogy that helped define this is that a stream is like a conveyor belt that allows items to be processed one at a time rather than all at once or in large batches.

**streaming media** Streaming media are multimedia that are constantly received by, and normally presented to (think: video) an end-user while still being delivered by a streaming provider The name refers to the delivery method of the medium and not the medium itself.

**SVG** Scalable Vector Graphics (SVG) is a family of specifications of an XML-based file format for describing two-dimensional vector graphics, both static and dynamic (which can mean interactive or animated).

**SXSW** SXSW stands for South by Southwest, an annual event that combines elements of traditional conference settings with music festivals. SXSW has become the place to showcase creative and emerging technologies, especially social media focused ones. The event combines learning experiences, business activities, and entertainment and is help each spring in Austin, Texas, USA

**tag** In the online environment, a tag is a word or words attached to a piece of information, such as a file, image, or blog post, that allows it to be found when the word is searched.

**tag cloud** A representation of the word content of a website or blog. Based on the frequency with which a word is used or tag applied, the words are arranged as a visual illustration, with the most frequent words appearing in a dominant color or large type size or color, while more infrequent usages appear in small type or weaker color.

**taxonomy** Taxonomy is the practice and science of classification. Providing contributors to a site with a set of categories under which they can add content is offering a taxonomy. Allowing people to add their own keywords is to endorse folksonomy.

**teleconference** A live meeting between at least two people at different locations using telephones. A teleconference can utilize telephones, speaker phones, or even bridging networks that allow larger numbers of people to participate. A more recent meaning of the term involves using the phone service to present a live session (seminar or conference) to multiple individuals at multiple locations at the same time. Also referred to as audio conferences, telephone conferences, or phone conferences.

**terms of services** Also referred to as terms of use, terms and conditions, or T&Cs, the terms of services are the license to use a site, service, or software. You often must click an agreement checkbox to indicate you have read and understood the terms before you are able to proceed. While many people blindly click and agree, you really should scan the terms to see what usage and content rights you are agreeing to.

**text messaging** The act of sending and/or receiving short written messages using cell phones or other mobile devices. Also referred to as "texting."

**thread** When comments are posted on news sites, blogs, discussion forums, and the like, and are all related to the topic at hand, the comments are referred to as forming "discussion threads." The term has two uses: one is that the thread is all of the comments on a single topic grouped together, and the other is that the thread is the topic of discussion itself.

**thumbnails** Small versions of pictures used to help identify and organize them. On websites, smaller image sizes help images load more quickly.

**topic** The subject of an online conversation.

**trackback** An automatic method of notification when one blog or article mentions and links to another blog or article. This helps the original writer keep aware of references to their sources and also acknowledges the mentions and sources.

**Transmission Control Protocol/Internet Protocol (TCP/IP)** The system that monitors and performs data transfer over the Internet. TCP sends data and IP receives it. On individual computers TCP/IP is the software component that enables users to access the graphical aspect of the World Wide Web.

**trending** On Twitter, there is an area on a user's home page that indicates a list of topics that are most popular (or most tweeted about) at that precise time. Trending topics are often reflective of what is going on in the news, such as celebrity deaths, political activity, new movies, and sports events, as well as popular hashtag memes.

**tribe** A group of people who share a similar interest or interests and who have connected via online communities, social media networks, and the like.

**troll** An Internet term for a person who purposely posts controversial or negative comments to blog posts and articles or online forums for the sole purpose of creating tension among readers and provoking retaliatory responses.

**tweet** A message posted on Twitter. Tweets are limited to 140 text characters and are displayed on a user's profile as well as on his or her followers' timelines.

**URL** The uniform resource locator (URL) is the Internet address of a company, service, or other information resource.

**User-generated content** Material that is contributed by the end user rather than the company itself. Examples of user-generated content on the Internet range from product reviews to Wikipedia entries to YouTube videos.

**viral** Although it comes from the term "virus" and shares the connotation that it is something meant to spread, in terms of marketing, the term "viral" indicates that something is popular or attention-getting in such a way that it compels viewers to share it and pass it along to friends.

**virtual world** An online community that utilizes a simulation of the real world in which community members can interact through the use of avatars. Second Life is a popular example of a virtual world community.

**Vlog** A video blog. A form of blogging on the Internet that makes use of video instead of just text, to transmit the message.

**vodcast** A shortened reference to a "video podcast." As the name implies, it is online delivery of a video broadcast.

**VoIP** Standing for "Voice over Internet Protocol," VoIP refers to the delivery of voice information over an IP data network, such as the Internet, rather than the traditional public telephone network. As such, an advantage of VoIP is that it is not subject to the toll charges of standard telephone service.

**wall** A Facebook construct, the Wall is the area where one's friends can post comments and messages directly for them. Wall posts are visible to the page owner and anyone the user designates, based on privacy settings. The Wall posts and status updates of a user's friends appear in chronological order on a News Feed on the platform.

**W3C** The World Wide Web Consortium (referred to as W3C, as well as WWW or W3) is an international community responsible for developing standards that support the long-term growth of the Web.

**Web 2.0** Indicating what is thought of as the "second generation" of the Web, Web 2.0 points to the more interactive and collaborative nature of the Internet, whereas the first generation involved only the ability to view static Web pages.

**web browser** A graphical or text-based utility that enables users to navigate the World Wide web. Safari, Internet Explorer, Google Chrome, Mozilla Firefox and Opera are popular graphical browsers. Lynx is a text-based browser.

**web feed** Content can be distributed beyond visitors viewing it on a website. Feeds allow subscriptions that automatically delivers new content to subscribers via a reader program or even email.

**webcast** As the name suggests, this is information that is "broadcast" via the World Wide Web A webcast can either be live or hosted on a server to be accessed on-demand. As the audio or video content is transmitted online, it differs from a podcast which is usually downloaded by the end user.

**widget** A piece of software or application embedded on a Web page that provides information or acts as a tool for the end user. Common examples are clocks, weather information, progress bars, etc.

**Wikipedia** A free online encyclopedia where the database of information is created, edited, monitored, and maintained by general Internet users. Anyone can add or edit a Wikipedia entry, although it is monitored for accuracy.

**Wikis** Collaborative sites that are open to allow any user to contribute, update, and correct content using the site's server software. Content on a wiki is essentially a living document, allowing anyone to add to it or change something and simplifying site organization, document history, markup, and link and page creation

**WYSIWYG text editor** Meaning "What You See Is What You Get, this is a system in which content appears, during the editing or creation process, the same as it will look in its final output.

**World Wide Web (WWW)** A hypertext program that allows users to access related documents across global networks by navigating a series of electronic links. Developed by scientists at CERN, the European Particle Physics Laboratory in Geneva, Switzerland, in 1989, the WWW was originally text-based. Introduction of the first graphical browser NCSA Mosaic in 1993 made it possible to access the color imagery, sound, and video that we take for granted today.

**worm** A worm is a program that can spread itself to other computer networks without being attached or transferred via an existing file. This is unlike a virus. However, a work is like a virus in that it can cause disruptions ranging from slowing the network to damaging files.

**XHTML** "XHTML (Extensible Hypertext Markup Language) is a family of XML markup languages that mirror or extend versions of the widely used web page language, Hypertext Markup Language (HTML). While HTML (prior to HTML5) was defined as an application of Standard Generalized Markup Language (SGML), a very flexible markup language framework, XHTML is an application of XML, a more restrictive subset of SGML. Because XHTML documents need to be well-formed, they can be parsed using standard XML parsers. HTML, on the other hand, requires an HTML-specific parser."

**XML** XML (Extensible Markup Language) is a set of rules for encoding documents electronically. It is defined in the XML 1.0 Specification produced by the W3C, as well as several other related specifications, of which are open standards. Although XML's design focuses on documents, it is widely used for the representation of arbitrary data structures, for example in web services.

## About the Authors

**Julie Shaffer** is Vice President, Digital Technologies at Printing Industries of America. She heads up the Digital Printing Council (DPC) as well as the Center for Digital Printing Excellence at Printing Industries headquarters in Sewickley, PA. In her position, Shaffer plays a lead role in developing programs and tools to help members grow their businesses with digital technologies.

Shaffer has a twenty-plus year background in premedia and print and is well known for her graphic production expertise. She is often called upon for training and presentations and to provide on-site consulting throughout the industry on a diverse range of topics, including PDF, color management, digital printing, social media, and web-to-print implementation. As an author, Shaffer contributes articles to industry publications as well as social media venues and pens white papers, case studies, and research reports. In additional to this one, Shaffer is co-author of several books, including *The PDF Print Production Guide* (1st, 2nd, and 3rd editions) and the *Web-to-Print Primer.*

As the Executive Vice President of Printing Industries of America, **Mary Garnett** is responsible for the direction and execution of programs, projects, and services of the organization. She serves as the senior staff member overseeing educational conferences and special interest groups. Garnett is a member of the executive management group of the association and is the chief planning officer for the organization. She oversees career/industry outreach projects including Printing Executive Networks (peer groups) and Skills USA. Garnett also serves as the publisher of *Printing Industries of America: The Magazine* and is responsible for the strategic direction of Printing Industries Press and the website.

Garnett earned a bachelor's degree in business education and a master's degree in counseling. Her previous professional experience has been with universities and colleges where she served as an administrator, instructor, and facilitator in U.S. military educational programs in Korea, Germany, and the USA.

## About Printing Industries of America

Printing Industries of America, along with its affiliates, delivers products and services that enhance the growth, efficiency, and profitability of its members and the industry through advocacy, education, research, and technical information.

Printing Industries of America developed from the 1999 merger of the Graphic Arts Technical Foundation (GATF), founded in 1924, and Printing Industries of America (PIA), founded in 1887. This consolidation brought together two powerful partners: the world's largest graphic arts trade association representing an industry with more than 1 million employees and $156 billion in sales and a nonprofit, technical, scientific, and educational organization dedicated to the advancement of the graphic communications industries worldwide.

Printing Industries of America's staff of researchers, educators, and technical specialists helps members in more than 80 countries maintain their competitive edge by increasing productivity, print quality, process control, and environmental compliance and by implementing new techniques and technologies.

In addition to striving to advance a global graphic communications community through conferences, Internet symposia, workshops, consulting, technical support, laboratory services, and publications, Printing Industries of America promotes programs, services, and an environment that helps its members operate profitably.

Many of Printing Industries' members are commercial printers, allied graphic arts firms such as electronic imaging companies, equipment manufacturers, and suppliers. Its special industry groups, sections, and councils were developed to serve the unique needs of specific segments of the print and graphic communications industries and provide members with current information on their specific segment, helping them to meet the business challenges of a constantly changing environment. These groups focus on web offset printing, label printing, binding, financial executives, sales and marketing executives, and digital printing.

Printing Industries Press publishes books on nearly every aspect of the field; training curricula; audiovisuals and digital media; and research and technology reports. It also publishes *Printing Industries of America: The Magazine,* providing articles on industry technologies, trends, business management practices, economics, benchmarks, forecasts, legislative and regulatory affairs, human and industrial relations issues, sales, marketing, customer service techniques, and management resources. The magazine represents the consolidation of *GATFWorld* and *Management Portfolio*, formerly bi-monthly publications of the association.

For more information about Printing Industries of America, special industry groups, sections, products, and services, visit www.printing.org.

## Printing Industries of America Affiliates

**Canadian Printing Industries Association**
Ottawa, Ontario
www.cpia-aci.ca

**Graphic Arts Association**
Trevose, PA
www.gaa1900.com

**Pacific Printing and Imaging Association**
Portland, OR
www.ppiassociation.org

**Printing & Graphics Association MidAtlantic**
Columbia, MD
www.pgama.com

**Printing & Imaging / Association of MidAmerica**
Dallas, TX
www.piamidam.org

**Printing & Imaging Association of Georgia, Inc.**
Smyrna, GA
www.piag.org

**Printing Association of Florida**
Orlando, FL
www.pafgraf.org

**Printing Industries Alliance**
Amherst, NY
www.pialliance.org

**Printing Industries of Arizona/New Mexico**
Phoenix, AZ
www.piaz.org

**Printing Industries Association of San Diego, Inc.**
San Diego, CA
www.piasd.org

**Printing Industries Association Inc. of Southern California**
Los Angeles, CA
www.piasc.org

**Printing Industries of Ohio • N. Kentucky**
Westerville, OH
www.pianko.org

**Printing Industries of Colorado**
Greenwood Village, CO
www.printincolorado.org

**Printing Industries of the Gulf Coast**
Houston, TX
www.pigc.com

**Printing Industries of Michigan, Inc.**
Southfield, MI
www.print.org

**PINE**
Southborough, MA
www.pine.org

**Visual Media Alliance**
San Francisco, CA
www.visualmediaalliance.org

**Printing Industries of St. Louis, Inc.**
Maryland Heights, MO
www.pistl.org

**Printing Industries of the Midlands**
Urbandale, IA
www.pimidlands.org

**Printing Industries of Utah**
West Jordan, UT
www.piofutah.com

**Printing Industries of Virginia**
Ashland, VA
www.piva.com

**Printing Industries of Wisconsin**
Pewaukee, WI
www.piw.org

**Printing Industry of Illinois/Indiana Association**
Chicago, IL
www.pii.org

**Printing Industry of Minnesota, Inc.**
Roseville, MN
www.pimn.org

**The Printing Industry of the Carolinas, Inc.**
Charlotte, NC
www.picanet.org

**Printing Industry Association of the South, Inc.**
Nashville, TN
www.pias.org

## Printing Industries Press Selected Titles

- *2010 Print Market Atlas,* compiled by Printing Industries of America Economic and Market Research Department, item no. 1847
- *Adding Value to Print,* by Manfred Breede, item no. 1786
- *Customer Satisfaction Surveys: Samples from the Industry,* compiled by Printing Industries of America Human relations Department, item no. 1861
- *Customer Service in the Printing Industry,* by Richard Colbary, item no. 1594
- *Glossary of Graphic Communications,* Fourth Edition, revised by Joe Deemer, item no. 13054
- *Hot Topics: Marketing Services Provider, Solutions Provider, or What?,* compiled by Deanna Gentile, item no. 18120
- *Marketing4Digital: A Guide to Print Markets,* by Frank Romano, et al. and Digital Printing Council, Set of 5 volumes: item no. 1852S
- *Playbook for Selling Success in the Graphic Arts Industry: A Sales Growth Workbook for Graphic Arts Sales Professionals,* by T.J. Tedesco and Dave Clossey, item no. 1788
- *Print Market Updates,* by Printing Industries of America Economic and Market Research Department, updated quarterly
- *Social Networking Primer for Printers*—Webinar Archive, hosted by Julie Shaffer, item no. WEB0909.
- *Win Top-of-Mind Positioning: Graphic Arts Sales and Marketing Excellence,* by T.J. Tedesco, Mike Stevens, and Henry Mortimer, item no. 1300

## Colophon

*Social Media Field Guide: A Resource for Graphic Communicators* was produced digitally as an on-demand publication at the Printing Industries of America headquarters in Sewickley, Pennsylvania. Content for this book was provided as Microsoft Word and Microsoft Excel files, went through the editorial process, and then were imported into Adobe InDesign CS4 for page layout. The typefaces used for the interior are Apple Casual, Futura, Marker Felt, Serifa, and Tiffany. The cover was created on an Apple Macintosh using Adobe InDesign and Adobe Photoshop.

Adobe PDF files were made from the InDesign files and then transmitted by internal network to Printing Industries of America's on-demand printing department. The interior and covers of the book were printed on a Ricoh C901S Graphic Arts Edition press. The RIP is a Fiery Command WorkStation 5. Finally, the book was bound offline using Wisdom Adhesive and the Bourg Book Factory.